- 国家自然科学基金面上项目（2019—2022）"基于旅游者时空行为规律的旅游活动空间生产与建构研究"（41871138）
- 山东省重点研发计划（重大科技创新工程）"关于山东智慧文旅云平台关键技术的研发及产业化应用"（2020CXGC010904）

普通高等学校"十四五"规划旅游管理类精品教材
旅游管理双语系列教材
总主编◎史 达

TOURISM RESOURCES

旅游资源学
（双语版）

TOURISM RESOURCES (BILINGUAL EDITION)

主　编◎黄潇婷
副主编◎黄琢玮
参　编◎孙晋坤　相沂晓　王素洁　韩若冰
　　　　汪佳慧　王志慧　郭秋琪　陈秋霞
　　　　邵卫芳　周彤昕

华中科技大学出版社
http://press.hust.edu.cn
中国·武汉

内容提要

"旅游资源学"是高等院校旅游管理专业必修的核心课程之一,旅游资源学内容具有涉及面广、操作性强、动态变化快等特点。本教材以传达清晰的概念、可操作性强的方法为教学目标,紧扣《旅游资源分类、调查与评价》最新国家标准。前三章着重于明晰旅游资源的概念和基本理论、旅游资源调查与评价的内容和方法、旅游资源开发与保护;第四章至第九章分别对地文景观资源、水文景观资源、生物和气候景观、遗产与建筑景观、人文活动和旅游商品等主要旅游资源类型的基本概念、保护与开发的方法等进行了系统阐述。

Abstract

Tourism Resources is one of the required courses for tourism management majors in colleges and universities. The content of tourism resources has the characteristics of wide coverage, strong operability, and fast dynamic changes. The current textbook closely follows the latest national standards of *Classification, Investigation, and Evaluation of Tourism Resources*, aiming to provide clear concepts and highly operable methods to the audience. In this textbook, Chap. 1 to Chap. 3 focused primarily on delineating the concepts and basic theories of tourism resources, the content and methods of tourism resources investigation and evaluation, as well as the development and protection of tourism resources. Chap. 4 to Chap. 9 systematically clarified the basic concepts, protection, and development methods of main tourism resources typology, respectively, such as geological landscape, water tourism‐ocean tourism, biological and climate landscape, heritage tourism, humanistic activities, tourism commodities.

图书在版编目(CIP)数据

旅游资源学:双语版/黄潇婷主编.—武汉:华中科技大学出版社,2023.8
ISBN 978-7-5680-9608-9

Ⅰ.①旅… Ⅱ.①黄… Ⅲ.①旅游资源-双语教学-教材 Ⅳ.①F590

中国国家版本馆CIP数据核字(2023)第153061号

旅游资源学(双语版) 黄潇婷 主编
Lüyou Ziyuanxue(Shuangyu Ban)

策划编辑:王 乾	
责任编辑:王雅琪 王 乾	
封面设计:原色设计	
责任校对:阮 敏	
责任监印:周治超	
出版发行:华中科技大学出版社(中国·武汉)	电话:(027)81321913
武汉市东湖新技术开发区华工科技园	邮编:430223

录 排:孙雅丽
印 刷:武汉科源印刷设计有限公司
开 本:787mm×1092mm 1/16
印 张:13.25
字 数:408千字
版 次:2023年8月第1版第1次印刷
定 价:59.80元

本书若有印装质量问题,请向出版社营销中心调换
全国免费服务热线:400-6679-118 竭诚为您服务
版权所有 侵权必究

总序

华中科技大学出版社出版的旅游管理类专业的双语教材，首套包含《旅游消费者行为》《旅游学概论》《旅游目的地管理》《中国旅游文化》《旅游资源学》五本教材，由分别来自东北财经大学、山东大学、云南大学、西安外国语大学、北京第二外国语学院等多所在旅游管理国际化办学方面有较多经验积累的高校的三十多名教师合作完成。

我们都知道，旅游业是中国1978年改革开放后，较早对外开放的一个行业。旅游业的特性也决定了它始终具有国际化发展的元素和内在动因。从行业发展和顾客服务的角度来看，这个行业与人，比如国际游客的直接接触频率很高；对英文信息，比如各境外旅游目的地或英文版的旅游网站的搜索量很大。从语言要求上来看，英语是为大多数国际游客所能听懂的语言。在国内的很多知名旅游景点，我们会经常看到用熟练的外语给外国游客介绍中国历史文化景点的导游；在很多城市的街头巷角，会有一些当地居民用外语为外国旅客指路或者推介家乡的风土人情。他们亲切友善的表达，不仅传递了信息，还展现了一个国家的包容度和自信。所以，与其他服务业业态和商业业态相比，旅游业的国际化程度相对较高，对国际化人才的需求也更多。要想做到准确地把握不同国家旅游者的行为，达意地传递旅游和文化信息，就需要旅游业的从业者能够掌握和使用专业外语。

高等教育机构作为人才的提供者，要想满足行业对于国际化人才的需求，就需要从教师国际化和课程国际化等方面提供支撑。从目前高校发展的情况看，在经过多年教育国际化发展后，越来越多的教师已经具备较强的国际化视野和国际化沟通能力。但是课程国际化的关键环节——教材国际化却成为木桶上的短板。在国际化教材的使用方面，高校主要通过中国图书进出口（集团）有限公司来引进教材，或者由教师自制课程讲义和幻灯片。引进的教材几乎都为国外学者所著，里面的案例多以国外企业为样本，中国学生甚至教师对很多国外企业并不了解。特别是在新的旅游业态方面,中国的旅游业有着其他一些国家所没有的运营形态,比如数字化等,在这个层面上,中国的旅游业与国外存在较大程度的差异性。

而教师自制的讲义对于学生而言,其在课后很难进行阅读和复习。此外,随着中国教育改革和对外开放的不断深入,越来越多的国际留学生选择来华学习。这个时候再拿着境外的教材讲中国企业的案例,就显得有点不合时宜了。因此,由中国教师编著一套讲述"中国故事"的双语教材,让境外的读者也能更便捷地了解中国旅游业的实践与发展,就成为一项非常紧迫且有意义的工作了。首套五本教材涵盖了旅游管理类专业的三门核心课程,同时还包括"中国旅游文化""旅游资源学"两门非常有特点的课程,希望能够满足大多数读者的需求。

华中科技大学出版社是国内在旅游管理类教材出版方面的佼佼者。因为工作的关系,编者与李欢社长、王乾编辑在多次交流中碰撞出火花,并很快确定出版书目,组建写作团队。从筹备到五本教材全部完稿用时一年半。经历了严肃的周例会讨论、外审等多个环节,克服了各种困难,该系列教材终于能够与读者见面了,编者在内心充满了喜悦的同时,也有担心不能如读者所愿的不安。

因此,也希望读者在阅读过程中,如发现其中的问题或不足之处,能及时与我们进行沟通。编者将不断吸取读者的意见和建议,不断完善本套教材,以便能为旅游管理教育提供更多、更好的教材。

史达

2023 年 3 月 19 日

Foreword

The first set of bilingual textbook on tourism management majors published by Huazhong University of Science and Technology Press includes five textbooks: *Tourism Consumer Behavior*, *Introduction to Tourism*, *Tourism Destination Management*, *Chinese Culture and Tourism*, and *Tourism Resources*, which were jointly written by over thirty teachers from such universities as Dongbei University of Finance and Economics, Shandong University, Yunnan University, Xi'an International Studies University, Beijing International Studies University as they have accumulated experiences of international education in the field of tourism management.

The tourism industry, as we know, was one of the earliest industries that opened up to the outside world after China put in place the policy of reform and opening up in 1978. The qualities of the industry determine that it always has attributes and dynamism from within to pick up an international characteristic in its development. From a perspective of industry development and customer service, this industry has a high frequency of direct contact with people, international tourists, for example; as for information in English on tourist destinations or travel websites, the search volume is large; when it comes to language accessibility, English is the language that most international tourists can understand. At many popular tourist attractions in China, it is common to see tour guides fluent in English or other foreign languages introducing historical and cultural sites to international tourists; locals give directions to international travelers or introduce local culture in the neighborhoods in English or other foreign languages. Their kind words convey more than information. They are showcasing openness and confidence of a nation. For all these reasons, the tourism industry has a higher degree of internationalization and demands more international talent than other service and business formats. It is required that industry employees be able to use a kind of foreign language for business purposes to effectively understand the behavior of tourists from different countries and precisely deliver tourism and cultural messages.

As talent suppliers, higher education institutions need to provide support by offering international faculty and courses to meet the industry's demand for international talent. Over the years of international practice, the current development of colleges and universities shows that an increasing number of teachers have gained global visions and international communication capabilities. Textbooks, however, turn out to be the short stave of the barrel, hindering international course development. The text materials in use were either imported from CNPIEC or handouts and slides produced by teachers themselves. Imported teaching materials were nearly all written by foreign scholars and packed with cases of foreign businesses, which Chinese students and sometimes even teachers have difficulty understanding very well. It is worth noting that the tourism industry in China has what is not common in other countries when it comes to a nascent business format, such as digitalization, where differences can be identified between China and other countries.

On the other hand, teachers' handouts make it hard for students to do extension reading and review after class. We also witness more international students coming to study with us when China's educational reform and opening up further advances. It is inconvenient to use foreign text materials while talking about cases of Chinese businesses. As a result, writing textbooks, telling Chinese stories and facilitating overseas readers to get insights into tourism practice and development in China has become an imperative and meaningful task for Chinese teachers. This initial five-volume set covers three core courses in the tourism management major and the two distinctive courses on "Chinese Culture and Tourism" and "Tourism Resources". We hope that these books can meet the needs of the majority of the readers.

Huazhong University of Science and Technology Press excels in publishing tourism management text materials. The inspiring work discussions between the authors, President Li Huan and editor Wang Qian kindled the spark to confirm the book list for publication and eventually have the writing team pulled together. It took one and a half years from preparation to completion of all five manuscripts. This textbook set finally made it to be put in print after we undertook discussions at weekly meetings, went through external reviews and overcame difficulties. While being full of joy, we are concerned about not being able to fulfil our readers' expectations.

We look forward to hearing from you if any mistakes or errors are spotted during your reading. Any of your opinions and suggestions will be welcome so that we will continue to improve and provide you with better textbooks.

Shi Da
March 19, 2023

前言

"旅游资源学"是高等院校旅游管理专业必修的核心课程之一,旅游资源学内容具有涉及面广、操作性强、动态变化快等特点。本教材以传达清晰的概念、可操作性强的方法为教学目标,紧扣《旅游资源分类、调查与评价》最新国家标准。

本教材以国家标准《旅游资源分类、调查与评价》为逻辑主线,全书分为两个部分共九章。第一部分为基本概念与基本理论,着重于明晰旅游资源的概念和基本理论(第1章)、旅游资源调查与评价的内容和方法(第2章)、旅游资源开发与保护(第3章);第二部分分别对地文景观资源(第4章)、水文景观资源(第5章)、生物和气候景观(第6章)、遗产与建筑景观(第7章)、人文活动(第8章)和旅游商品(第9章)等主要旅游资源类型的基本概念、保护与开发的方法等进行了系统阐述。

本教材是集体合作的结晶。根据各章内容撰写者的工作分工、参与程度与实际贡献,主编为黄潇婷,副主编为黄琢玮。本教材的章节贡献者如下:黄潇婷、汪佳慧、郭秋琪、邵卫芳、陈秋霞(第1章);黄潇婷、王志慧、郭秋琪(第2章);孙晋坤、郭籽萌(第3章);黄潇婷、汪佳慧、陈秋霞、邵卫芳(第4章);黄琢玮(第5章);相沂晓(第6章);王素洁、汪佳慧、王心珂、宋广鑫、石穆沙(第7章);黄琢玮(第8章);韩若冰(第9章)。

与国外同类教材相比较,本教材注重培养学生的系统思维,全面系统地构建学生旅游资源学知识体系,在案例选择方面注重体现中国文化自信,并将中国在生态文明建设和保护生物多样性等方面的做法融入教材内容中。此外,本教材与已经在中国大学慕课、智慧树和爱课程平台上线的《旅游资源学》全英文课程相匹配。

由于编者水平有限,本书仍有不少待完善之处,希望读者在使用过程中帮助我们发现问题,指出错误或不当之处,以便再版时修正、提高。

黄潇婷

2023年1月

Preface

Tourism Resources is one of the required courses for tourism management majors in colleges and universities. The content of tourism resources has the characteristics of wide coverage, strong operability, and fast dynamic changes. The current textbook closely follows the latest national standards of *Classification, Investigation and Evaluation of Tourism Resources*, aiming to provide clear concepts and highly operable methods to the audience.

The textbook follows the logical sequence of *Classification, Investigation and Evaluation of Tourism Resources*, and is structured into two parts with nine chapters. The first three chapters of Part Ⅰ cover the basic concept and basic theory, focusing on clarifying the concept and basic theory of tourism resources (Chap. 1), the content and method of tourism resources investigation and evaluation (Chap. 2), the development and protection of tourism resources (Chap. 3). Part Ⅱ systematically clarifies the basic concepts, protection, and development methods of the main tourism resources. Specifically, geological landscape (Chap. 4), water tourism‐ocean tourism (Chap. 5), biological and climate landscape (Chap. 6), heritage tourism resources (Chap. 7), humanistic activities (Chap. 8), and tourism commodities (Chap. 9).

This is a collaborative project. According to participation and contributions submitted by authors, the chief editor is Huang Xiaoting and the deputy chief editor is Huang Zhuowei. The chapter contributors are as follows: Huang Xiaoting, Wang Jiahui, Guo Qiuqi, Shao Weifang, Chen Qiuxia (Chap. 1); Huang Xiaoting, Wang Zhihui, Guo Qiuqi (Chap. 2); Sun Jinkun, Guo Zimeng (Chap. 3); Huang Xiaoting, Wang Jiahui, Chen Qiuxia, Shao Weifang (Chap. 4); Huang Zhuowei (Chap. 5); Xiang Yixiao (Chap. 6); Wang Sujie, Wang Jiahui, Wang Xinke, Song Guangxin, Shi Musha (Chap. 7); Huang Zhuowei (Chap. 8); and Han Ruobing (Chap. 9).

Compared with similar foreign textbooks, this book featured the following aspects:

focusing on cultivating the systematic thinking of students, constructing tourism resources knowledge system of students, reflecting Chinese culture when selecting cases, and integrating China's practice of ecological construction, biodiversity protection, and other aspects into the textbook. Besides, this textbook is supported by video resources *Tourism Resources*, an online English course that is available on the platforms such as Chinese University MOOC, Wisdom Tree, and Love Course.

Limitations existed in the current book due to the authors' ability. In order to see improvement in future editions, comments, criticisms, or corrections to any of the existing content will be gratefully appreciated.

Huang Xiaoting
January, 2023

目录
Contents

Chapter 1 Basic Concept and Theory of Tourism Resources / 001

1.1 Tourism Resources and NewTourism Resources View / 003
1.1.1 The Study of Tourism Resources Concept / 003
1.1.2 The Attributes of Tourism Resources / 007
1.1.3 New Tourism Resources View / 007

1.2 Tourism System and Tourism Products / 008
1.2.1 Tourism System and Tourism Resources / 008
1.2.2 Tourism Products / 012
1.2.3 Tourism Product Life Cycle / 014

1.3 Characteristics of Tourism Resources / 016
1.3.1 Diversity / 016
1.3.2 Territoriality / 017
1.3.3 Comprehensiveness / 019
1.3.4 Oriented Attractiveness / 020
1.3.5 Ornamental Value / 020
1.3.6 Cultural Value / 021
1.3.7 Sustainability / 022
1.3.8 Non-renewability / 023

Chapter 2 Content and Method of Tourism Resource Investigation and Evaluation / 025

2.1 Content of Tourism Resources Investigation / 026
2.1.1 Classification of Tourism Resources / 026

2.1.2 Content /035

2.2 Models, Procedures and Methods of Tourism Resources Investigation /037

    2.2.1 Models of Investigation /037
    2.2.2 Procedures of Investigation /039
    2.2.3 Methods of Investigation /041

2.3 Evaluation of Tourism Resources /042

    2.3.1 Purpose and Content of the Evaluation /043
    2.3.2 Evaluation Criteria and Principles /044
    2.2.3 Evaluation Methods /046

Chapter 3 Development and Protection of Tourism Resources /049

3.1 Tourism Resources Development /050

    3.1.1 Overview of Tourism Resources Development /050
    3.1.2 Theoretical Basis of Tourism Resources Development /057
    3.1.3 Tourism Resources Development Process /058

3.2 Protection of Tourism Resources /060

    3.2.1 Destructive Factors of Tourism Resources /060
    3.2.2 Tourism Resource Management /062
    3.2.3 Protection Measures for Tourism Resources /064

3.3 Sustainable Development of Tourism Resources /065

    3.3.1 Sustainable Development Concept of Tourism Resources /065
    3.3.2 Barriers to Sustainable Development of Tourism Resources /067
    3.3.3 Sustainable Development Path of Tourism Resources /070

Chapter 4 Geological Landscape /074

4.1 Overview of Geological Landscape /075

    4.1.1 The Definition of Geological Landscape /075
    4.1.2 The Features of Geological Landscape /076
    4.1.3 The Implications of the Geological Landscape /077

4.2 The Typology of Geological Landscape / 080
    4.2.1 Natural Landscape Complex / 081
    4.2.2 Geological and Tectonic Traces / 082
    4.2.3 Surface Morphology / 083
    4.2.4 Natural Markers and Natural Phenomena / 084

4.3 The Development and Utilization of Geological Landscape / 085
    4.3.1 Tourism Function of Geological Landscape / 085
    4.3.2 Geological Landscape Development / 088

Chapter 5   Water Tourism-Ocean Tourism / 092

5.1 Water Tourism-Ocean Tourism / 093
    5.1.1 The Definition of Water Tourism-Ocean Tourism / 093
    5.1.2 The Major Activities of Water Tourism-Ocean Tourism / 093
    5.1.3 Typical Issues and Concerns of Water Tourism-Ocean Tourism / 094

5.2 Water Tourism-Seaside Tourism / 095
    5.2.1 The Definition of Water Tourism-Seaside Tourism / 095
    5.2.2 The Activities of Water Tourism-Seaside Tourism / 095
    5.2.3 Typical Issues and Concerns of Water Tourism-Seaside Tourism / 095

5.3 Water Tourism-Lake Tourism / 096
    5.3.1 The Definition of Water Tourism-Lake Tourism / 096
    5.3.2 The Activities of Water Tourism-Lake Tourism / 096
    5.3.3 Typical Issues and Concerns / 097

5.4 Water Tourism-Wetland Tourism / 098
    5.4.1 The Definition of Water Tourism-Wetland Tourism / 098
    5.4.2 The Activities of Water Tourism-Wetland Tourism / 098
    5.4.3 Typical Issues and Concerns of Water Tourism-Wetland Tourism / 098

Chapter 6   Biological and Climate Landscape / 101

6.1 Biological Landscape as Tourism Resources / 102
    6.1.1 Definition of Biological Landscape / 102
    6.1.2 Biological Resources and Tourism / 103
    6.1.3 The Characteristics of Biological Resources / 103

6.1.4 Categorizing Biological Landscapes for Tourism / 108
6.1.5 Conservation Frameworks for Biological Resources / 117

6.2 Climate Landscape as Tourism Resources / 119

6.2.1 Defining Climate and Meteorology Tourism Resources / 119
6.2.2 Characteristics of Climate and Meteorology Tourism Resources / 120
6.2.3 Impact of Climate and Meteorology Elements on Tourism Activities / 121
6.2.4 Categories of Climate Landscape Resources / 122

Chapter 7 Heritage Tourism Resources / 127

7.1 Overview of Heritage Resources / 128

7.1.1 The Definition of Heritage / 128
7.1.2 The Implications of Heritage Resources / 130

7.2 The Typology of Heritage Tourism Resources / 132

7.2.1 Natural Heritage / 133
7.2.2 Tangible Cultural Heritage / 135
7.2.3 Assessment of World Natural and Cultural Heritage / 138
7.2.4 Intangible Cultural Heritage / 139
7.2.5 Mixed Heritage / 144

7.3 The Development and Protection of Heritage Tourism Resources / 146

7.3.1 The Development of Heritage Tourism Resources / 146
7.3.2 The Protection of Heritage Tourism Resources / 151

Chapter 8 Humanistic Activities / 157

8.1 The Concept of Humanistic Activities / 158

8.2 Personnel Records / 160

8.3 Art / 161

8.4 Folk Customs / 163

8.5 Modern Festivals / 166

8.6 Festivals and Events / 167

8.7 Hometown/Residence of Celebrities / 169
8.7.1 The Definitions of Hometown/Residence of Celebrities / 169
8.7.2 The Activities of Hometown/Residence of Celebrities / 170
8.8 Performance / 171
8.8.1 The Definitions of Performance / 171
8.8.2 The Activities of Performance / 171

Chapter 9 Tourism Commodities / 173

9.1 The Definitions and Attributes of Tourism Commodities / 174
9.1.1 The Definitions of Tourism Commodities / 174
9.1.2 The Fundamental Types of Tourism Commodities / 177
9.1.3 The Attributes of Tourism Commodities / 178
9.2 Tourism Handicrafts / 179
9.2.1 The Definitions of Tourism Handicrafts / 179
9.2.2 The Fundamental Types of Tourism Handicrafts / 180
9.2.3 The Attributes of Tourism Handicrafts / 181
9.3 Souvenirs / 182
9.3.1 The Definitions of Souvenirs / 182
9.3.2 The Fundamental Types of Souvenirs / 183
9.3.3 The Attributes of the Souvenirs / 184
9.4 Specialties / 185
9.4.1 The Definitions of Specialties / 185
9.4.2 The Fundamental Types of Specialties / 186
9.4.3 The Attributes of Specialties / 186
9.5 Tourism Supplies and Consumables / 186
9.5.1 The Definitions of Tourism Supplies and Consumables / 187
9.5.2 The Fundamental Types of Tourism Supplies and Consumables / 187
9.5.3 The Attributes of Tourism Supplies and Consumables / 187

参考文献 / 189

Chapter 1
Basic Concept and Theory of Tourism Resources

Learning Objectives

(1) Learn the definition and attributes of tourism resources.
(2) Understand the meaning of new tourism resources view.
(3) Understand the views of different scholars on the tourism system.
(4) Learn the components of the tourism system.
(5) Understand the concepts of tourism product and tourism product life cycle.
(6) Understand characteristics of tourism resources.
(7) Command the ability to discern characteristics of various tourism resources.

Technical Words

English Words	中文翻译
tourism resources	旅游资源
tourism resources attributes	旅游资源属性
new tourism resources view	新旅游资源观
tourism system	旅游系统
tourists generating regions	旅游客源地
transit routes	旅游通道
destination regions	目的地区域
nucleus	核心
marker	标识
generating marker	先入标识
transit marker	沿途标识
contiguous marker	亲临标识

Continue

English Words	中文翻译
tourist origin system	旅游客源市场
travel system	出行系统
destination system	目的地系统
support system	支持系统
tourism product	旅游产品
tourism product life cycle	旅游产品生命周期
diversity	多样性
territoriality	地域性
oriented attractiveness	定向吸引力
ornamental value	美学价值
cultural value	文化价值
sustainability	永续性
non-renewability	不可再生性

Knowledge Graph

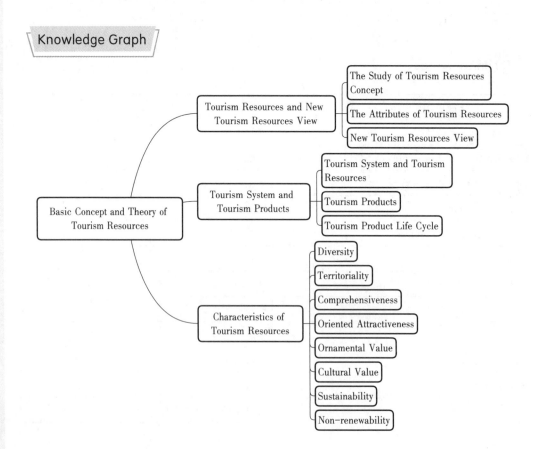

1.1 Tourism Resources and New Tourism Resources View

1.1.1 The Study of Tourism Resources Concept

With the development of tourism and the deepening of tourism research, people continue to discover new problems, put forward new insights, and try to achieve a more accurate grasp of tourism resources. At present, there are several representative definitions of tourism resources.

Before our discussion, it should be noted that western scholars and Chinese scholars working in this area have used two different terms to indicate tourism resources, namely "tourism attractions" in western countries, and "tourism resources" in China. There are three tips to explain the term "tourism attractions" in western countries. Firstly, tourism resources issues are generally understood as "resources utilized in tourism" or "resources in tourism" by western scholars, including but not only referring to "tourist attractions". Secondly, the term "tourism resources" is generally not used in western, and its meaning is different from the attraction resources we refer to in China, which is equivalent to "various resources in the field of tourism". Thirdly, tourism resources have not yet become a widely used phrase in English with a conventional meaning. To ensure the integrity of the contents, the terms "tourism resources" and "tourism attractions" were used interchangeably in this book.

1) International Definitions of Tourism Resources

Tourist attractions must be those things that give tourists positive benefits and characteristics, they can be seaside or lakeside, mountain scenery, hunting parks, interesting historical monuments and cultural activities, sports, as well as a pleasant and comfortable meeting environment (Holloway, 2001).

By definition, an attraction is magnetic. If it does not have the power to attract people to enjoy its value, it will fail to be an attraction (Gunn, 1972).

The tourist attraction is an empirical relationship among tourists, sights, and markers—some pieces of information about sights (Mac Cannell, 1976).

Tourist attractions do have some inherent unique quality which attracts tourists (Schmidt, 1979).

Attractions might be site attractions or event attractions, both of which exert gravitational influence upon non-residents (Burkart and Medlik, 1981).

Tourism resources are natural, technological, and socioeconomic factors that can be used to organize a tourism economy under existing technical and material conditions. This is a definition from the perspective of technology and economy (Preobrazensky et al., 1982).

Tourist attractions are defined as any attraction that can attract tourists (Lundberg, 1985).

In essence, tourist attractions consist of all those elements of "non-home" place that draw discretionary travelers away from their homes. They usually include landscapes to observe, activities to participate in, and experiences to remember (Lew, 1987).

A tourist attraction is a system comprising three elements: a tourist, a sight, and a marker (Leiper, 1990).

2) Domestic Definitions of Tourism Resources

Domestic research on tourism resources began in the late 1970s, which started at the same time as Chinese modern tourism and modern tourism education. With the continuous development of tourism, it is constantly required to explore the connotation and extension of tourism resources in practice, to conduct a scientific investigation, evaluation, development, and management of tourism resources, and promote the value realization and sustainable development of tourism resources. The main points are as follows.

Tourism resources are all the natural and social factors that are sufficient to attract tourists, that is, the object or purpose of tourists (Deng Guanli, 1983).

Tourism resources are all the objects and services that can provide people with touristic viewing, knowledge, fun, vacation and leisure, entertainment and rest, adventure and curiosity, investigation and research, friendly exchanges between the people and kill leisure time (Guo Laixi, 1985).

The so-called tourism resources refer to the part of the geographical environment with tourism value, that is, the environmental factors that tourists are interested in and the material conditions that can be used in the process of tourism (Zhou Jinbu, 1985).

Tourism resources are the raw materials of various things that attract people to visit and entertain. These raw materials can be material or immaterial. They are not the objects and attractions of tours, and they must be developed to become attractive things (Huang Huishi, 1985).

Tourism resources refer to the natural existence and historical and cultural heritage that are attractive to tourists, as well as artificial creation directly used for tourism purposes (Bao Jigang, 1993).

Tourism resources are the sum of various factors that can induce people to generate tourism motivation and carry out tourism activities under realistic conditions. It is the basis for the emergence and development of tourism (Chen Chuankang and Liu Zhenli, 1990).

Tourism resources are all the natural, social, or any other factors that can create an attractive environment for tourists(Li Tianyuan, 1993).

The definition of tourism resources is not the most important, the definition is open. If there is a standard or a core of definition, it should be tourism products. As long as it is a thing or phenomenon that has the potential to be developed as a tourism product, whether it is tangible or intangible, it can be regarded as a kind of tourism resource(Wu Bihu, 2001).

Tourism resources refer to the sum of all kinds of things and factors in nature or human society that can attract tourism and may be used to develop into tourism consumption objects. Generally speaking, tourism resources are the sum of many factors that can induce tourism motivation and implement tourism behavior. It is not only a tourist destination within a certain geographical space but also a place that tourists and various things that can convey information about the tourist destination(Su Wencai and Sun Wenchang, 1998).

Tourism resources refer to the objective existence that can attract tourists after development. It is the material conditions that can arouse the interest of tourists and make use of them in the natural and human environment. Specifically, tourism resources refer to the objects and services that provide tourists with sightseeing, viewing, knowledge, interest, vacation, entertainment, exploration, research, physical exercise, and friendly exchanges (Qian Jinxi, 1993).

Tourism resources are created by human beings, cultivated by culture, and have relatively stable geographical locations which can be visited by most people, or the mountains and rivers that are recognized by most people as having tourism value(Ban Wuqi, 1994).

All kinds of things and factors in nature and human society that can attract tourists, can be developed and utilized for tourism, and can generate economic, social, and environmental benefits, and can be regarded as tourism resources. The National Standard of the People's Republic of China *Classification, Investigation and Evaluation of Tourism Resources* issued by the General Administration of Quality Supervision, Inspection and Quarantine of the People's Republic of China in February 2003 and implemented in May, fully accepted the definition of tourism resources in the *Regulations on the Census of Chinese Tourism Resources* (Trial Draft),1992, (GB/T 18972-2003). This means that the definition has become an authoritative definition of tourism resources recognized by the domestic tourism industry.

3) The National Standards of the People's Republic of China Definitions (GB/T 18972-2017)

The General Administration of Quality Supervision, Inspection, and Quarantine of the People's Republic of China and Standardization Administration of the People's Republic of China have published the national standard *Classification, Investigation and Evaluation of Tourism Resources* (GB/T 18972-2017) in December 29, 2017. The standard has unified the technical definition of tourism resources in the field of practice. The officially accepted definition is that various things and phenomena in the nature and human society that can attract tourists can be used in tourism, and produce economic, social and environmental benefits. This definition has altered a little and replaced with the former standard (GB/T 18972-2003), in the former one, the subjects of tourism resources are "various things and factors" rather than "various things and phenomena".

This definition includes the following meanings.

First, tourism resources can attract tourists. Any product has its specific appeal to its consumers, and tourism products are no exception. As the source of tourism products, the attraction of tourism resources is directed to tourists. It is possible to become a tourism resource only if it has a certain attraction to tourists and can stimulate their tourism motivation. Any resource factor without such attraction will not become a tourism resource. Once the attraction from a different place is strong enough, this attraction can prompt tourists to realize the migration of different places, thus contributing to a special life experience in different places.

Second, tourism resources are the object of tourism development and the source of tourism products. On the one hand, tourism is an economic industry that produces, organizes, and sells tourism products. It develops and utilizes tourism resources through necessary auxiliary factors and means, converts resources into products, and pushes them to the market to achieve a healthy operation of tourism. Auxiliary factors and means cannot be counted as tourism resources. On the other hand, being able to be developed and utilized by the tourism industry is the value of tourism resources. Only through the development and utilization of the tourism industry and becoming tourism products, tourism resources can be connected with tourists, and provide unique experiences to realize their value. In addition, since the development of tourism resources and tourism products are both multi-level, tourism resources include not only the parts that have not been developed but have potential value, but also the parts that have been developed and can be combined into different tourism products.

Third, economic benefits, social benefits, and environmental benefits are the constraints of whether tourism resources can be developed and utilized for the tourism industry. The tourism products produced from a certain tourism resource must not only meet the market demand and bring economic profits to the tourism industry, but also conform to social norms and be conducive to the development and progress of the society. They must also follow ecological principles and be beneficial to the environment. This is the requirement of modern society for resource utilization, and it also becomes the condition for whether resources can be developed.

1.1.2 The Attributes of Tourism Resources

Analyzing the above definitions, we can see that although their respective starting points and emphases are different, the basic attributes of resources are generally the same, mainly in the following three aspects: attractive, economic, and non-economic.

From the analysis of tourism concept, the most basic attribute of tourism resources is "attraction", that is, attracting tourists, which is the basic criterion for judging whether a social phenomenon or something is a tourism resource.

At the same time, as the basis for the development of tourism, it is necessary to generate economic benefits for tourism development. After the tourism resources are converted into tourism products, they are used for an operation to obtain economic benefits. Therefore, the tourism resources themselves also have economic properties.

Under the utilitarian orientation of the development of tourism, people almost blindly emphasize the economy of tourism, and emphasize the unity of the three major benefits mostly, that is, to produce "economic benefits, social benefits, and environmental benefits". However, in reality, only those that produce social and environmental benefits under the premise of economic benefits were generally regarded as tourism resources. Those that simply produce social or environmental benefits but do not produce economic benefits are not considered as tourism resources. This understanding is one-sided, and it is also the inevitable result of the utilitarian orientation of the one-sided pursuit of economic benefits in the long-term development of tourism.

Therefore, from the perspective of tourism as a basic human right and the spiritual significance of tourism, tourism resources should also have non-economic attributes at the same time, that is, some attractive resources that do not produce economic benefits can also be used as tourism resources.

1.1.3 New Tourism Resources View

Tourism resources are all-encompassing and dynamic. Although we have established national standards for the identification and classification of tourism resources, it cannot be done once and for all. We still need to constantly discover new resources and new tourism value of traditional resources under the guidance of the new resources view.

First, because human tourism demand itself is developing and changing, in different stages of historical development, human tourism preferences and fashion will change, which also leads to the limitation of our cognition of tourism resources. In this case, the traditional perspective will be used to identify the type and value of tourism resources. This requires that the tourism industry practice and the tourism academic research can timely and accurately adjust the perspective of our cognition of tourism resources according to the development trend of human needs, constantly develop new tourism resources, and understand new tourism value of traditional resources.

For example, Zhejiang Province possesses various types of tourism resources, including natural and environmental resources, festivities, tourist services, cuisines, and tourism mementos. Although some of them belong to resource types, they have not appeared before in the practice of industrial development.

Second, because human society itself is developing and changing, new phenomena and new things emerge in an endless stream, which will inevitably lead to the generation of new resources. This means that we need to continue to develop, research, and update.

Therefore, the new view of resources emphasizes that we should use a developing and constantly changing perspective to discover new valuable resources and re-explore the new value and new functions of traditional resources.

1.2 Tourism System and Tourism Products

1.2.1 Tourism System and Tourism Resources

Tourism activities are social activities involving many aspects, including eating, transportation, accommodation, sightseeing, shopping, entertainment, and others. The main subject of tourism activities is tourists and the object of tourism activities is the tourism resources of tourism destinations. With the transportation, hotels, and all the other components that the tourism industry provides, tourists complete a tour cycle from home to destination and then back home. Therefore, tourism resources play a very important role in the tourism system.

1) Tourism System

From the perspective of system theory, tourism activities are a system (Wu Bihu, 1998). Many scholars have discussed the elements of the tourism system from different perspectives and developed their tourism system models to explain how the tourism industry operates. This chapter will introduce the models proposed by several scholars at different times.

Gunn put forward the concept of tourism system and the tourism function system model in 1972, and updated the model in 2002 (as shown in Figure 1-1). Gunn and Var said that virtually all the elements can be modeled as an interrelated demand and supply side. In the system, the demand side is about tourists and the supply side is composed of transportation, information, promotion, attraction, service. Only when supply and demand match, can tourism develop in an orderly and healthy way. Therefore, a tourist destination, as a supplier of tourism activities, must provide products and services that can meet market demand. This description of the supply subsystem reflects the characteristics of tourism products as a combined product well. In the 1972 model, Gunn focused on the classification of various elements, however, in the supply side of the new model, there is an interdependent relationship among five elements. They work together to provide tourism products in line with market demand, which reflects the characteristics of tourism products as a combined product and grasps the essential relationship of the tourism system well.

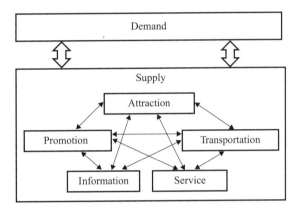

Figure 1-1　The tourism functioning system

Another kind of model is the geographic tourism system model, which is based on the spatial analysis of the tourism system. The most well-known one is the tourism system model proposed by Leiper in 1979(as shown in Figure 1-2). The elements of the tourism system are tourists generating region, transit route region, destination region, and the tourism industry. There is an origin or tourist generating region where tours begin and end. There is a tourist destination region or host locality where tourists stay temporarily. And there is a transit region or route which connects the two and through which tourists travel (Leiper, 1979). In addition, there are two factors interacting in the tourism process. One is the tourist, in search of experiences and needing support services and facilities. The other is the tourism industry which provides diverse kinds of resources. These elements which have the characteristics of an open system are arranged in spatial and functional connections, the organization of five elements operates within broader environments (Leiper, 1979).

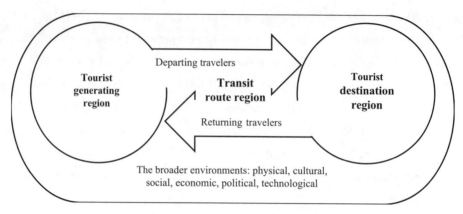

Figure 1-2 The tourism system

Leiper (1990) proposed the tourist attraction system (as shown in Figure 1-3), which is a systemic arrangement of three elements: a person with touristic needs, a nucleus (any feature or characteristic of a place they might visit), and at least one marker (information about the nucleus). In this model, tourism attraction is the nucleus. The marker is an important information medium. Tourists are pushed by their motivation towards the places where they expect their needs to be satisfied (Wu Jinfeng, 2014).

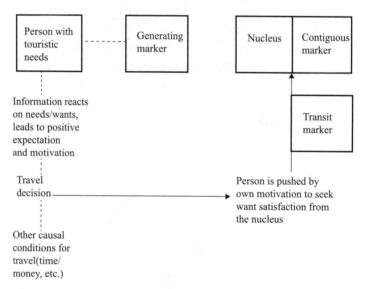

Figure 1-3 A model of tourist attraction

This model explains how a tourist attraction comes into existence, and what is involved in its operation. Different from the view that tourist attractions "pull" tourists to the destinations, Leiper(1990) believed tourists are never literally "attracted", "pulled" or "magnetized", but are "pushed" or motivated to experience a nucleus and its markers when a marker reacts positively with needs and wants. Tourists' expectations and needs will form a "push". When the information of tourism attractions meets the needs and wants of tourists, it will lead to positive tourism motivation.

Chinese scholar Wu Bihu (1998) also built the O-D tourism system model. "O" refers to the origin of tourist activities and "D" refers to the destination. In most cases, these two types of places do not overlap but are separated by a certain distance, and each has its operation law. In Wu's model, the tourism system framework includes four parts: tourist origin system, travel system, destination system, and support system (as shown in Figure 1-4).

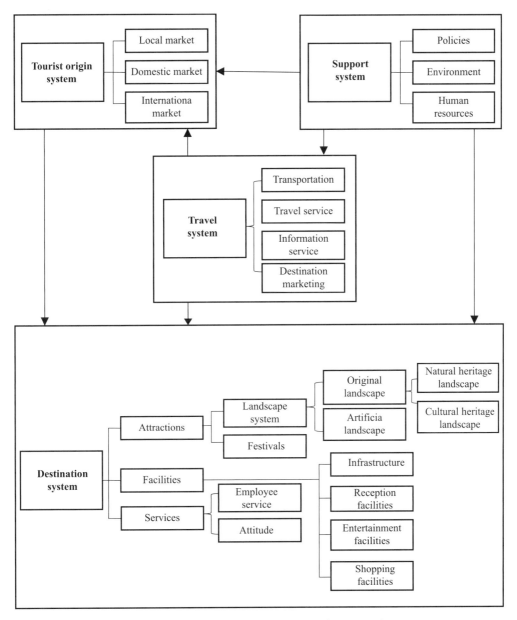

Figure 1-4 Recreation system (Tourism system)

Destination system mainly refers to a complex of various factors that provide for tourists who have reached the destination with tourism needs. Specifically, the destination system consists of three elements: attractions, facilities, and services. The attractions are formed through a certain degree of development based on tourism resources which generally include two parts: the landscape system and tourism festivals. Therefore, sometimes the attraction system can be roughly understood as a tourism resource system.

Support system is composed of policies, environment, human, and other factors at the periphery. It cannot exist independently, but is attached to the other three subsystems and plays an important role in the three subsystems.

2) The Status of Tourism Resources in the Tourism Activity System

Through the discussion of tourism models, we can find that most tourism models do not try to reflect the reality accurately, but recognize the complexity of tourism and try to explain the characteristics and relationships of different components of tourism. In addition, tourism resources play an important role in the tourism system and are one of the core elements of the tourism system.

(1) Tourism resources are the object of tourism activities. Tourism resources are the object that meet the tourists' inner demands for novelty and beauty and are the important material basis and conditions for attracting tourists and developing tourism activities (Yang Ali, 2016).

(2) Tourism resources are the foundation for the development of tourism in destinations. Tourism resources are the core elements of tourism products. The primary tourism products of most tourist destinations are formed by the original local tourism resources, such as Lijiang River of Guilin, the Great Wall of Beijing, and the Mausoleum of the First Qin Emperor in Xi'an. Differences in the quality and richness of tourism resources will affect the development of local tourism.

(3) Tourism resources are the key factor for the sustainable development of tourism destinations. In the development of tourism, tourism resources and environment are used passively, but they are the most important stakeholders of the sustainable development of tourism and all other industries, and they should be the beneficiaries of the principle of intergenerational equality and ecological sustainability. Excessive or improper low-level tourism development will destroy non-renewable tourism resources. Meanwhile, tourists' activities are also responsible for the destruction of resources and environment (Wang Degang and Wang Wei, 2011).

1.2.2 Tourism Products

Tourism products and tourism resources are closely related, but they also have great differences. Tourism products are developed based on tourism resources, which means that resources are the "raw materials" of tourism products. However, the same tourism resources can be developed and packaged into different types of tourism products. A tourism product can be based on one or more tourism resources.

The academic community has the following representative views on the concept of the tourism product.

Gunn and Var(2020) asserted that a tourism product is a complex human experience (not a simple, objective commodity) and that tourism product development must be an integrated process involving information service, transportation, accommodation, and attraction.

Middleton(1989) observed that the term "tourist product" is used at two different levels. One is the "specific" level, which is that of a discrete product offered by a single business such as a sightseeing tour or an airline seat. The other is the "total" level, which is the complete experience of the tourist from leaving home to returning.

Kotler(1997) claimed that the product is "anything that can be offered to a market for attention, acquisition, use or consumption that might satisfy a want or need. It includes physical objects, services, persons, places, organization, and ideas".

Shen Baojia(1995) stated that the concept of tourism products includes two parts: professional conditions (talent factor, material basis) and social conditions (security, social awareness, residents' attitude, community life, cultural element, and public facility).

Stephen L J Smith(1994) systematically presented a model that describes the product with five elements: the physical plant, service, hospitality, freedom of choice, and involvement(as shown in Figure 1-5).

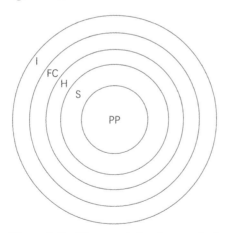

Figure 1-5　The generic tourism product

Note: PP = Physical plant; S = Service; H = Hospitality; FC = Freedom of choice; I = Involvement

Physical plant is the core of any tourism products. It can be a site, natural resources or facility such as waterfall and wildlife. It may be either fixed property such as a hotel, or mobile equipment such as a cruise ship. Service refers to the performance of specific tasks required to meet the needs of tourists. For example, A theme park needs management, actors, ticket selling, maintenance, food and beverage provisions to function. Hospitality is something beyond service. Consumers in almost every field expect "enhanced service" or "something extra". This expectation of "something extra" has been a part of tourism for a long time: it is hospitality. Whereas service is the technically-competent performance of a task, hospitality is the attitude or style in which the task is performed. Freedom of choice refers to the necessity that the traveler has some acceptable range of options for the experience to be satisfactory. The degree of freedom of choice will vary greatly, depending on whether the travel is for pleasure, business, family matter, or a combination. Involvement is not only physical participation, but also a sense of engagement focused on activites, whether for pleasure or business.

1.2.3 Tourism Product Life Cycle

The Tourism Product Life Cycle (TPLC) or Tourism Area Life Cycle (TALC) was systematically elaborated by R.W. Butler in 1980. TALC is one of the most cited and contentious areas of tourism knowledge for a long time. Not only can it convincingly explain the reality of tourism development, but also it is of great significance to the planning and development of tourism products and tourism destinations.

Some scholars suggest that the difference between tourism product and tourist area can be reflected in the size of geographical scope, but the more important difference is that tourist area can contain multiple tourism products. Therefore, from the perspective of the geographical area of the destination, what contains a geospatial attraction unit is a tourism product, while what contains multiple geospatial units is a tourism area.

Butler (2006) proposed TALC exactly based upon the product cycle concept in marketing research. Similarly, TALC is a process of development of tourist area generally including 6 stages: exploration, involvement, development, consolidation, stagnation, decline or rejuvenation. Although there are many modified models of TALC, in this part we will introduce the original hypothetical evolution model Butler put forward in 1980(as shown in Figure 1-6).

1) Exploration Stage

There are only scattered tourists, no special facilities, and its natural and social environment has not been developed and changed by tourism.

2) Involvement Stage

The number of tourists increases, tourism activities become organized and regular, residents provide some simple tourism services for tourists, local governments invest in improving facilities and traffic conditions, and tourism advertisements begin to appear.

3) Development Stage

Tourist reception increases rapidly, tourism advertisements appear in large numbers, foreign investment increases sharply, simple accommodation facilities are gradually replaced by large-scale, modern facilities, and the natural appearance of tourist sites has changed significantly.

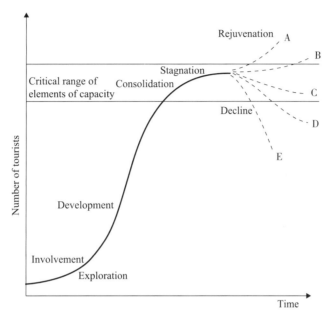

Figure1-6 Hypothetical evolution of a tourist area

4) Consolidation Stage

The number of visitors continues to increase but the growth rate declines. Tourism function zoning is obvious, local economic activities and tourism are closely linked. Residents are beginning to resent tourism.

5) Stagnation Stage

The natural and cultural attractions of tourism destinations are replaced by artificial facilities, the image of tourism destinations is weakened, and the market volume is difficult to maintain. Problems related to the overload of tourism environmental capacity occur quickly.

6) Decline or Rejuvenation Stage

Tourism market declines, tourism infrastructure dilapidates, tourism investment withdraws. Ultimately, the area may become a veritable tourist slum or lose its tourist function completely.

Tourism destinations take measures such as increasing the artificial landscape and developing new tourism resources to enter the recovery stage and replace the original tourism products. The direction of the curve after the period of stabilization illustrated in Figure 1-6 is open to several interpretations.

1.3 Characteristics of Tourism Resources

As is known to all, any concept should be the unity of commonness and individuality. Tourism resources not only belong to the concept of resources which have the general commonalities, but also have their own individual characteristics. Therefore, understanding these characteristics is also of great significance for the development of the tourism industry, especially for the development and utilization of tourism resources, tourism marketing, and the protection of tourism resources in a country and region.

It is undeniable that the characteristics of tourism resources are the multi-dimensional display and extension of the essential attributes of tourism resources. Definitely, studying the characteristics of tourism resources should start from their essential attributes so as to reflect their basic connotation. It should be able to provide a basis and guidance for the practical work of the tourism industry and lay a solid foundation for revealing the special laws of tourism development and perfecting the theoretical system of tourism.

For the individual characteristics of tourism resources, the academic community has been constantly studying and discussing, and no consensus has been reached. As a consequence, there are many different versions of the characteristics of tourism resources. However, researchers usually analyze and summarize the characteristics of tourism resources from the perspective of the scope, use, existence model, and the value of tourism resources. Although the expressions are quite different to some extent, there are no major differences. Thus, more consensus has been reached in academic community. To be frank, we should know that these theoretical achievements can serve the specific tasks and requirements of the tourism industry very well and have played an important guiding role.

Combined with the essential attributes of tourism resources, its basic characteristics mainly include the following eight aspects: diversity, territoriality, comprehensiveness, oriented attractiveness, ornamental value, cultural value, sustainability, and non-renewability.

1.3.1 Diversity

Diversity primarily indicates that the various types of tourism resources are a bit abundant. Moreover, the existing forms of tourism resources are fairly diverse, which is from nature to humanity, from material to spirit, from crude or man-made to virtual, from objects and events to phenomena and activities. To be brief, all things in the world can be regarded as tourism resources as long as they are attractive enough to tourists. In the official *Classification, Investigation and Evaluation of Tourism Resources* (GB/T 18972-2017), there are 8 main categories, 23 subcategories, and 110 basic types of tourism resources. The diversity of tourists' social composition and psychological characteristics determines the universality of tourism resources as the core source of tourism products. Generally speaking, common resources have specific material content and distribution features whereas tourism resources are totally not. Its types and manifestations are particularly diverse and its material content is intricately complex. It is not exaggerated that its scope of existence is omnipresent and boundless, which is quite incredible. It can even be said that any objective existence in the world may be considered as a kind of tourism resource.

Tourism resources may be available for development and utilization in any area that human beings can reach. There are a lot of factors in the formation of tourism resources, including not only natural factors such as geology and landform, meteorology and climate, land and ocean, soil, animals and plants, but also human conditions such as history, culture, nationality, religion, urban and rural areas, and industry. The joint action of various factors makes tourism resources be available in all aspects of nature and society so that its diversity and universality are absolutely superior to other resources. This merit of tourism resources is actually the product-driven by tens of thousands of different tourism needs. As a result, it can meet the requirements of the continuous development of the tourism market quite well. To the best of our knowledge, the more types of tourism resources a region has, the greater it attracts the most tourists here.

1.3.2 Territoriality

A considerable number of things in the world have regional features, forming the differences of things which are characterized by "geography", especially in the field of tourism resources.

First of all, though there are many kinds and complex types of tourism resources, they are rationally distributed in a certain spatial range and reflect the characteristics of the local geographical environment.

There are obvious regional differences in the geology, landform, climate, hydrology, animals, and plants of each region, as well as the material culture and spiritual culture created by human beings in the long-term struggle with nature. For instance, the architectural art, religion, and folk customs are obviously different with regard to each region, which forms a geo-culture with distinct characteristics. This evident regional difference makes tourism resources be equipped with different characteristics based on region. Furthermore, it also makes tourism resources have obvious regional characteristics. For example, the most attractive "3S" resources and landscapes in the world are mainly distributed on the sandstone coast of medium latitudes and low latitudes; Karst landscape is mainly distributed in tropical and subtropical limestone generation areas. To be concrete, the gardens in the world can be roughly divided into three types: oriental gardens, Western gardens, and Western Asian gardens. China's gardens include southern types, northern types, and Lingnan types, among which the bright and beautiful gardens in the south, the magnificent gardens in the north, and the gardens with subtropical scenery in Lingnan are obviously different. As we all know, China has a vast territory, intricate and diverse natural environment, distinct social and cultural regional characteristics, therefore, the tourism resources formed naturally have their own features.

Second, the essential attributes of tourism activities and tourism resources fundamentally determine that only things and factors with distinctive regional characteristics can become tourism resources.

Tourism activities are the special life experiences in other places which are far away from tourists' homes under the influence of different attraction factors. Tourism resources are the crucial source of tourism products and the main attraction force in different tourist destinations with sufficient potential to attract a lot of tourists. The charm of different attraction factors comes from the difference between these tourists' destinations and the tourists' own habitual living environment. Therefore, the unique natural scenery, cultural customs and production practice are the main factors to attract more tourists. Without any doubt, it is doomed to cause a great waste of local human, material, and financial resources due to repeated blind development and construction instead of making good use of local characteristics in the practice of tourism development. The gradual disappearance of regional characteristics and the increasing homogeneity among regions are severe problems in the development and utilization of tourism resources in recent years, which has attracted much attention from academic circles.

Third, the regional traits which are basically determined by the geographical characteristics of tourism resources are the main criteria for the division of tourism areas. The regional distribution of tourism resources has formed tourism areas with distinguishing features in the world, which has a profound impact on the spatial flow of tourists. The combination of tourism regional characteristics and tourists' needs is the key to the success of tourism marketing.

Tourism resources are always formed in a specific space and distributed in a specific geographical space in a certain form and change in accordance with a certain law. That is, tourism resources are rather fixed in the region to some extent. Moreover, thanks to the different natural conditions, historical causes, and social development levels, the tourism resources in different places also have displayed quite different features and forms. By and large, with the regional changes of natural location, longitude, and latitude, there are certainly regional differences in tourism resources, such as tropical scenery, temperate scenery, and landscape in the cold zone, which are closely related to different geographical locations. Not only the distribution of natural tourism resources but also the distribution of cultural and social tourism resources are affected by geographical location. As the old saying goes, each place has its streams in from all over the country. In the long-term development process, in order to survive and live a better life, human beings must give full play to their subjective initiative and adapt to nature. The transformation of nature, the various cultural landscapes, and the splendid cultures created by people living in various environments must also be influenced by the specific environment, which can be on behalf of the specific region and reflect the obvious geographical differences.

1.3.3 Comprehensiveness

No tourism resources can exist separately. In most cases, tourism resources greatly depend on and interact with other kinds of tourism resources to form a harmonious organic relationship. All kinds of tourism resources exist in specific regions to realize their tourism value as an organic whole by appealing to a large number of tourists. This can be deemed as the comprehensiveness of tourism resources. Generally speaking, the more kinds of tourism resources in a region there are, the closer the connection is, so the stronger its vitality will be. The more prominent the overall landscape effect of the region is, the greater the potential of comprehensive development and utilization will be. For instance, marvelous mountains and rivers in Guilin, the West Lake in Hangzhou, and scenic spots and historic sites in Beijing have all become famous traditional tourist attractions at home and abroad because of their wide variety of resources and outstanding comprehensive traits.

The comprehensiveness of tourism resources shows that tourism resources are mostly complex composed of different elements of mountains. For example, the mountain landscape is composed of towering mountains, forest land, and clouds. The canyon landscape is composed of valleys, rivers, and forest land. The two meteorological and celestial landscapes are the result of the joint action of sunset, rainbow, and "Buddha light". There is no doubt that humanistic tourism resources also have comprehensive characteristics. For instance, as a kind of tourism resources, ancient villages are formed under the joint result of a variety of material or non-material elements, which can be summarized as ecological, physical, cultural and other elements. The comprehensiveness of tourism resources is also explicitly reflected in the development of tourism resources. The development of single tourism resources often plays a limited impact on tourists. In the process of practice, different types of tourism resources are often combined to form complementary advantages so as to attract more tourists. For example, though the West Lake scenic spot is primarily dependent on lakes, it also contains a series of resource types such as mountains, forest lands, ancient buildings, ancient bridges, local traditional legends.

1.3.4 Oriented Attractiveness

Attraction to tourists is the essential attribute and core value of tourism resources. Without this function, tourism resources can not be regarded as tourism resources any longer. This essential attribute is inherently rooted in the usefulness and foundation of tourism resources as general resources. It is because tourism resources can meet the tourism and leisure needs of tourists from different aspects and have practical value. And the practical value of tourism resources and their compatibility with tourists' needs determine the attractiveness of tourism resources together. For example, there are thousands of Buddhist temples in China, so a considerable number of Buddhist believers and ordinary people go to pray for blessings, worship Buddhas, and make wishes. But strictly speaking, not all temples can be considered as tourism resources since some small temples are only places of worship for local residents with a small space. Sometimes, there are some tourists passed by.

In addition, the attractiveness of each temple to tourists is also different on account of historical influence, temple construction, architectural style, and other reasons. The distinctly renowned Buddhist holy places and Tibetan Buddhist holy places in China are of high tourism resources grade, while the tourism resources grade of other Buddhist temples is relatively general. Therefore, attractiveness has become the fundamental standard to judge whether one place is a kind of tourism resource or not. What's more, the strength of attraction has become a pivotal benchmark to judge the grade of a kind of tourism resource.

Therefore, the attractiveness to tourists is the essential feature of all tourism resources. However, no matter how excellent tourism resources are, the attraction orientation often only points to some people rather than all tourists owing to the different aesthetic preferences, aesthetic experiences, aesthetic abilities, cultural and artistic cultivation of tourists, and limitations of various objective factors. For example, for some adventurous, religious tourism resources, or tourism resources with special functions, it may be very attractive to corresponding tourists. It can be the main purpose and activity object of these tourists. Nonetheless, it can not be attractive or even completely unattractive to other groups of tourists. In terms of the scope of attractiveness, the attractiveness of sightseeing tourism resources is slightly greater, while the attractiveness of thematic tourism resources is relatively smaller. Understanding the orientation of the attractiveness of tourism resources is of great significance for tourism operators in combining tourism product and enlarging tourism market.

Case 1-5

1.3.5 Ornamental Value

The biggest and most common significance of tourism resources lies in aesthetic appreciation by large, which is mainly reflected in that tourism resources can mold people's temperament, improve people's aesthetic taste, and cultivate aesthetic sense, as well as the exterior aesthetic value, momentum and interior aesthetic characteristics of tourism resources. There are many elements of beauty, among which history is one of the important factors (Xie Mengyun, 2021). Large quantities of historical sites and natural landscapes in China have long historical origins and rich connotations, such as the Great Wall of China. The most important value of the historical landscape is the cognitive value of their cultural relics. It is a silent history or historical witness (Chen Wangheng, 2015). The main difference between tourism resources and other resources lies in its aesthetic value. Tourists will not only pay attention to the landscape design of scenic spots but also pay more and more attention to the ecological environment of scenic spots (Yu Bing, 2022).

Although people's tourism motivation varies from person to person and tourism content and forms are diverse, appreciation activities are almost indispensable to all tourism processes. All kinds of tourism resources have not only the beauty of grandeur, danger, novelty, seclusion, openness, and wildness but also have the morphological beauty of movement and stillness. It has the colorful beauty of the blue sky, white clouds, green mountains, green water, and blue sea. There are also the rhythmic beauty of stormy waves, slow-flowing mountain springs, gurgling streams, and vast pines. For example, Yuntai landform with magnificent mountains and rivers is characterized by lofty mountains, steep cliffs, deep canyons, wonderful streams, and various peaks and rocks. It has a high aesthetic appreciation value (Zhang Zhonghui, 2002).

1.3.6 Cultural Value

Tourism itself is a subjective human activity, and human tourism activity innately also has been equipped with cultural attributes, which is the perception and experience of culture. Therefore, tourism resources condense human spiritual culture and are the concentrated embodiment of social and cultural environment. Even for natural tourism resources, their aesthetic essence is also the expression of their cultural attribute, which condenses people's wisdom and efforts in the process of development and utilization. Humanistic resources contain rich culture as well. Some other emerging tourism resources can also not be separated from the mapping scope of social culture.

The cultural nature of tourism resources comes from the spiritual needs of tourists. Therefore, tourism is a spiritual activity of mankind, tourism demand is a high-level demand, and tourism activity is a high-level consumption activity. As you can see, no other resource has such a significant cultural attribute as tourism resources. You may wonder why they can be tourism resources. To be frank, whether human or natural resources, the fundamental reason why they can become tourism resources and the object of people's tourism is that they provide a special experience for tourists and meet people's high-level spiritual needs, which is the specific expression of the cultural attribute of tourism resources. For example, the towering mountains make people feel majestic; the vast oceans make people feel unrestrained; streams on mountains and valleys give people a strong and quiet feeling; museums, aquariums, and research bases provide visitors with opportunities and conditions to explore and understand their own unknown knowledge and information. In addition, cultural heritage and cultural relics have cultural and educational significance to some extent.

The cultural nature of tourism resources has different connotations for different tourists, which is related to the cultural heritage, historical origin, and formation conditions of tourism resources, as well as the tourists' age, gender, interest, occupation, education level, life experience, religious belief, and other factors. In addition, different tourists have different cultural needs for tourism resources. Various history museums can help people review and understand history comprehensively and thoroughly. People can understand the laws of social development from the rise and fall of history. What's more, they can learn the truth of being a gentleman from the fate of historical figures. Various national handicrafts let us understand the essence and characteristics of other national culture, enhance mutual understanding and promote national unity. Tourism is also a process of acquiring knowledge and enlightening the mind. Similarly, to obtain such knowledge and cultural enjoyment is often closely related to the cultural cultivation and spiritual realm of tourists. Tourism developers should deeply study the cultural connotation of tourism resources and take reasonable measures to fully display its cultural connotation in front of tourists, so as to increase the attractiveness to tourists and benefit more and more people.

1.3.7 Sustainability

Sustainability means that tourism resources can be reused again and again. Unlike oil, minerals, forests, and other tangible resources which will decrease because of the continuous utilization of mankind, tourism products are intangible products. Tourists need to pay a certain amount of money to buy such products, which is actually just a kind of experience and feeling, not the tourism resources themselves. Therefore, in theory, tourism resources can be reused for a long time or even forever.

Some renewable resources such as forest resources will be consumed in the process of utilization or need to be supplemented by natural reproduction, artificial feeding and cultivation. However, tourism resources are not. Tourists can only use these resources in tourism activities to get the specific emotion and make themselves relax to get rid of daily trifles. Tourists can only take away the impression and tourism experience left during the tourism process, but cannot take away the tourism resources themselves. From this point of view, tourism resources are indeed sustainable in use.

However, the sustainability of tourism resources is relative, which is actually based on the rational use of tourism resources so as to protect resources better. If tourism developers make improper use of tourism resources, the quality of tourism resources may decline or even be completely destroyed. Once the development and utilization of tourism resources exceed its carrying capacity, the quality of tourism resources will be greatly reduced, so it's difficult to provide tourists with high-quality aesthetic experience. For example, Ciqikou ancient town in Chongqing has a low sense of experience for tourists due to too many tourists on holidays at the same time.

1.3.8 Non-renewability

Just as natural ecology and cultural heritage are vulnerable to damage, improper use of tourism resources will also result in damage, and the vast majority of tourism resources are easy to damage and difficult to regenerate. Therefore, their continuity of use is not absolutely tenable. As is known to all, tourism resources are the remains of nature and human history. They are produced under certain conditions as time passes by. Although they are rich in types, the number of tourism resources is a bit limited for the sustainable development of tourism. They are different from the inexhaustible and renewable resources such as sunshine and air, as well as the abundant resources such as land, forest, and grassland. As a consequence, tourism practitioners are required to be responsible when carrying out the development work of tourism resources. It must be very good for them to carry out the development work in an orderly manner on the basis of scientific and reasonable tourism planning. At the same time, it is also essential to rely on practical economic and legal means to effectively strengthen the protection and management of tourism resources.

Along the Silk Road, there are many cultural relics that attract many visitors, especially the religious grottoes. In ancient times, Buddhists made caves on the remote mountains into shrines filled with carvings, sculptures, and other religious art to practice their religion. These caves were developed as places for Buddhist pilgrimage. The caves have witnessed the development of the Silk Road. The elegant statues and fantastic mural paintings can definitely show tourists the high level of art in ancient China.

Case 1-6

Case 1-7

Reading time

Chapter Review

This chapter mainly introduces the basic concept and theory of tourism resources.

Firstly, the officially accepted definition of tourism resources comes from the national standards of the People's Republic of China, that is, various things and phenomena that can attract tourists, be developed and utilized by the tourism industry, and industry, and generate economic, social, and environmental benefits in nature and human society. And the basic attributes of tourism resources are attractive, economic, and non-economic.

Second, tourism is an organic and integrated system. Based on the different views of various scholars on the tourism system model, it can be found that all elements in the tourism system are in different positions and play different roles. Each element influences each other and forms a closed loop of tourism activities together. As an important part and core element of the tourism system, tourism resources play a vital role in the tourism system. Readers should also understand the definition and content of tourism products, tourism product market, and tourism area life cycle theory.

Finally, combined with the essential attributes of tourism resources, its basic characteristics mainly include the following eight aspects: diversity, territoriality, comprehensiveness, oriented attractiveness, ornamental value, cultural value, sustainability, and non-renewability.

Questions for Discussion

Exercises

1. What's the national standards of the People's Republic of China's definition of tourism resources?
2. What are the attributes of tourism resources?
3. What are the two sides of the tourism functioning system proposed by Gunn analyzed?
4. What are the components of Wu Bihu's tourism system model?
5. What's the definition of a tourism product?
6. What are the stages of a tourist destination's life cycle?
7. Do all tourist destinations have the life cycle curve of tourist destinations proposed by Butler? Please find a case to illustrate your point of view.
8. What are the characteristics of tourism resources?

Chapter 2
Content and Method of Tourism Resource Investigation and Evaluation

Learning Objectives

(1) Learn the classification and investigation of tourism resources.

(2) Understand characteristics of national standards.

(3) Command the ability to investigate and evaluate various tourism resources.

(4) Learn the procedures and methods of tourism resources investigation.

(5) Master the criteria, index system and evaluation methods of tourism resources evaluation.

(6) Learn the basic procedures and principles of tourism resources evaluation.

(7) Be able to apply the theories learnt in the development of tourism resources to guide development practice.

Technical Words

English Words	中文翻译
tourism resources	旅游资源
tourism resources investigation	旅游资源调查
tourism resources grade	旅游资源等级
object of tourism resources	旅游资源单体
environment of tourism resources	旅游资源环境
broadly investigation	概查
general investigation	普查
detailed investigation	详查
tourism resources evaluation	旅游资源评价
tourism resources charisma	旅游资源魅力度
tourism product	旅游产品

Knowledge Graph

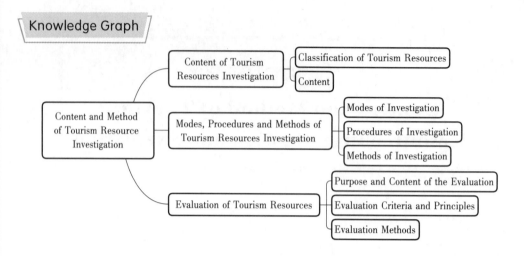

2.1 Content of Tourism Resources Investigation

2.1.1 Classification of Tourism Resources

Tourism resources are the material basis for the sustainable development of tourism and the potential for tourism productivity growth, and the correct classification of tourism resources is the premise for determining the direction of tourism development. General investigation, classification and evaluation of tourism resources are the three steps before the development and utilization of tourism resources, and they are usually indispensable. General investigation is the basis for the preparation of tourism development planning, tourism resources classification system is the purpose of resource general investigation, tourism resources general investigation, classification and evaluation need to be carried out on the basis of determining the connotation and extension of tourism resources. Due to the diversity of tourism resources and the inconsistencies among different resources, it is determined that any classification will not be able to exhaust or cover all types of resources. Therefore, at present, there is no unified classification standard and classification method for tourism resources in various countries in the world.

The practical work of tourism development and planning is not only satisfied with the guiding significance of the theoretical research on the classification of tourism resources, but also needs a standardized classification system that is for the purpose of general investigation, oriented to evaluation and development, and can be used for operation. Due to the short history of tourism development, tourism resources have been in a state of rich diversity, continuous updating and spreading, and at present, all countries in the world

Chapter 2 Content and Method of Tourism Resource Investigation and Evaluation

have not formed a unified classification standard and program yet. This method is commonly used in our country—*Classification, Investigation and Evaluation of Tourism Resources*(GB/T 18972-2017).

This standard fully considers the research and practice results of the tourism industry, value and application of tourism resources since the promulgation of GB/T 18972-2003, and focuses on the revision of the type division of tourism resources, so that the standard is more prominent in practical operation. The classification and basic types are explained in Table 2-1.

Table 2-1 Basic types and interpretation of tourism resources

Main Class	Subclass	Basic type	Brief description
A Geographical landscape	AA Natural landscape complex	AAA Mountain-type landscape	The overall landscape or individual landscape in the mountains and hills that can be visited for sightseeing
		AAB Mesa-type landscape	The overall landscape or individual landscape on the edge of the mountain or the platform between the mountains that is available for sightseeing
		AAC Gully-type landscape	The overall landscape or individual landscape in the valley for sightseeing
		AAD Beach-type landscape	The overall landscape or individual landscape in the gentle beach that is available for sightseeing
	AB Geological and tectonic traces	ABA Fracture landscape	The landscape formed by the stratum fracture on the ground surface
		ABB Folded landscape	The distortion and deformation of the formation under the action of various internal forces
		ABD Stratigraphic profile	A typical section of scientific significance in the stratum
		ABG Biological fossil sites	The excavation sites of biological remains and activity relics preserved in the strata during the geological period
	AC Surface morphology	ACA Terraced and hilly landscape	The landforms in the shape of terraces and hills

Continue

Main Class	Subclass	Basic type	Brief description
A Geographical landscape	AC Surface morphology	ACB Peak-column landscape	Peak-like stone bodies protruding from mountains, hills or flats
		ACC Ridge-like landscape	Karst landforms formed by dissolution for a long time under the control of tectonic traces
		ACD Ravines and caves	Ravines, inferior lands formed by internal or external forces, and natural caves located inside and on the rock surfaces of the bedrock
		ACE Strange and pictographic rocks	Mountains or rocks with strange shapes and anthropomorphic shapes
		ACF Lithospheric catastrophe relics	The surface traces left by natural disaster changes in the lithosphere
	AD Natural markers and natural phenomena	ADA Bzarre natural phenomenon	The peculiar phenomena that occur on the surface of the earth that generally have no reasonable explanation.
		ADB Natural landmarks	The locations that mark special geographical and natural areas
		ADC Vertical natural zone	The phenomenon that the mountain natural landscape and its natural elements (mainly landform, climate, vegetation, soil) change with altitude
B Water landscape	BA River system	BAA Recreation river section	Sections of the river that can be used for sightseeing
		BAB Falls	The river falls vertically from a high altitude as it flows through faults, depressions, etc.
		BAC Passages of ancient river course	Extant passages of the historical river that have disappeared
	BB Limnology	BBA Recreation lake district	Sightseeing area with section of the lake water body
		BBB Pond pool	A place surrounded by small areas of water with shores

Continue

Main Class	Subclass	Basic type	Brief description
B Water landscape	BB Limnology	BBC Wetlands	Natural outcrops of groundwater in shallow areas with still or flowing water bodies, such as natural or artificially formed swamps
	BC Groundwater	BCA Springs	Natural outcrops of groundwater
		BCB Buried water bodies	Buried in the ground at a suitable temperature, with mineral elements of underground hot water and hot steam
	BD Snowy land	BDA Snow	Snow accumulation surface that does not melt for a long time
		BDB Modern glacier	Modern glacial reservoir
	BE Sea surface	BEA Recreation sea	A sea area for sightseeing and recreation
		BEB Surge and crash phenomenon	The scene of the tide rushing in when the sea is high, and the phenomenon of the shore hitting the shore when the waves are advancing
		BEC Small island reef	Small open reefs or reefs that appear in rivers and seas
C Bio landscape	CA Vegetation landscape	CAA Woodlands	A large group of trees that grow together
		CAB Solitary trees and bush trees	A group of plants consisting of individual plants or small patches of woods that grow together
		CAC Meadows	An area composed of plant communities consisting of perennial herbaceous plants or small semi-shrubs
		CAD Floral floor	A group of one or more flowers
	CB Wildlife habitat	CBA Aquatic habitat	A place where one or more aquatic animals inhabit year-round or seasonally
		CBB Land animal habitat	A place where one or more terrestrial wild mammals, amphibians, reptiles, etc., inhabit all year round or in season
		CBC Bird habitat	A place where one or more birds live year-round or seasonally

Continue

Main Class	Subclass	Basic type	Brief description
C Bio landscape	CB Wildlife habitat	CBD Butterfly habitat	A place where one or more species of butterflies live year-round or seasonally
D Celestial phenomena and climatic landscapes	DA Celestial landscape	DAA Space scene viewing ground	A place to observe various sun, moon, stars, auroras and other space phenomena
		DAB Surface light phenomenon	Natural or artificial light phenomena that occur on the ground
	DB Weather and climate phenomena	DBA Cloud-prone area	Where clouds and rime appear more frequently
		DBB Extreme and special climate indications	Areas or locations prone to extreme and special climates, such as typical locations with windy, rainy, hot, cold, and arid areas
		DBC Phenological view	The germination of various plants spreads leaves, flowers, fruits, and leaves change color; seasonal phenomena such as leaf fall
E Buildings and facilities	EA Cultural landscape complex	EAA Social and business event venue	A place for social interaction activities and commercial trade activities
		EAB Military sites and ancient battlefields	Remains of ancient places used for warfare, buildings and facilities
		EAC Teaching and research experimental site	Various types of schools and educational institutions, institutions carrying out scientific research, and places engaged in sightseeing, research, and internship in engineering and technology test sites
		EAD Construction and production sites	Economic development projects and entity units such as factories, mining areas, farmland, pastures, forest farms, tea gardens, farms, processing enterprises and various production sectors
		EAE Cultural event venue	A place for cultural activities, exhibitions, and popularization of science and technology

Continue

Main Class	Subclass	Basic type	Brief description
E Buildings and facilities	EA Cultural landscape complex	EAF Recreation and leisure resort	A place with recreational, fitness, leisure, recuperation, vacation conditions.
		EAG Place of religious and sacrificial activities	A place where religious, ritual, and ceremonial activities are performed
		EAH Transportation depot	Ground yard stations, etc. for transport traffic
		EAI Memorial sites and places of commemorative events	A museum or venue to commemorate the deceased or to carry out various religious sacrifices and ceremonial activities
	EB Practical buildings and core facilities	EBA Featured neighborhood	Streets that reflect the architectural style of a certain era, or operate specialized goods and commercial services
		EBB Featured houses	A house with a viewing tour function
		EBC Independent halls, rooms, pavilions	Landscape architecture with ornamental tour function
		EBD Independent field, institute	Cultural and sports venues with the function of viewing and touring
		EBE Bridges	Overhead passages built across rivers, valleys, barriers, or other lines of communication
		EBF Channel, canal section	A human-honed waterway section in operation
		EBG Paragraph	Waterproof; water-blocking structure section
		EBH Ports, ferries and terminals	Located in rivers, lakes, seashores for shipping, transition, trade, fishing activities

Continue

Main Class	Subclass	Basic type	Brief description
E Buildings and facilities	EB Practical buildings and core facilities	EBI Caves	Underground voids which can enter formed by the dissolution, erosion and wind erosion of water
		EBJ Mausoleum	Tombs of emperors, princes and martyrs
		EBK Landscape farmland	Farmland with a certain ornamental tour function
		EBL Landscape ranch	A ranch with a certain ornamental tour function
		EBM Landscape forest farm	A forest farm with a certain ornamental tour function
		EBN Landscape farm	A farm with a certain ornamental and tour function
		EBO Featured stores	A shop with a certain sightseeing function
		EBP Featured market	A market with a certain sightseeing function
	EC Landscape with sketch architecture	ECA Image marker	A symbol that reflects the image of a certain place of tourism
		ECB Viewpoint	A place for landscape viewing
		ECC Pavilions, terraces, buildings	A building for visitors to rest, cool off or take in the scenery
		ECD Paintings and calligraphy	Calligraphy and painting works with a certain degree of popularity
		ECE Sculpture	Ornaments and monuments that are carved and shaped for beautification or commemoration, with certain allegories, symbols or pictograms
		ECF Monument, forest of steles, scripture building	Group carved or polygonal stone pillars that record texts and scriptures
		ECG Arch, shadow wall	In recognition of their meritorious service, the buildings erected by Kedi, Dezheng, and Zhongxiao Jieyi, as well as the walls used to obscure the view in Chinese architecture

Chapter 2   Content and Method of Tourism Resource Investigation and Evaluation

Continue

Main Class	Subclass	Basic type	Brief description
E Buildings and facilities	EC Landscape with sketch architecture	ECH Doorways, corridors	The front silhouette is an ornament, unlike the narrow strip of the base on both sides.
		ECI Tower building	Upright buildings with monuments, town objects, indicating Fengshui and certain practical purposes
		ECJ Landscape trail, yong road	A path made of paving for sightseeing tours
		ECK Flower lawn	Natural or artificial ground full of flowers and plants
		ECL Wells	Water extraction facilities for living and irrigation
		ECM Fountain	Man-made water spraying equipment from the ground to the ground
		ECN Rock pile	Landscapes formed by stones piled up or filled in
F Historical sites	FA Material cultural relics	FAA Architectural remains	Remains of historic buildings with local style and historical overtones
		FAB Movable artifacts	Important objects, works of art, documents, manuscripts, library materials, representative objects, etc. of each era in history are divided into precious cultural relics and general cultural relics.
	FB Intangible cultural relics	FBA Folklore	Literary and artistic works created by the people to summarize the image of social life
		FBB Local customs	Fashions, etiquette, habits and taboos that have been formed for a long time in social culture
		FBC Traditional costume decoration	Clothing with local and ethnic characteristics
		FBD Traditional performing arts	Folk various traditional performance methods
		FBE Traditional medicine	Local traditions of medicine and treatment
		FBF Traditional sporting events	Sports competitions are held regularly in the local area.

Continue

Main Class	Subclass	Basic type	Brief description
G Travel shopping	GA Agricultural products	GAA Plantation products and products	Locally produced plantation products and products with cross-regional prestige
		GAB Forest products and products	Locally produced forest products and products with cross-regional prestige
		GAC Livestock products and products	Locally produced livestock products and products with cross-regional prestige
		GAD Aquatic products and products	Locally produced aquatic products and products with cross-regional prestige
		GAE Aquaculture products and products	Aquaculture products and products with cross-regional prestige
	GB Industrial products	GBA Daily industrial products	Locally produced daily industrial products with cross-regional prestige
		GBB Travel equipment products	Locally produced outdoor travel equipment and items with cross-regional prestige
	GC Handmade crafts	GCA Stationery supplies	The main stationery of the study room
		GCB Dyeing and weaving of fabrics	Textile and dyed printed fabrics
		GCC Furniture	Utensils for people to sit, lie down, or support and store in life, work, or social practice
		GCD Ceramics	It is made of porcelain stone, kaolin, quartz stone, mullite, etc., and the surface is coated with glass glaze or painted objects.
		GCE Goldstone carvings, sculptures	Crafts carved from materials such as metal, stone, or wood
		GCF Goldstone	An ornamental artifact made of metal and stone

Chapter 2 Content and Method of Tourism Resource Investigation and Evaluation

Continue

Main Class	Subclass	Basic type	Brief description
G Travel shopping	GC Handmade crafts	GCG Paper art and light art	A flat or three-dimensional work of art made of paper and lighting materials
		GCH Paintings	Handmade paintings with certain ornamental value
H Humanities activities	HA Personnel activity records	HAA Local characters	Local historical and modern celebrities
		HAB Local events	Historical and modern events that have taken place locally
	HB Season	HBA Religious activities and temple fairs	Ceremonial events organized by religious believers, as well as gatherings held near temples or at established locations on festivals or prescribed days
		HBB Farm time festival	Local traditional festivals closely related to agricultural production
		HBC Modern festival	Local regular or irregular cultural, trade, sports activities, etc.
8	23	110	

2.1.2 Content

Tourism resources survey is the preliminary preparation for tourism development, and it is the basic work of "finding out the bottom of the family" before the development of tourism industry and tourism development.

Tourism resources survey can be a corresponding work carried out before the development of tourism resources, and it can also be an important part of the daily work of tourism management departments.

1) The Significance of Tourism Resources Survey

Tourism resources are widely distributed, the reasons for their formation are diverse, and the tourism resources themselves are constantly developing and changing, mainly manifested in two ways. On the one hand, the developed and realistic tourism resources with the change of time and the implementation of development measures, the own constituent factors and the status in the surrounding environment constantly change; on the other hand, with the continuous improvement of human productivity and the enhancement of cognitive ability, the depth and breadth of tourism resources development have expanded. Therefore, it is important to investigate the resources before development.

Through the investigation of tourism resources, it is possible to understand the current status, characteristics, categories, scale and development potential of tourism resources in the survey area, so as to identify the taste and value of resources, lay the foundation for evaluation and development, and provide direct and accurate data.

Through the basic information obtained through the investigation of tourism resources, information archives can be established and connected to the regional information database, so as to play a role in finding out the family background and understanding the current situation, which has great reference value for regional economic development and tourism management.

Through the in-depth investigation of the tourism resources themselves and their external development conditions, it is possible to fully grasp the current situation and existing problems of development, protection and utilization of resources, so as to provide detailed and reliable materials for determining the development orientation, development timing, development focus and corresponding management measures of resources.

Through the regular investigation of tourism resources, it is possible to dynamically and systematically grasp the progress of tourism resources development and detect their protection, so as to provide conditions for tourism management departments to obtain relevant information in a timely and accurate manner, respond quickly, and make their work scientific and modern.

In short, tourism resources survey is the first step in the development of tourism resources. The results of the survey are of positive significance for the scientific planning, rational development, modern management and environmental monitoring and protection of tourism resources.

2) The Content of the Tourism Resources Survey

Due to the wide variety of tourism resources, different causes and complex constituent elements, the investigation should pay attention to the various situations of tourism resources themselves, and also pay attention to the current situation and development trend of the external environment. Therefore, there are special technical requirements for the content of tourism resources survey and the collection of data.

3) Individual Survey of Tourism Resources

Individual survey includes the individual nature, morphology, structure, generation process, evolutionary history and composition of tourism resources. During the investigation, it is necessary to provide the distribution maps, photos, videos and other relevant materials of the tourism resources in the investigation area, as well as major historical events, celebrity activities, literary and artistic works related to the main tourism resources.

4) Tourism Resources and Environmental Investigation

Environmental investigation includes two parts: natural environment survey and human environment survey. The natural environment includes the rocks, strata, structures, landforms, hydrology, animals and plants, meteorological climate, etc. of the area; the human environment includes the historical evolution of the region, the economic environment, the social and cultural environment, the policy and regulation environment, etc.

5) Investigation on the Current Situation of Tourism Resources Protection and Development

The current status of protection refers to the preservation, protection measures and facilities of tourism resources in the region where the individual tourism resources are located; the development status refers to the current development status, projects, types, time, tourist trips, tourism revenues, and the development comparison and development plans of similar tourism resources in the surrounding areas.

2.2 Models, Procedures and Methods of Tourism Resources Investigation

2.2.1 Models of Investigation

According to the detailed degree of survey, tourism resources investigation can be divided into three types: broadly survey, general survey and detailed survey. These three investigation models are different in the purpose, scope and accuracy.

Broadly survey refers to a general survey of tourism resources in tourism regions based on the analysis and sorting of second-hand data limited by time, capital, human and material resources (Wang Degang, 2011). Broadly survey can simplify the working procedures. In particular, investigation teams may not be established if they are not needed, but the investigators should be appointed by the project organizations which they participate in. The collection of information is limited to the scope required for specific purposes. The filling of "questionnaire of object of tourism resources" is optional but not necessary. The sources of the broadly survey is numerous and complex, so it may be wrong or inaccurate, which is easy to cause deviation to the evaluation of resources in the region.

General survey refers to a detailed and comprehensive investigation of specific areas in order to provide necessary and scientific basis for the rational protection, development and utilization of tourism resources (Wang Degang, 2011). The data from general investigation are comprehensive and accurate, involving many aspects, but the workload is very large. Therefore, it takes a lot of manpower, material resources, financial resources and time.

Detailed investigation refers to the comprehensive investigation of tourism resources for the comprehensive purpose of regional tourism development (Yin Zesheng, 2006). The scope of detailed investigation is relatively small, but the goal is clear and the investigation is in-depth(as shown in Table 2-2). Thematic studies and discussions on key issues and locations are usually conducted through direct measurement, verification and the collection of basic information (Xiao Xing, 2013). Detailed investigation shall complete all the investigation procedures of tourism resources, including investigation preparation and field investigation. The objects of investigation include all objects of tourism resources, and the "questionnaire of object of tourism resources" of all objects should be submitted. The scope of data collection includes: ① various written description materials related to tourism resources objects and their environment, including local chronicles, local teaching materials, introduction of tourism areas and tourist spots, planning and special reports, etc.; ② various graphic materials related to the tourism resources survey area, especially thematic maps reflecting the tourism environment and tourism resources; ③ various photos and image materials related to the tourism resources survey area and tourism resources objects.

Table 2-2 Comparison of broadly investigation, general investigation and detailed investigation of tourismresources

Type	Broadly investigation	General investigation	Detailed investigation
Nature	Thematic	Regional	Regional
Purpose	Services for one or a few specific purposes of regional tourism development (e.g., tourism planning, project setting, resource protection, regulatory construction, marketing)	Lay a foundation for the evaluation and development of regional tourism resources	Serve the comprehensive purpose of regional tourism development, such as establishing a tourism resource database
Technical support	National standards or self-determined investigation technical regulations	The national standard	The national standard
Scope of application	It is applicable to the investigation of tourism resources in specific regions or special types.	It is applicable to the formulation of regional tourism development objectives, the planning and development of tourism resources, etc.	It is applicable to the investigation of tourism resources to understand and master the overall situation of tourism resources in the whole region.

Continue

Type	Broadly investigation	General investigation	Detailed investigation
Organizational form	Generally, there is no need to set up a special investigation team.	Set up a special investigation team with complete professional members	Set up a special investigation team with complete professional members
Operation model	Operate in accordance with the relevant procedures specified in the investigation; determine the investigation object and carry out the investigation according to the actual needs; It can simplify the working procedure.	Conduct a comprehensive survey of all tourism resources and implement all procedures set out in the survey	Conduct a comprehensive survey of all tourism resources and implement all procedures set out in the survey
Documents submitted	Some relevant documents and drawings	All documents and drawings required by the standard	All documents and drawings required by the standard
Use of results	The results directly serve the special task.	It lays the foundation for formulating the development goal of tourism and provides the basis for the planning and development of tourism resources.	It lays the foundation for formulating the development goal of tourism and provides the basis for the planning and development of tourism resources.

Source: Classification, Investigation and Evaluation of Tourism Resources (GB/T 18972-2017)

2.2.2 Procedures of Investigation

In order to ensure the efficiency and investigation quality, the tourism resources investigation must go through standardized procedures. Specifically, it generally includes the following three stages: the preparation stage, the implementation stage and the collation stage.

1) The Preparation Stage

The first step is to set up an investigation team. Members of the investigation team should have professional knowledge related to the tourism environment, tourism resources and tourism development in the investigation area. The investigation team generally includes professionals in tourism, environmental protection, geology, biology, architecture, landscape architecture, history and culture, etc. Team members should carry out technical training according to the requirements of investigation standards, and prepare various equipments needed for field investigation, such as location instruments, measuring instruments, cameras.

Secondly, the plan of tourism resources survey should be made, and the classification system and questionnaire of tourism resources should be drawn up. The investigation team can draw up a classification system of tourism resources and compile "questionnaire of object of tourism resources" based on the *Classification, Investigation and Evaluation of Tourism Resources* (GB/T 18972-2017).

2) The Implementation Stage

First, we should determine the investigation area and investigation route. The whole investigation area can be divided into several small investigation areas (zones). Investigation areas are generally divided by administrative districts (for example, investigation areas at the provincial level can be divided into small investigation areas according to the administrative districts at the prefecture-level division; investigation areas at the regional level can be divided into small investigation areas according to the administrative districts at the county-level division; investigation areas at the county level can be divided into small investigation areas according to the small administrative areas at the township-level division), or it can be divided according to the existing or planned tourism area. The investigation route shall be set up according to the actual requirements and shall run through all the investigation areas and the locations where the main objects of tourism resources are located.

Secondly, we should select the investigation objects. The following objects should be selected for key investigation: tourism resources monomers with tourism development prospects and obvious economic, social and cultural values; the representative part of the object of collective tourism resources; tourism resources objects representing the image of the survey area. The following objects of tourism resources should not be investigated temporarily: those with obvious low grade and no value for development and utilization; those in violation of the current laws and regulations of the state; those leading to environmental problems; those affecting the national economy and the people's livelihood; those located in specific areas.

Finally, we should fill in the "questionnaire of object of tourism resources". According to the requirements of the investigation plan and the arrangement of the work plan, the investigation of tourism resources should be carried out, primary and secondary data should be collected systematically, and a "questionnaire of object of tourism resources" should be filled out for each object.

3) The Collation Stage

First of all, the text, pictures, videos and data obtained through the investigation should be summarized and analyzed.

Secondly, according to the data, the detailed investigation of tourism resources should be filled in the actual data table of tourism resources investigation area, we should also draw the tourism resources map which reflects the current distribution of tourism resources, and compile the tourism resources investigation report. For the compilation content and requirements of the above documents (maps), please refer to the *Classification, Investigation and Evaluation of Tourism Resources* (GB/T 18972-2017).

Finally, the most important work in this stage is to complete the compilation of the tourism resources survey report, which is the analysis and summary of the investigation theme. Through the report, the outside world can understand the overall characteristics of the tourism resources in the investigation area and obtain important documents of special information and data. Tourism resources investigation report is an important basis for tourism planning.

2.2.3 Methods of Investigation

1) Literature Survey

This method is an indirect survey method. It is a method that collects various existing data and information of tourism resources and extracts the content related to resource survey items for analysis and research. The scope or sources of data generally includes local chronicles, folk customs, scenery and facts records, cultural relics, documents describing local culture, scenery and specialties, various planning and design materials, etc. Among them, local historical records are the documents that must be checked in the investigation of tourism resources.

2) Interview Survey

It is an auxiliary method of tourism resources investigation by visiting or holding a symposium, including two ways: direct and indirect interview. Direct interview refers to the direct conversation between the investigators and the relevant local departments, professional researchers, residents and tourists; indirect interview is a survey conducted to residents or tourists who are familiar with the situation through questionnaires and cards, and the results are provided in writing.

3) Field Survey

This method is the most basic method of investigation. Through observation, reconnaissance, measurement, recording, mapping, photographing and other forms, investigators can directly contact tourism resources, obtain valuable first-hand information and more objective perceptual knowledge of professionals. The results are detailed and reliable. Investigators are required to be diligent in observation, good at discovery, and record, fill in maps, photograph and summarize in time.

4) Remote Sensing Survey

The application of modern science and technology has brought a lot of convenience to the investigation of tourism resources. At present, some computer technology such as "3S" high-tech has been applied to the tourism resources survey, which improves the efficiency and accuracy of the survey. Specifically, "3S" high-tech includes geographic information systems (GIS), remote sensing (RS) and global positioning systems (GPS), which are often abbreviated to "3S" technologies in China. The GPS is basically a series of satellites that orbit the earth broadcasting signals picked up by a system of receivers. By triangulating the data received from at least four satellites, it is possible to determine a receiver's location. The GIS is a system that creates, manages, analyzes, and maps all types of data. The GIS connects data to a map, integrating location data (where things are) with all types of descriptive information (what things are like there). It helps users understand patterns, relationships, and geographic context. The RS is the process of detecting and monitoring the physical characteristics of an area by measuring its reflected and emitted radiation at a distance (typically from satellite or aircraft). Special cameras collect remotely sensed images, which can help researchers "sense" things about the earth. GPS and RS provide regional information and spatial positioning to GIS, while GIS can carry out corresponding spatial analysis at the same time. These three technologies are visual, scientific and efficient, so they play an important role in tourism resources investigation.

2.3 Evaluation of Tourism Resources

The investigation and evaluation of tourism resources are prepared for development and utilization, and their practical significance is ultimately reflected in the development of the tourism industry.

Tourism resources evaluation is to scientifically determine and evaluate the value of tourism resources themselves and the value of tourism development and utilization according to certain standards and principles on the basis of resources survey. Tourism resources evaluation directly provides a theoretical basis for tourism resources development and planning and serves the development practice of tourism industry, and it is an important link in the development and utilization of tourism resources. Scientific and accurate evaluation is an important means to overcome the blindness of tourism resource planning and construction, and enhance the efficiency of resources development and utilization. The scientific and practical evaluation directly affects the degree of regional tourism development and long-term development.

Chinese tourism resources evaluation began in the early 1980s, after more than 20 years of development, it has formed a set of evaluation theories and methods. However, theoretical evaluation can not really be effectively connected with practice because tourism

Chapter 2 Content and Method of Tourism Resource Investigation and Evaluation

practice and theoretical research have always been in the process of continuous change and improvement.

2.3.1 Purpose and Content of the Evaluation

1) Purpose of Evaluation

Tourism resources evaluation is a necessary step for the development of tourism resources, and the results of tourism resources evaluation will have a direct impact on the direction of tourism resources development and utilization, and construction and development of tourism destinations, which is an important basis for judging whether the project is feasible or not. The evaluation of tourism resources must first determine the purpose of the evaluation, usually, the purpose of tourism resources evaluation includes the following aspects.

First, through the evaluation of the basic physical attributes, potential functions and development environment of tourism resources in a certain area, development value and development goals are determined.

Second, through the specific evaluation of a certain type or a certain region of tourism resources, scientific development and management decisions are determined.

Third, through the comprehensive evaluation of tourism resources in a certain area, feasibility demonstration and specific planning are carried out, and the leading resources of this area are determined, as well as the goals, scale and sequence of tourism development.

Fourth, through the comprehensive evaluation and characteristic analysis of tourism resources in a certain region, the image design and marketing planning of regional tourism are carried out, and the promotion strategy and target market are determined.

2) Evaluation Content

The specific content of the tourism resources evaluation varies depending on the purpose of the evaluation. However, in general, the content of the evaluation of tourism resources basically does not exceed the following scope.

(1) Basic physical properties.

The basic physical properties of resources vary depending on the types of resources, generally speaking, including the types and characteristics of tourism resources, structure and quality, scale and capacity, preservation status and other factors. The basic physical properties of resources determine the appropriate product form, degree of development and scale of tourism resources.

(2) Attractiveness.

Attractiveness includes the beauty of tourism resources, pleasure, culture, peculiarity, popularity and other factors. The value of tourism resources lies in the fact that they can be developed into tourism products, so the evaluation of their value should not only include their own attributes, but also combine their own attributes with the psychological scale of tourists. The attractiveness of tourism resources determines the value of their suitable development.

(3) Functional characteristics.

The potential function of tourism resources is the basis of tourism development, and the important content of tourism resources evaluation is to determine the functional characteristics of tourism resources themselves to provide a realistic basis for tourism development.

(4) Source market conditions.

Source market conditions include the actual distance from the main source of tourists, the traffic conditions and communication conditions of the source area, the population and travel level in the source area, the relationship with the neighboring tourist places, the tourism demand of tourists in the source area and other tourist source conditions. The market conditions of tourist sources are also an important decision-making basis for the development of tourism resources.

(5) Regional tourism development environment.

Regional tourism development environment includes regional economic, social and environmental conditions, such as finance (investment), human (labor), material resources (property and material supply), infrastructure and construction land, construction conditions, existing service facilities, leadership and economic decision-making departments which attach importance to tourism development, regional development degree and foreign exchange traditions, health and health conditions, public security conditions, ecological environment carrying capacity, the stability of the current ecological environment, tourism economy development, social and environmental benefits and other factors. Tourism is a highly relevant and dependent industry, and tourism resources are the basic basis for the development of tourism in a region, the effect of tourism resources development directly affects the development of local tourism, so it is necessary to comprehensively consider all relevant factors to ensure the good benefits of tourism resources development in the process of tourism resources development planning.

2.3.2 Evaluation Criteria and Principles

1) Evaluation Criteria

From the perspective of tourism development, the evaluation criteria of tourism resources mainly include three aspects: professional standards, tourism development standards and market standards.

(1) Professional standards.

Professional standards are the evaluation of the value of tourism resources in a particular area.

Since tourism resources have different natures and types, and these resources are usually the more excellent, prominent and distinctive parts of each field, they are usually evaluated first in their field of value, and their value is determined with a professional perspective.

For natural tourism resources, it is necessary to evaluate them according to aesthetic standards first, and then evaluate the value of their sightseeing tours by analyzing the aesthetic characteristics and aesthetics of the landscape environment and scenery.

For humanistic tourism resources, it is necessary to measure through social standards and historical standards, which determines the value of the resources themselves contained in the historical weight and social and cultural content. In general, the value is higher because of the more social representative things and the longer history resources. For new humanities industry tourism resources such as public facilities, buildings, factories, gardens, it needs to be evaluated according to its characteristics, excellence, and function within the scope of its original ownership.

The level of professional standard evaluation is not completely equivalent to the value of tourism development, because the evaluation criteria in some professional fields are often not completely coupled with the value orientation pursued by tourism development.

(2) Tourism development standards.

Tourism resources are the source of tourism products and the objects of tourism activities, tourism resources value assessment needs to be based on the degree and effect of their development and utilization for tourism. Although some resources are unique in the field and have a high value, their tourism value may be greatly reduced because of their professional characteristics that are not suitable for tourism development.

The value orientations highlighted in tourism development standards include: ① the function of tourism resources; ② the possibility of transforming tourism resources into tourism products; ③ policies and economic conditions for the development of tourism resources.

(3) Market standards.

Market standards, that is, the attractiveness of tourism resources relative to tourists, are evaluated from the perspective of tourists' psychological induction. Although the professional value of some resources is very high and suitable for tourism development and utilization, they limit the development of the source market after developing tourism products because of excessive professionalism and the narrow range of attractive groups, so that their value is greatly discounted. The value of resources depends on the value of the product, the attractiveness of tourism resources to tourists is an important measure of their value evaluation, the greater the attraction, the higher the value. Therefore, from the perspective of tourism development, professional standards in the evaluation of tourism resources should be subordinate to market standards.

In the early stage of tourism evaluation research, the evaluation of tourism resources is only the evaluation of the physical attributes of the resources themselves, that is, professional evaluation, and later, many scholars and experts are more inclined to combine the physical attributes evaluation of tourism resources with the psychological evaluation of tourists. Combining the above standards and comprehensively evaluating tourism resources from a professional, developmental and market perspective can we truly face development and benefit practical work. At the same time, we should also note that due to the different purposes of evaluation and the different contents of evaluation, the evaluation criteria will also be different, so it is not possible to generalize easily.

2) Evaluation Principles

(1) The principle of seeking truth from facts.

Only according to the actual situation and objective evaluation, the evaluation results can be true and effective, which can really guide the tourism development planning smoothly, otherwise, they can only increase the tortuous degree of development, resulting in a huge waste of materials, manpower and funds, and may even lead to the complete failure of resources development. And redevelopment work is difficult to carry out, resulting in irreparable losses.

(2) The principle of scientific norms.

Generally speaking, the evaluation of tourism resources is a highly technical work, which must pay attention to scientific norms and be carried out in an orderly manner according to scientific methods and means and standardized procedures.

(3) Development-oriented principles.

The evaluation of tourism resources should serve the development practice of tourism resources, so the methods and systems of tourism resources evaluation must follow the development-oriented principles and pay attention to practicality and effectiveness, which is conducive to the smooth progress of development.

2.2.3 Evaluation Methods

The evaluation of tourism resources is an extremely complex work. On the one hand, because tourism resources themselves are all-encompassing, it is difficult to adopt unified evaluation standards; on the other hand, due to the influence of subjective factors, people of different nationalities, occupations, ages and cultural backgrounds often have different aesthetic standards. Nevertheless, people are still working tirelessly to study and develop optimized evaluation methods, so that the evaluation of tourism resources continues to make progress. At present, there are many methods of evaluation of tourism resources, but in general, there are no more than two types: qualitative evaluation and quantitative evaluation.

In the early stage of the evaluation of tourism resources in China, there are mainly empirical evaluation and one-factor evaluation, and in the near future, the main evaluation mathematical models will be established, considering the combination of qualitative and quantitative multi-factors. The early empirical evaluation method includes the "three-three-six" evaluation method, and the one-factor evaluation includes climate suitability evaluation, beach and bathing evaluation, cave evaluation and ski evaluation, etc.; in the later stage, there are mainly hierarchical analysis methods, fuzzy mathematical methods, index evaluation methods, comprehensive scoring methods, value engineering methods, etc.

1) Qualitative Evaluation Method

The so-called qualitative evaluation refers to the qualitative description of the quality of tourism resources made by the evaluator according to his subjective impression and inherent value after investigation. The subjective color and empirical color of qualitative evaluation are stronger, and its scientificity and accuracy are therefore limited, but this method has the advantages of saving time and effort, simplicity and ease, and is more suitable for those projects with small investment, small scale and short cycle.

2) Quantitative Evaluation Method

Quantitative evaluation is an evaluation made after conducting in-depth and meticulous investigation and analysis of tourism resources and related actual conditions and using mathematical methods to quantitatively calculate. Compared with qualitative evaluation, quantitative evaluation can make a scientific evaluation of tourism resources more objectively, so it is the development trend and research direction of tourism resources evaluation, but at the same time, this method is more complex and difficult, the technical requirements of evaluators are higher, and its development history is relatively short, which determines that the work of quantitative evaluation has a long way to go. In practice, it is necessary to prevent the breeding and influence of a bad tendency, that is, the blind pursuit of quantification and digitization. In fact, quantitative evaluation is based on qualitative evaluation, and the two evaluation methods cooperate and complement with each other. The tourism resources are first qualitatively described, and then the quantitative indicators are quantified through quantitative analysis, and finally the quantitative calculation results are converted into qualitative conclusions, that is, the so-called "qualitative-quantitative-qualitative".

Case 2-1

Chapter Review

This chapter mainly introduces the content and method of tourism resources investigation and evaluation.

Tourism resources survey is the first step in the development of resources of tourist places. The results of the survey have positive significance for the scientific planning, rational development, modern management, environmental monitoring and protection of tourism resources.

Case 2-2

Broadly investigation, general investigation and detailed investigation are three types of tourism resources investigation. Tourism survey mainly includes three stages: the preparation stage, the implementation stage and the collation stage of tourism resources investigation.

The central content is the criteria, evaluation system, evaluation level and evaluation basis of tourism resources evaluation, which is the premise of tourism resources development and provides a reliable basis for the preparation of tourism planning. The ultimate aim is to develop and utilize tourism resources effectively and make the development more effective.

 Questions for Discussion

1. What are the models of tourism resources investigation? What are the characteristics of each?

2. What are the objectives and principles of tourism resources evaluation and what are the criteria?

3. How are tourism resources evaluated?

4. How to view the importance of tourism resources survey?

Chapter 3
Development and Protection of Tourism Resources

Learning Objectives

(1) Understand the principles, characteristics and content of tourism resources development.

(2) Understand the basic theory of tourism resources development.

(3) Understand the development model and procedure of tourism resources.

(4) Understand the destructive factors of tourism resources.

(5) Learning tourism resources management.

(6) Understand the protection measures and resources restoration of tourism resources.

(7) Understand the sustainable development of tourism resources.

Technical Words

English Words	中文翻译
tourism resources development	旅游资源开发
destructive factors of tourism resources	旅游资源破坏性因素
sustainable development	可持续发展
tourism environmental capacity	旅游环境容量

Knowledge Graph

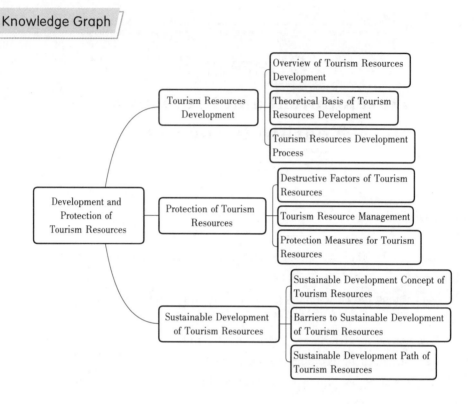

3.1 Tourism Resources Development

There are various types of tourism resources and various formation mechanisms which are closely related to the natural and social environment, and they have their own development and evolution laws. Only by mastering and understanding the causes, development and evolution laws of various types of tourism resources, can it be possible to carry out a reasonable and deep development of tourism resources, so tourism resources can fully and sustainably serve the development of tourism(Wu Bihu and Yu Xi, 2010).

3.1.1 Overview of Tourism Resources Development

Tourism resources are the object of tourism activities and the material basis on which tourism development depends. As the basis of tourism development, tourism resources need to be developed into tourism products in order to play its economic and social benefits. With the development of tourism, the number of tourists is gradually increasing, and the demand for tourists is becoming more diversified and personalized. Tourism resources development refers to the economic and technological system engineering that takes tourism development as the main purpose, takes market demand as the guidance, and uses tourism resources in an organized and planned way by improving and enhancing the attractiveness of tourism resources to tourists. The purpose of tourism resources development is to develop tourism, and the essence is to deeply tap the connotation value of tourism resources, improve its attractiveness, and make tourism resources become a real tourist attraction.

1) Principles of Tourism Resources Development

(1) Ecological principle.

Since the emergence of mankind, it has not been able to deal with the relationship between resources development and environmental protection. Tourism resources are rooted in the natural and social ecosystem where they are located, and only tourism resources that coordinate with the ecological environment can be sustainable development.

First of all, the tourism resources development that does not affect or less affect the ecological environment of tourism projects, especially in the fragile ecological zone of tourism resource development, should put the ecosystem balance and environmental protection in the first consideration.

Secondly, attention should be paid to the coordination between the development of tourism resources and the surrounding social and ecological environment, so as to maintain its original atmosphere and environment and protect the charm of attracting tourists. Otherwise, the process of tourism resources development is the process of tourism resources destruction.

(2) Coordination principle.

The principle of coordination is the rational requirement of tourism resources development. The comprehensive and coordinated development requires the tourism resources developers to correctly handle the relationship between the reality and the future, economic development and resource and environment protection, tourism and other industries. It requires that the tourism resources development must emphasize the overall benefits, the ecological environment and social welfare, and must comprehensively coordinate the complex relationship among economic benefits, social benefits and environmental benefits, so that the tourism industry can develop in an all-round way. Tourism is not only a cultural economic industry, but also an economic cultural industry and a resource consumption industry closely related to the environment and ecology. This requires that the economic interests pursued by tourism resources development should be controlled within a certain limit, that is, it should not only focus on economic benefits, but also ensure the stability and harmony of the living order of residents and tourists in the tourist area, and more importantly, protect the environment and ecology of the tourist area.

(3) Aesthetic principle.

Tourism is an aesthetic activity. The development of tourism resources is a process of discovering beauty, displaying beauty and creating beauty. In the design and development, the principle of aesthetics should be fully used to organically integrate the natural beauty, artistic beauty and conceptual beauty, create a poetic tourism environment to let tourists stay there, get a full range of aesthetic enjoyment and spiritual pleasure, and strive to achieve a harmonious layout of the tourism area, smooth tourism line and harmonious tourism atmosphere.

(4) Market principle.

The market is the driving force of tourism resources development. The development of tourism resources should be market-oriented. In tourism planning, it is necessary to fully study the economic feasibility, the risk of investment and the expected benefits. We should follow the law of supply and demand in market development and determine the level, scale and direction of development. On the basis of thorough market research, we should understand the needs of tourists and the development trend of the macro tourism market. We should also understand the current and future interest points of tourists(Zhao Yuan, 2013).

(5) Characteristic principle.

Characteristics are the life of tourism resources development. Seeking difference is one of the main reasons for tourists' tourism motivation. The tourist attractions with personality are more attractive to people than those without personality, and can achieve better economic and social benefits under the same conditions. In fact, characteristics have become the first vitality of the survival and development of tourist attractions. In the development of tourism resources, it is necessary to constantly explore new and unique natural or cultural things for tourism, highlight local characteristics and give full play to local advantages; it is necessary to highlight the characteristics of the times and the historical characteristics; it is necessary to highlight the aesthetic characteristics of art, the distinctive ethnic customs, and the unique culture and art to occupy the market(Liu Junmei, Tian Xiaoxia and Yan Min, 2012). In addition, the pursuit of characteristics does not require a single development. In view of the diversification of tourism consumption structure, when developing tourism resources, we should diversify from form to content on the basis of highlighting characteristics.

(6) Cultural principle.

Culture is the soul of tourism resources development. On the one hand, whether tourism products can attract tourist depends on whether the resources themselves have a high value; on the other hand, it depends on whether the culture it shows can bring tourists beautiful enjoyment and pleasure. The development of human tourism resources should take culture as the core, and the development of natural tourism resources also requires to improve its cultural grade(Liu Wei and Lü Bing, 2018). In the process of development, it is necessary to tap the cultural connotation of the resources, enrich the cultural content of the resources, enhance the cultural atmosphere of the tourism area, improve the viewing, education and enlightenment functions of the scenic spots, and create a high-quality tourism culture that can shake the hearts of the people.

2) The Characteristics of Tourism Resources Development

In addition to retaining the general characteristics of traditional tourism resources, the development of tourism resources should also show the characteristics of tourism resources value, tourism resources utilization, tourism resources development, tourism resources efficiency and tourism resources space.

(1) Characteristics of tourism resources value.

In the new era, the tourism consumption model is developing from sightseeing to sightseeing, leisure, vacation, recreation and so on. The rationality of tourism resources allocation, the transformation and upgrading of industrial structure, the realization of cultural value and the protection of the ecological environment are increasingly prominent (Jin Yingruo, 2004). It has become a strategic pillar industry of the national economy. Compared with other single forms of natural resources, tourism resources are a complex concept. The elements in the tourism resources system are interdependent and interact with each other, forming an organic whole with complex structure and comprehensive value. Under the background of the new era, different space-time structures and different combinations of elements will produce different economic values, social values and ecological values, resulting in the gradual transformation of tourism resources into tourism assets and tourism assets into tourism capital(Yao Lan, 2014).

(2) Characteristics of tourism resources utilization.

Tourism resources have a life cycle, and different economic and social development stages have different demands on tourism resources, so the development, allocation, utilization and value of tourism resources are limited by time. Only timely development can tap the maximum effectiveness of tourism resources. With the changes of the external environment, the characteristics of tourist demand and market competition, tourism resources are changing in the process of "innovation and renewal". They are always developing and changing. They have the open attributes of creativity, transformation and expansion(Li Qinglei, Xu Lei and Wang Yu, 2012). In addition, people's tourism needs are increasingly diversified and personalized, and their understanding of tourism resources is also changing. Tourism resources are constantly being created while they are being developed and utilized(Yan Yingna, Zhou Xianshu and Liu Likui, 2016). Only through reasonable development, utilization and protection of tourism resources can we improve the efficiency of resources utilization and give full play to greater comprehensive benefits. Governments at all levels should adhere to the equal emphasis on the development, utilization and protection of tourism resources, and promote the intensive, efficient, rational use and effective integration of tourism resources through the innovation of ideas, systems and technologies, so as to achieve the sustainable development of tourism(Han

Fang and Parhati Azimu, 2006).

(3) Characteristics of tourism resources development.

Any "combination and integration" of economic resources, social resources and tourism resources is likely to breed new tourism products, tourism formats, business models and lifestyles, and the tourism industry will drive the comprehensive development of regional economy and society(Yuan Chunqing, 1998). There is symbiosis among cultural resources, scientific and technological resources, agricultural resources, ecological resources and tourism resources. Using the new generation of information technology to develop tourism resources in depth, deepening the "tourism +" cross-border integration, and cultivating new tourism formats and new kinetic energy are the inevitable requirements for the transformation and upgrading of the tourism industry, the upgrading of tourism products, and the improvement of tourism service quality(Wu Guoqing, 2022). With the in-depth development of the tourism industry, new tourism models such as virtual tourism and novel tourism are emerging. The integration of tourism, culture, sports, transportation, industry, agriculture and medicine has become an inevitable trend.

(4) Characteristics of tourism resources efficiency.

Consumer demand is the main engine of economic growth, and the release of consumer potential and expansion of consumer demand are important means to promote high-quality economy development. Under the background of building a new dual cycle development pattern, the importance of promoting consumption and expanding domestic demand is further enhanced, and it is urgent to cultivate new economic growth points. Tourism has economic attributes, social and ecological functions, with the characteristics of great driving effect, high industrial relevance and low input-output ratio. With the rapid development of tourism, the role of tourism in promoting economic development is constantly improving. It is an important industry for stable growth, promoting consumption, expanding domestic demand and benefiting people's livelihood. The development of tourism can change people's consumption concept, consumption habit and consumption structure, promote the continuous increase of social employment, promote the optimization and upgrading of industrial structure and improve the ecological environment. In a word, improving the ability of sustainable development and utilization of tourism resources and accelerating the development of tourism industry can achieve greater economic, social and ecological benefits.

(5) Characteristics of tourism resources space.

Tourism resources are regional and immovable in space. Natural and traditional tourist attractions in many places are not popular. Tourism resources in various places have no complementary effect in a certain area(Li Qinlei, Sun Shengnan and Sun Ruitao, 2018). The flow of tourism resources is the process of realizing the space-time allocation of tourism resources, including the geographic spatial displacement of tourism resources under the effect of resource potential energy, and the transformation process of tourism resources form, function and value. The rapid development of modern vehicles such as airplanes, G-series High-speed train and expressways has accelerated the cross regional flow of tourism resources, shortened the distance between scenic spots, and accelerated the reasonable flow of population, materials and information (Meng Aiyun, 2013). In addition, the rapid development of the new generation of information technology has broken through the limitation of traditional time and space, reduced the dependence on traditional tourism resources, accelerated the visual expression of tourism resources information, broken the traditional spatial organization model of tourism elements, formed a new regional spatial organization form, and finally realized the replacement of place space by mobile space(Li Minghan, Liang Hua, Bao Guikun, 2013).

3) Contents of Tourism Resources Development

(1) Analysis of the background conditions.

It includes the geographical locations, natural conditions, historical evolution, social and economic basis and constraints of the tourism resources.

(2) The evaluation of tourism resources.

According to the survey of tourism resources, qualitative and quantitative evaluation is carried out, and the nature, type, scale, characteristics, value and development conditions of tourism resources are obtained.

(3) Tourism market demand forecasting and expansion planning.

The development of the tourism market includes the real market and the potential market. It is necessary to dynamically forecast the scale, quantity, source area and attraction radius of the tourism market demand, and formulate corresponding marketing strategies to expand the source area and develop various tourism markets.

(4) Determining the theme and image of tourism development.

On the basis of the above planning, the basic principles of the guiding ideology, nature, characteristics, creativity, planning and overall concept of the development planning of the tourism area, and the theme of the development planning of the tourism area are determined. And a distinctive tourism image is formed.

(5) The division of functional areas of land use structure and the organization of lines.

The tourism land structure organization is divided into three categories, namely, directly providing service land for tourists, tourism media construction land, and indirectly providing service land for tourists. The principle of functional area division is to highlight the functions and characteristics of the landscape, and the area is generally divided into landscape viewing area, leisure and entertainment area, field activity area, recuperation and holiday area, service center area, professional park, non-staple food supply area, natural protection area, etc. And then we can design these functional areas and their routes to contact with the outside world. The design needs to consider the organization of the tour, the choice and demand of the transport, the arrangement of the tour time and the arrangement of the tour route.

(6) Tourism service facilities planning.

It includes the evaluation of the current situation of travel agencies, tourist hotels, medical care, commercial services, and recreational facilities, and the planning of hierarchical distribution, scale and prediction.

(7) Tourism infrastructures planning.

It includes tourism transportation planning, power and energy planning, post and telecommunication planning, water supply and drainage planning, sewage treatment planning, green lake planning, flood control planning, etc.

(8) Tourism environment capacity analysis and environment planning.

It includes capacity analysis of tourism environment, environmental protection and sustainable development, division of protected areas and key points of protection, etc.

(9) Tourism products development planning.

The development of tourism products should adapt to the market demand and the sustainable development level of the local economy, and seize the opportunity to promote. The development should have a sense of advance, to do "others do not have and I have", "others also have, I do better than others", and "others have advantages, but I have my own characteristics".

(10) Training plan for employees.

It includes the current situation of human resources, demand forecasting, and guiding ideology and objectives of talent training. In the planning, the number and type of tourism service personnel needed should be considered.

(11) Tourism information network planning.

It includes the guiding ideology of information network development, project planning and development strategy.

(12) Divided planning and investment benefit evaluation.

It includes stage planning and construction projects, tourism investment planning, investment benefit analysis, and comprehensive evaluation.

(13) Tourism management planning.

It includes the management system of investment, development and operation of tourism areas, the setting of management institutions, management functions and the formulation of policies and laws, which can ensure the smooth development of tourism resources.

(14) The map of tourism planning.

It generally includes tourism resources distribution map, traffic location map, development status map, overall planning map, land use planning map, protection planning map, green space planning map, tour route map, project pipeline map, tourism service facility map, staged planning map, and detailed planning map.

3.1.2 Theoretical Basis of Tourism Resources Development

1) The Theory of Tourism Destination Life Cycle

The development process of tourism destination generally includes 6 stages: exploration, start, development, stability, stagnation and decline or recovery. The development of tourism economy or tourism destination itself is affected by the objective life cycle law. The essence of the life cycle of tourism destination is the life cycle of tourism product. How to break the destiny of the life cycle is the key and difficult point in the process of tourism resources growth and development. What's more, the life cycle of tourism destination is an objective phenomenon(Xie Zeming, 2022).

2) The Theory of Location

Location refers to the location of relevant objects, including natural geographical location, traffic geographical location and economic geographical location. Location factors include natural factors, economic and technological factors, social and political factors(Zhu Guiping, 2012). After introducing the location theory into tourism development research, its principle plays an important role in guiding the development of tourism resources. Many regional factors, such as competition and cooperation, accessibility and tourist resources market of tourist destinations, affect the development level, development type, tourism transportation route layout, tourism spatial layout and other important issues of tourism resources. Therefore, the study of location status in tourism development planning is an important work.

3) The Theory of Competitiveness

In the 1980s, Professor Michael Porter of Harvard Business School proposed the theory of competitive advantage. Competitiveness refers to the ability of economic entities to provide products and services with high cost and satisfaction to the market by occupying resources with comparative advantages and creating more competitive production factors and production environment on this basis, and also to obtain higher income. The theory mainly includes: the core of competition is industrial competition; industrial structure and industrial positioning are strategic elements; the basic competitive advantages include low cost and differentiation; the areas of competition include product specifications, varieties, circulation, customer types and sales areas; if an enterprise focuses its competitive field on an industrial sector, it will be likely to gain a competitive advantage; enterprises gain competitive advantages through innovation; the sustainability of competitive advantage lies in the level, the type and the update of advantage. The theory of competitiveness plays an important role in dealing with the competition and cooperation of tourism products in the development of tourism resources(Yang Zhenzhi, Chenjin, 2008).

4) The Theory of Landscape Aesthetics

As an objective natural resource, landscape is composed of shape, line and color and presents different aesthetic characteristics. Landscape aesthetics is the demand of people for the environment(Chen Yan'guang and Wang Yiming, 1997). Different people have different aesthetic standards for the understanding of beauty, and people's aesthetic views in different times are also different. With the improvement of material living standards, people's aesthetic requirements for the landscape environment gradually improve. How to fully tap the beauty of nature, history, culture, science and place in scenic spots, world cultural and natural heritage sites, forest park, geopark, important wetlands and cultural relics protection units, etc. is an important topic for tourism resources development.

3.1.3 Tourism Resources Development Process

The development process of tourism resources generally includes three main links: tourism resources investigation and evaluation, tourism resources development planning and tourism resources development and implementation.

1) Tourism Resources Investigation and Evaluation

(1) The significance of tourism resources investigation.

Through the investigation of tourism resources, the system grasps the current situation of tourism resources, completes the basic work for the development of tourism resources, and grasps reliable first-hand materials; through the investigation of tourism resources, a large number of survey data and information can be scientifically analyzed, the false and the true can be removed, and the nature and authenticity of tourism resources can be restored; through the in-depth investigation of tourism resources and its external development conditions, it can provide detailed and reliable materials for determining the development direction, development focus and corresponding management measures of the resources; through the investigation of tourism resources, the utilization status of tourism resources and some relevant data are mastered, and the tourism resources that have the development and utilization potential and meet the needs of tourists are developed in a timely and scientific way; through the investigation of tourism resources, the basic information obtained is of great reference value to regional economic development and tourism management; through the regular survey of tourism resources, we can dynamically grasp the development and utilization of tourism resources, so that the local tourism management department can timely and accurately provide the decision-making basis for the development of the tourism industry.

(2) The significance of tourism resources evaluation.

Through the evaluation of tourism resources, it clarifies a number of factors and external conditions affecting the development and utilization of tourism resources, accurately reflects the overall value of tourism resources, and provides scientific basis for the rational development and utilization, planning and construction(Ren Xi, 2014); through the evaluation of tourism resources, it highlights the characteristics of tourism resources, promotes competitive products, and sets up the tourism image of famous brand products in the market; through the evaluation of tourism resources and playing geographical advantages, the tourism resources are screened, the design and planning ideas are designed, and the order of tourism project development is determined(Li Jingyi, 1997).

2) Tourism Resources Development Planning

On the basis of tourism resources investigation, evaluation and development feasibility study, tourism resources planning is formulated first, and then the feasibility of development can be demonstrated. The content of the planning may vary according to the nature of resources, the purpose of utilization, and the way of development, but the basic content is generally the same, mainly including the nature of the tourist area, the scope and scale of the planning, the phased implementation goals of the planning, the overall project layout, the special planning of infrastructure services, the analysis of the tourist market, the estimation of investment benefits and many other aspects(Ma Yaofeng, Song Baoping and Zhao Zhenbin, 2017).

3) Tourism Resources Development and Implementation

First of all, in the stage of tourism resources planning, it puts forward measures, programs and steps for the implementation of the plan, including policy support, management system, publicity and promotion, financing methods, education and training.

Secondly, it writes the draft of the planning text, notes and attachments, and analyzes the overall investment of the planning implementation, including the investment and output analysis of tourism facilities construction, supporting infrastructure construction, tourism market development, human resources development and other aspects.

Thirdly, it puts forward the implementation steps, measures and methods of the master plan, as well as the management opinions in planning, construction and operation.

Fourthly, after the tourism planning text, map and attachment are discussed and approved by the planning review meeting, and revised according to the review comments, the entrusting party shall report for approval and implementation according to the relevant procedures.

3.2 Protection of Tourism Resources

Tourism resources are the basis for the development of tourism. The sustainable development of tourism must do a good job in the protection of tourism resources. The protection of tourism resources not only includes the protection of tourism resources themselves, which can ensure that they are not damaged and their characteristics are not weakened, but also involves the protection of the natural ecological environment around them(Liu Yanglin, Liu Shuyun and Chen Xihong, 2010). If the tourism resources are not effectively protected or even damaged, the tourism industry will become a water without source and a tree without roots. To protect tourism resources is to protect tourism. Tourism resources are fragile, they are mostly precious heritage left by nature and human culture, which is not only vulnerable to destruction, but also has the non‑renewable characteristics(Chen Yi, 2007). At present, while developing and utilizing tourism resources, all countries in the world attach great importance to the protection of tourism resources and regard it as the fundamental guarantee for the sustainable development of tourism.

3.2.1 Destructive Factors of Tourism Resources

1) Natural Destructive Factors

(1) Geological disasters.

Earthquakes, landslides, collapses, subsidence, mudslides, volcanoes and so on are all geological disasters. Among them, the influence range of earthquakes and volcanoes is large, and the probability of geological disasters in mountain tourism areas is large.

(2) Natural weathering.

Under the influence of solar radiation, atmosphere, water and biology, the form and nature of tourism resources will be changed slowly, that is, natural weathering. There are mainly two forms: mechanical weathering and chemical weathering which have a destructive effect on tourism resources.

(3) Air pollution.

Due to the serious coal dust in the air and the excessive acid substances in the rainfall, the tourism resources suffer from serious pollution and erosion.

(4) Meteorological disasters.

Typhoon, rainstorm, hail, fog, flood, sandstorm and other meteorological disasters will damage tourism resources and tourism environment.

(5) Biological hazards.

Some animals and plants will also have a certain destructive effect on tourism resources. For example, termites harm houses, cultural relics, dams and human safety.

2) Human Destructive Factors

(1) War damage.

The war's damage to cultural relics is devastating. The Old Summer Palace burned by the British and French allied forces was known as the "garden of ten thousand gardens". It was a treasure of the world's garden art. Unfortunately, after the treasure was ransacked in 1860, only a few remains are left.

(2) Economic and urban constructive damage.

In the process of economic development and urban construction, many buildings that are not in harmony with cultural relics and historic sites have been built, damaging the tourism landscape and atmosphere, and even directly demolishing and damaging tourism resources.

(3) Damage caused by improper tourism development and planning.

In the economic activities of tourism development, improper planning will also damage the ecological balance, affect the tourism landscape and lose the characteristics of tourism resources(Zhang Lanxia, Wang Zhiwen, 1997). For example, Dali in Yunnan is a relatively complete ancient city in China, which is the first batch of historical and cultural cities announced by the state. But in the process of its tourism development, due to one-sided consideration of the stone floor of the ancient city, which is not conducive to the travel of tourist vehicles, the stone road was changed to asphalt road, which is incompatible with the style of the ancient city and destroys the characteristics of the ancient city. Some famous scenic mountains have obviously shown a trend of urbanization, for example, buildings of Lushan Mountain have been covered everywhere, just like a mountain city. A large number of artificial landscapes were set up in some caves, which destroyed the natural atmosphere.

(4) Destruction of tourists themselves.

Due to the arrival of a large number of tourists, especially in the tourist peak season, the dust they bring in, their breath, feet, the touch of their hands, the camera flash and so on cause harm to tourism resources. For example, the color of the murals in the Mogao Grottoes of Dunhuang gradually faded, or even peeled off.

(5) Damage caused by poor management.

When building houses, roads and laying lawns in the scenic area, the natural landscape will be damaged, soil erosion will be intensified, and biological communities will be reduced, forming a simple and fragile artificial ecosystem. Due to the poor management and protection of the scenic spots, the cultural relics and historic sites are artificially destroyed.

(6) Tourism destinations are negatively affected in terms of humanities and social environment.

Tourism activities are essentially a social and cultural phenomenon. There are big differences between tourists and local residents in terms of speech and behavior, dress, religious beliefs, and life concepts(Ren Chanjuan, 2008). The interaction between the two is both positive and negative. The influx of a large number of tourists will damage the peaceful social living environment of local residents, causing traffic congestion, price hikes, and disruption of daily life, all of which cause local residents' dissatisfaction and aversion to the tourism industry. Due to the cultural penetration brought by tourists, it will also change the local folk customs, and even be assimilated by foreign cultures, and the mystique that attracts tourists is also gradually disappearing. Living habits have been changed, the simple folk custom has become a strong commercial atmosphere, and the national culture and art gradually lose their characteristics(Yu Juan, 2013).

3.2.2 Tourism Resource Management

1) Tourism Resource Information Management

Tourism resources information refers to all kinds of information generated in the process of people's investigation, research and management of tourism resources, which has the characteristics of regional differences, timeliness, comprehensiveness and hierarchy. Tourism resources information management is a strategic management of tourism resources background, evaluation, development, planning, control, integration, utilization and other related information. Its essence is the decision-making, planning, organization, coordination and control of information production, information resources construction and allocation, information integration and development, transmission services, absorption and utilization of various information elements (personnel, funds, technical equipment, institutional environment, etc.), so as to effectively meet the needs of tourists, tour operators and tour managers for tourism resources and information.

2) Quality Management of Tourism Resources

Joseph M.Juran, a famous quality management master in the United States, believes that quality is applicability, that is, the extent to which customers' requirements are successfully met in the process of product use. Quality is the combination of the characteristics and quality of a product or service, which will affect the ability of a product to meet various obvious or implied needs. And quality management is to command and control the coordinated activities related to quality, including the development of quality policies, quality objectives, quality planning, quality control, quality assurance and quality improvement. The quality of tourism resources refers to the degree to which the inherent characteristics of individual or combination of tourism resources meet the needs, including three elements of tourism resources type characteristics, structure and scale, and mechanism functions. It can be divided into completeness, aesthetics, strangeness, value, combination and scale. The quality management of tourism resources is the core of tourism quality management, which includes the protection and development of tourism resources, including the analysis of the quality elements, quality characteristics and quality levels of tourism resources, as well as the process (or program) of tourism resources development and utilization.

3) Tourism Resources and Environment Management

Tourism environment should be an intermediary connecting subject and object. Tourism environmental management often reflects the characteristics of comprehensiveness, extensiveness and regionality. It needs to start from the perspectives of science, legal system, ecology and cultural management to really play its due role. Tourism environment management can be roughly divided into the management of natural ecological tourism environment and the management of human and social tourism environment. Tourism cities collect many tourism attractions, especially cultural relics, they often integrates the natural ecological environment and human and social environment, therefore, tourism environment management should also take tourism city environmental management as a separate aspect. It is juxtaposed with natural eco-tourism environmental management and humanistic and social tourism environmental management, and the three constitute the basic content of tourism environmental management together.

4) Stakeholder Management of Tourism Resources

Stakeholder is a concept from management, which first appeared in the 1960s. But it was established in the 1980s in the theory of corporate governance. The stakeholder in the stakeholder theory refers to any group or individual that can influence the realization of the organizational goal or be affected by the goal. With the development of tourism industry becoming more and more mature, the role of various stakeholders is also gradually emerging. In order to achieve sustainable development of tourism destinations, we must pay attention to the strength of stakeholders and their interest requirements, and improve their participation. The application of stakeholder theory in the tourism industry began with Walle. Walle pointed out that as a comprehensive industry, the tourism industry involves more stakeholders than most other industries. Therefore, when analyzing the political, social and moral problems of tourism, the stakeholder model will be used. One of the main reasons for the failure of many eco-tourism destinations is that they failed to include key stakeholders. Therefore, bringing stakeholders into the planning and decision-making process is the key to ensure the sustainable development of eco-tourism (Huang Yanping, 2008).

3.2.3 Protection Measures for Tourism Resources

1) Slowing Down Natural Damage

The development and change of nature will affect the change of tourism resources and destroy them, which is the natural decline of tourism resources. In 1997, the oldest Puukohola Heiau temple on the island of Hawaii was completely submerged by the lava from Kilauea volcano, a historic site of 700 years was destroyed in an instant. The sudden natural decline of tourism resources caused by earthquakes, volcanoes, tsunamis and other natural disasters is called disaster damage of tourism resources.

(1) Reduce the rate of weathering.

It is impossible for the tourism resources exposed on the surface to completely stop natural weathering, but it is completely possible to change the environmental conditions to a certain extent and slow down the weathering process. For example, the tourism resources exposed to the wind and the sun should be covered or built to protect.

(2) Eliminate the cause of disaster.

The increasing trend of natural disasters in modern society is closely related to the impact of human activities. The reduction of forests and the excessive reclamation of land resources are the main inducements for aggravating soil erosion, landslides, mudslides and other mountain disasters, accelerating the deposition of rivers and lakes, reducing the capacity of flood regulation and storage, and frequent floods and droughts. The excessive exploitation of groundwater resources leads to a series of problems such as land subsidence, sea water intrusion, the reduction of urban flood control engineering standards, and the aggravation of waterlogging. The world's greenhouse gas emissions accelerate climate warming and lead to extreme climate, which makes island countries, especially small island countries, face "catastrophe".

2) Damage Caused by Man is Strictly Prohibited

The man-made destruction refers to the man-made destruction of tourism resources, which is multi-faceted and serious. The root cause of the destruction can be divided into constructive destruction and managerial destruction.

(1) Constructive destruction.

Constructive destruction refers to the destruction of tourism resources caused by improper planning in industrial and agricultural production, town construction and tourism resources development and construction.

(2) Management damage.

The tourist area is for tourists, if the management is not good, it will also cause damage to tourism resources. We should strengthen publicity and education to improve the relevant awareness and professional knowledge, and formulate relevant laws and regulations to strictly prohibit the artificial destruction of tourism resources.

3) Tourism Resources Digitization

Tourism resources digitization is an important means to protect, develop, and inherit tourism resources. We should be deeply aware that the purpose of digital protection of tourism resources is not only to collect and store, but also to enhance the social value of tourism resources in the context of the current tourism development (Wang Qian, 2017). At the same time, we should also be aware that the application and development of digital information technology will weaken the regional characteristics of tourism resources to different degrees. Therefore, how to fully use digital technology to protect and develop tourism resources, inherit and develop the wisdom and spirit of national culture, and promote the innovation and development of social culture.

3.3 Sustainable Development of Tourism Resources

3.3.1 Sustainable Development Concept of Tourism Resources

1) The Concept of Sustainable Development

The core of sustainable development is to meet the needs of contemporary people without endangering the ability of future generations to meet their needs. It is not only to achieve the goal of economic and social development, but also to protect the natural education resources and environment such as the atmosphere, fresh water, ocean, land and forest that we rely on for our own survival, so that future generations can develop sustainably, live and work in peace and contentment. Economic and social development cannot exceed the carrying capacity of resources and environment. The core of sustainable development is still development. But at the same time, it must be restrained to meet the needs of contemporary people, that is, the concept of development contains constraints. The concept of development also has constraints, including population, environment, resources, technical conditions and social organizations. Among them, the most important limiting factors are the material basis for human survival natural resources and environmental conditions.

2) The Concept of Sustainable Development of Tourism Resources

The essence of sustainable development of tourism resources is that the development of tourism resources should be coordinated with the natural, social, cultural and ecological environment. The sustainable development of tourism is not only a slogan for environmental protection, but also an action programmer for political, economic, technological, cultural and social development. It is a revolution that challenges the traditional way of tourism, value and scientific methods. The sustainable development of tourism resources emphasizes the development of tourism resources in a systematic, equal, global and coordinated way. The core of sustainable development of tourism resources is to coordinate the interests of the four aspects of resources, environment, tourists and society. The sustainable development of tourism resources is mainly reflected in three aspects: fairness, sustainability and commonality.

(1) The fairness of tourism resources.

The development of tourism equity includes the contemporary equity of tourism development, the equity between generations, the equity of tourism resources distribution and use. Contemporary people's equity refers to the development of tourism, the promotion of world economy and cultural exchange, the promotion of the development of economically backward countries and regions, the elimination of poverty, and the alleviation of polarization. Generation equity refers to that while meeting the needs of contemporary tourism development, the ability of future generations to meet tourism needs cannot be reduced, ensuring that the conditions for future generations to develop tourism resources will not be destroyed. Fair use of resources means that countries enjoy the sovereignty of resources development and utilization and are not interfered by other countries. *The Rio De Janeiro Declaration on Environment and Development* adopted by the United Nations Conference on environment and development pointed out that "each country has the sovereignty to develop its natural resources in accordance with its own human environment and development policies, and is responsible for ensuring that activities within its jurisdiction or under its control do not damage the environment of other countries or areas beyond the jurisdiction of each country." In addition, due to the particularity of the tourism industry, the idea of fair use of resources is also permeated with the idea of sharing. The global natural beauty is the common wealth of the people of the world, which can be shared by the whole world and tourism.

(2) The sustainability of tourism resources.

The sustainability of tourism resources emphasizes that the development of tourism resources and tourism industry cannot exceed the bearing capacity of natural resources and ecological environment, and it should maintain the ecological support system and biodiversity and ensure the sustainable use of renewable resources. At the same time, the consumption of non-renewable resources is minimized, because the consumption of non-renewable tourism resources by the development of tourism industry is absolute. In order to make future generations enjoy these resources fairly, it is necessary to put forward the boundary between the intensity and scale of tourism development. This is the difference between sustainable development and any previous development ideas. It opposes the predatory development of tourism resources for short-term interests.

(3) The commonality of tourism resources.

Due to the great differences in the level of culture, history and socio-economic development of various countries, the specific goals, policy measures and implementation steps of sustainable tourism development cannot be unique. However, as the general goal of global development, sustainable development embodies the spirit of fairness and sustainability, which is jointly abided by. And to achieve this general goal, it is necessary to take global joint action, and respects the characteristics and interests of all parties. It is also necessary to take international action in the protection of the global environment and development system, further develop common understanding and common sense of responsibility, oppose narrow political views, regional development views and the lack of common national views. It is closer to treating the earth as a whole, reflecting the common interests and development needs of all mankind. Fundamentally speaking, the implementation of sustainable development is to promote the harmony between human beings, and between human and nature. If the tourism industry of all countries can follow the common development principle, then human tourism can maintain a mutually beneficial relationship between man and nature, so as to realize the sustainable development of tourism.

3.3.2 Barriers to Sustainable Development of Tourism Resources

1) Climate Change

Tourism is an industry that depends on natural resources, ecological environment and climate conditions heavily. Climate change has a real and potential impact on global and regional tourism. Compared with other economic sectors such as agriculture, forestry and fishery, the impact of climate change on tourism is often ignored. To explore how to control greenhouse gas emissions in tourism and how to deal with the impact of climate change on tourism, the Second Global Warming and Tourism Conference held by the World Tourism Organization of the United Nations (UNWTO) in 2007 stressed that "climate change is the most serious threat to the sustainable development of tourism and the Millennium Development Goals for the 21st century. All sectors should take urgent action to face climate change seriously". And the theme of World Tourism Day 2008 was determined as "Tourism: responding to the challenge of climate change".

China has many excellent tourism resources with regional characteristics, and tourism resources are the material basis of China's tourism industry system that is first affected by climate change. Global climate change will lead to changes in the quantity, quality and spatial distribution of many types of tourism resources in China, especially the water, biological, architectural and cultural tourism resources (Huang Ying, Zhai Fudong and Long Liangfu, 2006). These changes are often achieved by affecting the generation and occurrence environment of tourism resources.

(1) Water tourism resources.

On the one hand, global climate change will change the spatial and temporal distribution of water resources to a certain extent by accelerating the atmospheric circulation and hydrological cycle, and then aggravate regional floods and droughts. On the other hand, the impact of climate change on ice and snow has been verified by countries around the world, and ice and snow tourism is facing severe challenges. Climate change will have a significant impact on the quality and development of water tourism resources.

(2) Biology tourism resources.

Climate change in the past few decades has had a great impact on the distribution and richness of species. China is one of the countries with the richest biodiversity in the world, with about 32,800 species of higher plants and about 104,500 species of animal species, accounting for 12 percent and 10 percent of the world's species respectively. Climate change is likely to lead to gradual changes in the characteristics and layout of China's biology tourism resources, including changes in the living environment of biology groups, and then affect the change of biological individual phenotype characteristics and internal physiological structure, as well as the change of the overall landscape pattern of the community.

(3) The culture tourism resources of architectural sites.

Global climate change will have a significant impact on the modern and future building environment including architecture design, building maintenance, building construction, building materials and many other factors. Climate change has become one of the most important factors threatening world heritages. Many world natural and cultural heritages are facing major threats due to rising temperatures, melting glaciers, sea level changes, meteorological disasters and severe droughts. In recent years, extreme weather disasters have affected the safety of China's cultural heritages. How to promote the protection of heritages under the background of climate change has become a problem for heritage workers. Under the guidance of the National Cultural Heritage Administration, Beijing started to deal with climate change from three aspects: first, change the concept of protection and actively respond to climate risks; second, strengthen disaster assessment and capacity building to ensure that dangers and hidden dangers are eliminated; third, establish an inter-sectoral cooperation mechanism to improve the effect of heritage protection.

2) Environmental Pollution

(1) Pollution of tourism area by industry.

Industrial development will cause a series of pollution to tourism resources. The air pollution causes acid rain, which corrodes and destroys tourism resources. For example, the Palace Museum, Tiantan and other white marble fences, stone sculptures, copper products are threatened by acid rain. Xi'an is a city with the best ancient style in China. The Ancient City Wall, the Drum Towers, the Giant Wild Goose Pagoda, the Terracotta Army of Qin Shi Huang and other landscapes attract Chinese and foreign tourists. However, Xi'an is suffering from the pollution of national defense industry, aircraft industry and textile industry, which will cause irreversible erosion of historical sites.

(2) The pollution of tourism activities on the ecological environment of tourism areas.

In tourism cities and scenic spots, the entry of tourists, the development of tourism activities and the basic living needs of tourists will have an impact on the tourism ecological environment. For example, the waste steam and oil discharged by tourism and transportation vehicles pollute the air and water; a large number of domestic sewage and garbage will be discharged into the environment if the accommodation facilities meet the needs of tourists(Li Qinglei, Dong Peihai, 2016). Taking HuangShan as an example, in a year, tourists discharge 40,000 tons of sewage, 3,000 tons of feces, 2,800 tons of garbage and 3,000 tons of coal cinders. If no measures are taken for these wastewater, waste gas and garbage, it will lead to serious environmental pollution.

3) Social Unrest and Epidemic Diseases

Tourism is increasingly important to the economy of the world, and has become a pillar industry in some countries. However, contrary to the general trend of the world's tourism industry, the tourism industry of some Middle East countries, such as Egypt, suffered heavy losses due to the turbulence and social unrest. The Middle East is one of the regions with good momentum of tourism development in recent years. Around 2010, the number of foreign tourists in the region reached 79 million, which is the fastest growing region. But since the political turmoil and the resulting social unrest, the number of foreign tourists has decreased by about 7 million. The downturn in the tourism industry has also seriously affected other related industries, such as the operating profits of airlines. Yemen has attracted a large number of tourists from all over the world for vacation and tourism every year with its rich cultural relics, strong Arabia regional style and long coastline. It was an ideal destination for the rich people in Arabia peninsula. But with the continuous violent conflicts in recent years, the number of tourists in Yemen has decreased significantly, and tourism investment has basically stagnated. The serious security situation, the backward tourism infrastructure, the lack of funds and the inability to develop tourism resources are the main obstacles to the development of tourism industry.

4) Over Development and Utilization of Tourism Resources

The development of tourism resources is prone to excessive problems, which leads to the destruction of scenic spots, and even cause environmental degradation. The emergence of these problems will not only limit the development of tourism itself, but also produce some negative benefits. Therefore, over development has become an important problem hindering the development of tourism. The main reasons for the excessive development and utilization of tourism resources include three aspects as follow.

(1) The lack of systematic, holistic and overall development concept.

In the development of tourism resources, many local governments did not uphold the concept of system, entirety and overall situation, which made their planning concept deviate from the concept of the overall development of the country, and also violated the natural law of resource development. At the same time, it also made tourism resources unable to achieve sustainable development.

(2) Blind development and unreasonable utilization.

Before the development of tourism resources, some local governments did not do a scientific survey in advance, and did not carry out a comprehensive and reasonable demonstration, evaluation and planning, which made the development very hasty. Especially, some new discoveries in order to achieve economic benefits as soon as possible, the developers began to develop tourism resources before scientific and reasonable demonstration and planning. Such development is bound to be blind and extensive. This kind of development focuses on benefits but neglects protection typically, which will inevitably lead to the destruction and waste of tourism resources. For example, the Terracotta Army of Qin Shi Huang in Shaanxi, due to technical reasons, the original bright colored pottery of No.1 pit has begun to fade, and the luster has also gradually disappeared. It can be seen that blind development of tourism resources will lead to serious damage to the resources, environment and ecology of the tourism area.

(3) Super scale reception of tourists.

For a long time in the past, most of China's tourist attractions lacked a sound management system, and passenger flows exceeded their tolerance for a long time. Most of the scenic spots are in the overload stage in the two golden tourism periods of May Day and National Day. The people in the scenic area are suffering, the air is polluted, and the quality of tourism is also reduced. There are many beautiful sculptures, strange mountains and water, rare different trees, etc., becoming "ferocious" due to the number of tourists. Many natural and cultural landscapes have been damaged to varying degrees(Wagar J L, 1964).

3.3.3 Sustainable Development Path of Tourism Resources

1) System Construction and Policy Restriction

For a long time, people have always argued about "protection" and "use". *The Law on the Protection of Cultural Relics* and related laws are important measures to improve China's cultural heritage protection system and tourism resources, and also point out the direction for us to use tourism resources and develop tourism. "Protection first, rescue first, reasonable utilization and strengthening management" are the basic principles throughout *the Law on the Protection of Cultural Relics*. According to the theory of sustainable development of tourism and the theory of harmonious coexistence between human and nature, we should adhere to the principle of "protection is the premise of utilization, and utilization is the purpose of protection". Although the changes caused by natural disasters can't be avoided, protection measures can be taken to delay the process. As for the man-made damage, it can be stopped through laws and regulations, policy publicity and strengthening management. For the damaged tourism resources, according to the degree of damage, certain repair and reconstruction measures can be taken to maintain the original styles and features as far as possible, and maintain the "old as the old". For those that cannot be restored, the site park can be built on the original site.

The state has taken a series of measures to strengthen the protection and management of tourism resources, such as legislation, the establishment of protection and management system, and the establishment of management institution. Scenic spots, cultural relics protection units, historical and cultural cities, natural reserves and forest park, which belong to the category of tourism resources, have achieved great development and achievements after more than 50 years. Since the liberation of China, the National People's Congress and the State Council have issued a series of relevant laws and regulations, such as the *National Park Law* (Draft), *the Law of the People's Republic of China on the Protection of Cultural Relics*, *the Provisional Conditions for the Management of National Scenic Spots*, *the Regulations of the People's Republic of China on Natural Reserves*, and *the measures for the management of Forest Park*. It plays an important role in the protection of tourism resources. However, just after the implementation of these laws, tourism resources are still artificially destroyed, mainly because the publicity and popularization of the protection law are not enough(Chen Xialin, Cui Wushe, 2002). In depth, many people don't know the protection law at all or don't know that what they do violates the laws and regulations. There are also some law enforcers who, due to lax law enforcement, only focus on immediate economic interests at the expense of long-term interests and ignore the law. Therefore, we should not only formulate laws, but also strictly enforce the law and widely publicize, so as to truly establish and improve the legal management system of tourism resources.

2) Tourism Education Popularization

The main reason for the serious man-made destruction of tourism resources is that the masses are not aware of the protection of tourism resources. So, to protect tourism resources, first of all, we need to improve the protection awareness of the masses, let the masses understand the historical and cultural value and scientific investigation value of tourism resources, strengthen publicity and education, strengthen science popularization, improve the sustainable development awareness of tourists and tourism managers, and gradually form a social atmosphere of civilized tourism, scientific tourism and health tourism.

The introduction of relevant laws and regulations on the protection of tourism resources has played a very important role in the protection of tourism resources. However, after the promulgation of these laws and regulations, tourism resources are still being artificially damaged, and the scope and circumstances of the damage are extremely serious. There are two main reasons. One is lack of understanding of the side effects of tourism resources and environment on the development of tourism. For a long time, there has been a misunderstanding that tourism is a "smoke-free industry" in propaganda, resulting in a deviation in people's understanding, causing obvious damage to tourism resources and environment, affecting the sustainable use of tourism resources and the sustainable development of tourism. The other reason is that the publicity of laws and regulations on tourism resources and environmental protection is not deep and extensive.

3) Tourism Environment Capacity Control

Tourism environmental capacity refers to the number of tourists that a tourist destination can withstand in a certain period of time under the premise that the existing state and structural combination of the tourism environment system does not occur harmful changes to contemporary people, including tourists, local residents, and future people, such as the loss of environmental aesthetic value, the destruction of the ecosystem, environmental pollution, and the weakening of comfort(Brush S, 1975). That is to say, on the premise of sustainable development of tourism environment, the maximum activity and passenger flow of tourism and related activities that the natural environment and social environment in the region can bear(O'Reilly A M, 1986). Based on the principle of system dynamics, this paper explores the problems in the sustainable development of tourism capacity, which lays a foundation for the sustainable research of tourism capacity. Generally speaking, with the proposal of sustainable development, the content of the concept of tourism environmental capacity is also constantly enriched(Cole D N, Stankey G H, 1997). Although the premise is diverse, the focus is on tourist satisfaction, scenic area environmental quality and tourism system benign interaction.

4) Dynamic Real-Time Monitoring and Evaluation

Tourism resources real-time monitoring and early warning are based on the distribution characteristics of tourism resources and the current situation of development and utilization, to monitor and warn the tourist information, weather conditions and ecological environment protection of scenic spots, and establish an emergency response plan system for emergencies. Tourism resources have double characteristics of nature and humanity. The introduction of GIS technology and computer visualization methods to the research of tourism safety early warning can promote the quantitative, scientific, standardized and dynamic prediction of tourism safety early warning, which is the future development direction of tourism safety early warning. The real-time monitoring system queries the monitored road sections according to the needs, and monitors the number of tourists passing through in real time. What's more, it can carry out real-time statistics of the total number of tourists in the scenic area, and control the total number of tourists according to the ecological warning line and safety warning line of the scenic area formulated in advance. If it exceeds the ecological warning line of the scenic spot, the ecological recovery period should be arranged. If the safety line is exceeded, tourists should be arranged to move to their destination or wait outside the scenic area, and then guide the tourists in the scenic spot to keep a good order, and organize and arrange the tourists who have finished visiting the scenic spot to leave the scenic spot as soon as possible.

Chapter Review

This chapter mainly introduces the relevant concepts and implementation methods of tourism resources development.

First of all, we learned the concept of tourism resources development and the basic theory that tourism resources development should follow, and clarified the principles, characteristics and development content of tourism resources development.

Secondly, we learned the main factors of tourism resources destruction, the importance of tourism resources protection and protection measures.

Finally, we learned the concept of sustainable development of tourism resources and the importance of adhering to the concept of sustainable development. While understanding the obstacles faced by the sustainable development of tourism resources, we should grasp the effective paths for the sustainable development of tourism resources.

Questions for Discussion

1. Brief introduction to the characteristics of tourism resources development.
2. Briefly describe the contents of tourism resources investigation and evaluation.
3. Describe the connotation of sustainable development of tourism resources.

Case 3-1

Case 3-2

Reading time

Exercises

Chapter 4
Geological Landscape

Learning Objectives

(1) Grasp the definition of geological landscape.
(2) Understand the values of geological landscape.
(3) Command the typologies of geological landscape.
(4) Understand and being familiar with the function and development of landscape tourism products.

Technical Words

English Words	中文翻译
geological landscape	地文景观
natural landscape complex	自然景观综合体
geological and tectonic traces	地质与构造形迹
surface morphology	地表形态
natural markers and natural phenomena	自然标记与自然现象
tourism function	旅游功能
tourism development	旅游开发

Chapter 4   Geological Landscape

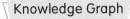

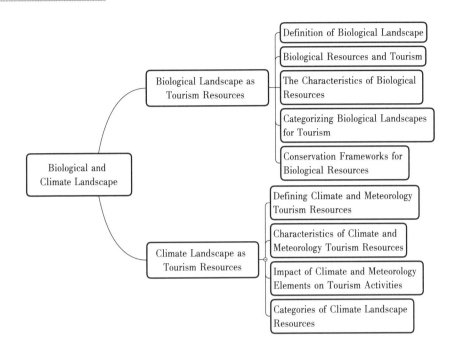

4.1 Overview of Geological Landscape

4.1.1 The Definition of Geological Landscape

The term "landscape" first appeared in some of the works of the German geographer Humboldt, and it referred to the fact that surface scenery seen from a perspective or the area unit of scenery is essentially the same. There are three annotations on the landscape in Cihai. The general concept refers to the specific area of surface scenery. Then, the given concept indicates the initial or basic regional unit in the division of physical geography, which is relatively consistent in occurrence and has the same morphological structure, namely, the physiographic region. Finally, the concept of type means the isolated areas are classified into the same type units according to the similarity of their external characteristics, such as prairie landscape and forest landscape. The interpretation of landscape in *the Dictionary of Geography* is the same. The general concept of landscape is interpreted as the natural complex, which adds meaning to the overall concept of landscape in geography: nature and humanity coexist.

The formation and evolution of various landscapes are directly influenced and controlled by strata and rocks, geological structures, and geological dynamics. Thus, the geological landscape is the combination of internal and external forcing in the earth's lithosphere and form the floorboard of all sorts of things and phenomena, including typical strata, rocks, fossils, structural features, earthquake sites, mountains, caves, coast, and a variety of special geological landscape. They are elements in the lithosphere of the landscape with landscaping function and ornamental value, which is an important place to carry out tourism activities.

According to *Classification, Investigation, and Evaluation of Tourism Resources*(GB/T18972-2003), tourism resources are divided into eight main categories which include geological landscape, water landscape, bio landscape, celestial phenomena and climatic landscape, historical sites, buildings and facilities, travel shopping, and humanities activities.

Geological landscape refers to various types of natural resources formed by long-term geological processes and retained on the surface or shallow surface.

4.1.2 The Features of Geological Landscape

1) Natural Endowment

From the perspective of genetics, all natural landscapes are the product of long-term development and change of the nature, and are carved by its magic, with the characteristics of natural endowment. That's to say, it is innate and natural.

2) Regional Attribute

Natural landscape is formed by the interaction of various natural elements of the natural environment, which has obvious regional characteristics. For instance, the merits of grand northern part and pretty southern part reflect the total difference between north and south natural landscape. As is known to all, Mount Tai which is located in Shandong is so towering that it is famous from home and abroad. While the South is renowned for its rivers, streams, and lakes, the Yangtze River must be a household name not only because of its contributions but also owing to its tourism value.

3) Scientific Property

Elements of natural landscape have a variety of complex and diverse causal relationships and interconnected features, which in turn reflects in all aspects of the natural landscape. Therefore, we should know that the specific causes, characteristics, and distribution of the natural landscape are all scientifically justified.

4) Integrated Beauty

From the perspective of tourism aesthetics, natural landscapes are all inherently beautiful in characteristics of properties. When it comes to the beauty of natural landscape, a single natural scenery is inevitable, due to the composition of monotonous consisting factors. In general, its beauty is monotonous and tedious. However, most of the natural landscape is composed of a variety of landscape factors which cooperate with each other, integrate, and coordinate with the environment. Thus, it can reflect the characteristics of integrated beauty.

5) Difference in Attractive Value

Though the natural landscape is the product of nature itself, thousands of mountains can only exhibit partial merits and millions of rivers can merely show partial splendor. Only with the natural landscape that can arouse visitors' aesthetic awareness can they enjoy the beauty of that part of the landscape. Thus, it is the representative of natural beauty with true beauty of natural landscape. In addition, the natural landscape can be regarded as the object of aesthetic, which is closely correlated with the level of development of society and people's overall quality.

4.1.3 The Implications of the Geological Landscape

The formation of the landscape is closely related to geological processes. Since its formation, the earth's crust has been in motion and change, and it still retains its appearance without fixed rock, structure, or landform. The so-called "seas change into mulberry fields" is a description of this great change. The constant changes in surface morphology, geological structure, and crustal material composition are called geological processes. According to its energy sources, geological processes can be divided into two types: the endogenetic force and the exogenetic force. It is universally acknowledged that a variety of geological landscapes formed by the geological process have peculiar values and appeal, which can attract a great number of tourists and scholars from different disciplines. It is of vital significance for scholars to study those geological landscapes, such as their functions, values, and benefits that people can have.

Generally speaking, the geological landscape has distinct values so that it can be charming and attractive to hundreds of thousands of tourists. There is no doubt that only on account of its values can it arouse scholars' awareness to study it. As is known to all, aesthetic value, educational value, sports value, as well as cultural and tourism value are all the most extraordinary values, which will be illustrated in the following sections. We should learn to appreciate values of geological landscape so that we can get a good understanding of the essence of geological landscape.

1) Aesthetic Value

The geological landscape shows its unique aesthetic value with its morphological beauty and various color beauty which make it an important aesthetic object in tourism. The morphological beauty of the landscape exhibits the comprehensive beauty of geological and geomorphic forms and spatial forms, which also includes the physiological and psychological feelings generated by the subject during the experience process. From ancient times, people hold different appraisals of the beauty of the natural landscape and summarize the image characteristics to describe people's feelings about the beauty of the various landscape. With the change of seasons, the natural scenery reflects each other, presenting a rich and fantastic color. The color of the landscape can not only be formed by the color of the rock mass itself, but also be rendered by vegetation, meteorological conditions, and other factors. Color beauty endows landscape with changes and vitality, allowing people to appreciate the beauty of different styles and get different aesthetic feelings.

Morphology is the first impression of things presented to people, and it is often deemed as the first criterion for visitors to judge whether a resource is a kind of tourism resources or not. Generally speaking, morphological beauty refers to the integrated beauty of the overall form and spatial form of geological landscape. A lot of geological types and geomorphological forms can be considered as tourism resources and have appealed to a large majority of tourists on account of their beautiful or special forms, especially several specific kinds of geomorphology. What's more, it can exceed in its form compared with others.

2) Educational Value

Geological landscape tourism resources are the comprehensive product of the earth's endogenetic and exogenetic forces, which can be regarded as the masterpiece of nature. Their formation and development obey latent rules and contain a certain scientific principle. In the process of viewing, visitors can not only get the feeling of beauty but also understand some scientific objects. They are able to learn scientific knowledge and get the enlightenment of education thoroughly and conveniently. It is not unusual that people will be amazed at various landscapes in China since China has a wide range of land and enjoys a bit long history. With the commodification of education and associated rapid growth in the number of exclusive schools since the 1990s, many schools have added international educational tourism (IET) opportunities to their curricula in order to remain competitive (Kenway and Fahey, 2014; Rizvi, 2014). Pitman et al. (2010) described educational tourism as "involving a deliberate and explicit learning experience", requiring active participation on the part of the educational tourists. As you can see, educational tourism is quite popular and important for students, the educational value of geological landscapes is also of great significance. Students can not only visit such grand landscape, but also learn basic knowledge of geological landscape.

For example, Danxia landform has become a popular tourist destination mainly because of its peculiar characteristics. Danxia landform refers to the special landform developed on the giant thick red sandstone represented by Danxia Mountain in Renhua County, Guangdong Province. This kind of landform is as colorful as haze, shaped like an embroidery, and its distribution is rare, so it has strong peculiarity. Because of its formation and appearance, Danxia landform can present visitors a wonderful sightseeing while it can let tourists compliment the omnipotent nature. Especially, after students experience and visit Danxia landform in person, they will be more familiar with such landform. They might be interested in its formation and be active in learning more about it.

3) Sports Value

The main peak of famous mountains and the depths of gully caves are filled with a breathtaking place, which can often attract some people with adventurous and challenging spirit to challenge, especially young people. Different geomorphic conditions can provide particular conditions for sports activities, for example, steep cliffs can be used for field climbing competitions. Relatively complex terrain can be used for cross-country activities.

Sport is, like tourism, a socially constructed phenomenon (Andrews, 2006), sports and tourism developed and evolved rapidly in many societies from the 1960s (Weed and Bull, 2012). These trends included an expanding demographic profile of sport participants, increasing interest in active living, health and fitness, and increasing demand for active engagement in recreational sports during leisure and holiday time (Glyptis, 1989; Higham and Hinch, 2018).

As we all know, there are plenty of sports events, especially global mega sports events, amongst which are the Olympic Games and FIFA World Cup, and locally unique recurring hallmark events such as Wimbledon where locale and sport are indivisible. They have been a primary focus of tourism scholarship in this field (Weed, 2007). The democratization of sport (Standeven and De Knop, 1999) was at the same time mirrored by revolutionary change in the production and consumption of tourism (Hall, 2004). These sports and tourism development trajectories have become increasingly integrated (Glyptis, 1991) and convergent over time (Higham and Hinch, 2018). To the point that in February 2001, the United National World Tourism Organisation (UNWTO) and International Olympic Committee (IOC) hosted their first international conference on sports and tourism in Barcelona, Spain.

The functions of sport in society have increased and diversified over time. Indeed, the IOC now claims sport to be a human right, and the United Nations considers sport to be a tool for humanitarianism and human development (United Nations, 2017). As a result, sports become an integral part in our daily life.

4) Cultural and Tourism Value

The landscape is not only a mere natural landscape but also contains profound, historical and cultural connotations which provide opportunities for the deep development of natural landscape tourism resources. China's ancient literati have special affection toward nature, with the help of painting and calligraphy, they could express their feelings and aspirations. Therefore, all famous mountains and rivers have been leading actors in numerous poetry and prose. Many magnificent masterpieces handed down from ancient times add unique spirit and artistic conception to the geological landscape. Mount Lushan (29°28'-29°40' N, 115°50'-116°10' E) is located in Lushan District, Jiujiang City, Jiangxi Province, China. The mountains, rivers, and lakes of Mount Lushan blend into landscape tapestry, and Buddhism, Taoism, Christianity, Catholicism, and Islam coexist here. It is known as a mountain of culture, education, and politics. Historically, it has inspired artists, philosophers, and thinkers and inspired many famous works of art. These elements fully demonstrate the cultural and natural elements of the Mount Lushan World Heritage Site. Mount Lushan is listed as one of the top ten most famous mountains in China in 2003 and was rated as a national 5A tourist attraction (5A is the highest level of China's tourist scenic spots, representing the level of China's world-class quality scenic spots) in 2007. As a consequence, it is undeniable that natural landscape can be treated as appealing tourist destinations. The cultural and tourism value of geological landscape can not only benefit the tourists but also the local residents as a great number of tourists and visitors come to famous scenic spots and they will consume in this destination.

In addition, China's scenic spots are often closely related to religious culture, which also makes some mountains a gathering place for religious followers. For example, Wudang Mountain and Huashan Mountain are famous Taoist mountains, while Wutai Mountain in Shanxi and Songshan Mountain in Henan are famous Buddhist mountains. As a place of worship and sacrifice for nature since ancient times, Mount Tai occupies a unique position in ancient Chinese mountain culture. At a global scale, mountain areas cover about 20 percent of the earth's land and represent areas that were less exploited in the past (Walther, Kohler and Imbach, 2002). There is no doubt that mountains can be a kind of main tourism resources because of their cultural value and tourism value. For example, Mount Tai enjoys both cultural fame and attraction that appeals to a vast majority of tourists.

4.2 The Typology of Geological Landscape

According to the classification in the national standard *Classification, Investigation and Evaluation of Tourism Resources*, the geocultural landscape is divided into four sub-categories and seventeen basic types. The four typologies are natural landscape complex, geological and tectonic traces, surface morphology, natural markers and natural phenomena.

4.2.1 Natural Landscape Complex

Natural landscape complex refers to a tourist destination with internal relative consistency formed by the natural elements on the earth's surface, these elements are mutual interrelated and interdependent, equipped with rich and colorful resources, mountains, water, forests and caves are relatively concentrated. Natural landscape complex destination mainly includes four basic types: mountain-type landscape, mesa-type landscape, gully-type landscape, and beach-type landscape.

1) Mountain-type Landscape

Mountain-type landscape refers to the overall landscape or individual landscape in the mountains and hills that can be visited for sightseeing. Famous mountains are of special significance in mountain-type tourism resources. The so-called famous mountain refers to the mountains and hills with excellent mountain environment, unique shape and beautiful natural scenery, which can be viewed and visited by tourists. Generally, these famous mountains have experienced the long-term human history and been influenced by religious culture and other activities. Mountain-type landscape are beautiful natural entities with typical research value in science, with a long history of development and rich cultural heritage. Usually, natural landscapes and human landscapes are integrated with each other in mountains. In China, famous mountain-type tourist destinations include "the Five Great Mountains", namely Mount Tai, the East Mountain; Mount Hua , the West Mountain; Mount Heng , the South Mountain; Mount Heng, the North Mountain; Mount Song, the Central Mountain.

2) Mesa-type Landscape

Mesa-type landscape refers to the overall landscape or individual landscape on the edge of the mountain or the platform among the mountains that are available for sightseeing. A mesa is a raised, flat terrain with a larger area and a lower elevation. The slope in the center of the mesa is gentle and steep on around sides, standing upright on the surrounding lowland hills.

3) Gully-type Landscape

Gully-type landscape refers to the overall landscape or individual landscape in the valley for sightseeing, which can be divided into two kinds, plain valley and mountain valley respectively. The plain valleys are generally relatively wide and shallow, with flat terrain and rich species. Human activities have been carried out since ancient times, and a large number of humanistic and historical activity relics have been left accordingly. The mountain valleys often have the characteristics of deep gorges, turbulent water, and beautiful natural scenery. In China, famous gully-type tourist destinations include the Three Gorges of the Yangtze River, Baofeng Lake in Zhangjiajie, Bifeng Gorge in

Sichuan, the Jiuqu River in Wuyi Mountain in Fujian, and the wide valley on the Yarlung Zangbo Plateau in Tibet.

4) Beach-type Landscape

Beach-type landscape refers to the overall landscape or individual landscape in the gentle beach that is available for sightseeing. Beach-type tourist destinations can be divided into river floodplain type, coastal beach type, lakeside beach type, etc. The typical feature is that the beaches are flat and submerged under water bodies, and most of them have unique biological resources (most of the river beaches have plants and birds, coastal beaches have animals). The Yellow River Delta is a famous river floodplain type beach in China. Coastal beaches are very rich in our country, including Dalian seaside beach, Beidaihe seaside beach, Qingdao seaside beach, Xiamen seaside beach, Sanya Seaside Beach, etc.

4.2.2 Geological and Tectonic Traces

Geological and tectonic traces refer to various relics left in the process of crustal movement which mainly include four basic types: fractured landscape, folded landscape, stratigraphic section, and biological fossil sites.

1) Fractured Landscape

Fractured landscape refers to the landscape formed by the stratum fracture on the ground surface. In the crustal movement, the rock is deformed by the force. When the force reaches or exceeds the capacity of the rock, it will cause the rock to break or move along the fracture surface. This kind of tectonic change that destroys the continuous integrity of the rock is called fracture structure. It is the result of brittle deformation of rock under the action of tectonic stress, and is one of the widely developed geological structural forms in the crust, including joints, cleavage and faults. Fault sites generally make people feel steep, majestic and beautiful, forming a unique tourist landscape. Famous fault landscapes in China include Dianchi Lake in Xishan, Yunnan; Mount Tai; Mount Huashan; Hongguozigou and Suyukou fault cliffs in the northwest of Yinchuan, Ningxia, etc.

2) Folded Landscape

Folded landscape refers to the distortion and deformation of the formation under the action of various internal forces. Folded structures can be large or small. China's Himalayas, Qinling Dabie Mountains, and the European Alps are all typical folded landscape. Large fold structures and small fold structures can be seen almost everywhere.

3) Stratigraphic Section

Stratigraphic section refers to a typical section of scientific significance in the stratum. There are many standards and complete stratigraphic sections in China, some of which have international academic value, and some of which have domestic and regional significance. The famous stratigraphic sections include the Precambrian stratigraphic section of Meishu Village, Jinning, Kunming, Yunnan (the first international geological section in China), the Three Gorges of the Yangtze River (Sinian-third Ji) and so on.

4) Biological Fossil Sites

Biological fossil sites refer to the excavation sites of biological remains and activity relics preserved in the strata during the geological period. China is also rich in ornamental fossil sites, such as insects, fish, birds, beasts and ancient human fossils unearthed in various places. Among them, the famous biological fossil sites include Zhoukoudian Ape-Man Site in Beijing, Yuanmou Ape-Man Site in Yunnan, Zigong Dinosaur Fossil Site in Sichuan (Jurassic), Shanwang Fossil in Linqu Mountain in Shandong (Tertiary), Paleontological Fossils in Western Liaoning (Late Mesozoic), etc.

4.2.3 Surface Morphology

Surface morphology refers to the crustal structure and various forms of the earth's surface produced during the formation and evolution of the earth, which mainly includes six basic types: terraced and hilly landscape, peak-column landscape, ridge-like landscape, ravines and caves, strange and pictographic rocks, lithospheric catastrophe relics.

1) Terraced and Hilly Landscape

Terraced and hilly landscape refers to the landforms in the shape of terraces and hills.

2) Peak-column Landscape

Peak-column landscape refers to the peak-like stone bodies protruding from mountains, hills or flats.

3) Ridge-like Landscape

Ridge-like landscape refers to the karst landforms formed by dissolution for a long time under the control of tectonic traces.

4) Ravines and Caves

Ravines and caves refer to the inferior lands formed by internal or external forces, and natural caves located inside and on the rock surfaces of the bedrock.

5) Strange and Pictographic Rocks

Strange and pictographic rocks refer to mountains or rocks with strange shapes and anthropomorphic shapes. The strange and pictographic rocks are widely distributed, and the lithology is limestone and granite mostly. The formation mechanism is that the rock has undergone crustal movement, weathering, water erosion, etc., and has been weathered in a long geological age. It gradually cracked and collapsed, forming a peculiar and pictographic rock landscape with strange shapes, various poses, and jagged edges.

6) Lithospheric Catastrophe Relics

Lithospheric catastrophe relics refer to the surface traces left by natural disaster changes in the lithosphere which include gravity deposits, debris flow deposits, earthquake relics, sinkholes, volcanoes and lava, glacial deposits, and glacial erosion relics.

4.2.4 Natural Markers and Natural Phenomena

Natural markers and natural phenomena refer to a certain condition in nature that is formed spontaneously due to the laws of nature's operation, which is completely unaffected by human subjective factors, which mainly includes three basic types: bizarre natural phenomena, natural landmarks, and vertical natural zone.

1) Bizarre Natural Phenomena

Bizarre natural phenomena refer to the peculiar phenomena that occur on the surface of the earth that generally have no reasonable explanation. The concept of bizarre natural phenomenon is relatively broad and intuitively understood, natural phenomena include not only the surface, but also the bizarre underground landscapes and the bizarre natural phenomena in the basic types such as astronomical and climatic landscapes in the classification below.

2) Natural Landmarks

Natural landmarks refer to locations that mark special geographical and natural areas. To protect natural landmarks is to maintain significant natural features because they have special significance or typical characteristics. Natural landmarks have the characteristics of relatively small area, highly scientific significance, and specific protection functions. After reasonable tourism development, it will inevitably bring multiple benefits such as social and environmental benefits. The more typical natural landmarks in China include provincial and national boundaries. For example, the effect of different water colors forms a "clear" water flow, that is, the dividing line between the Yellow Sea and the Bohai Sea.

3) Vertical Natural Zone

Vertical natural zone refers to the phenomenon that the mountain natural landscape and its natural elements (mainly landform, climate, vegetation, and soil) change with altitude. The main resources characteristic of vertical natural zones is that their ecological environment changes significantly with altitude. Most of them are located in high-altitude mountainous areas in low-latitude regions. If the height difference is 1,500 meters, there will be a more obvious bottom-up natural landscape and species replacement. Hengduan Mountains, Sigu'niang Mountain and Hailuogou Area in Sichuan, Tianshan Mountains in Xinjiang, Himalayas, Tainan Mountains in Taiwan, Huangshan Mountains in Anhui, Changbai Mountains in the northeast China, Andes Mountains in South America, Kilimanjaro Mountains in Africa, Alps in Europe and other mountains all have obvious vertical natural zonal distribution. Taking the Himalayas, the highest mountain in the world as an example, the southern slope of the subtropical evergreen broad-leaved forest at an altitude of 2,000 meters at the bottom presents a temperate coniferous and broad-leaved mixed forest (2,500 meters), coniferous forests (3,100 meters), alpine shrub forests (3,900 meters), alpine meadows (4,500 meters), cold deserts (4,800 meters), and alpine snow-covered glaciers (above 5,500 meters) is like going from the low latitudes of the earth to the high latitudes.

4.3 The Development and Utilization of Geological Landscape

4.3.1 Tourism Function of Geological Landscape

Geological landscape tourism resources, in short, are geological types and geomorphic forms with landscape making function and tourism value. This kind of tourism resources is the basis for the formation and landscape construction of other natural tourism resources, so it is often of decisive significance for the formation of a region's natural scenery. Geographical landscape tourism resources have the characteristics of spatiotemporal invariance, non renewability, prominent scientific significance, professional development and utilization, multi-type and multi-level spatial combination structure, which determines its unique tourism function.

1) Landscaping Function

Landscaping function refers to the aesthetic characteristics of things and the value that can be viewed by people. Landscaping function is a thing or phenomenon. As the basic function of tourism resources, things or phenomena without landscaping function are difficult to be called tourism resources.

2) Fitness Function

Fitness function is an important function of geological landscape tourism resources. Resources with fitness function are mainly distributed in comprehensive natural tourism destinations such as mountains and hills. Fitness function focuses on two aspects: recuperation function and function of physical exercise. In terms of recuperation function, it mainly uses the coordinated combination of mountain and other natural elements such as climate, water area and forest to provide tourists with recuperation services such as summer vacation, fitness and rest, and health preservation. For example, Lushan Mountain, Mogan Mountain, Jigong Mountain and other places with pleasant climate and elegant environment are famous summer resorts in China. The function of physical exercise mainly refers to the use of the surface fluctuation in mountainous and hilly areas, coupled with other necessary natural elements, such as ice and snow, streams to provide tourists with places for mountaineering, rock climbing, skiing, exploration, rafting and other activities, so as to enable tourists to achieve the purpose of exercising and strengthening their physique. Mount Everest in Tibet, Yunfo Mountain in Beijing and Chuanlong Gorge in Nankun Mountain in Huizhou, Guangdong are ideal places for mountaineering, skiing and rafting. The recuperation function mainly attracts middle-aged and elderly tourists, while the physical exercise function mainly attracts young tourists.

3) Basic and Background Functions

The geological landscape tourism resources play a basic and foil role to other natural tourism resources. It can be said that any natural tourism resources are the products of the comprehensive landscape construction of natural elements such as geology, landform, hydrology, meteorology and climate, biology and so on. We just divide the natural tourism resources into geographical landscape tourism resources, water landscape tourism resources, weather and climate landscape resources and biological tourism resources according to the most prominent landscape construction elements. In other words, any natural tourism resources are dominated by one natural element and formed against the background of other natural elements. However, compared with other natural elements, the background function of geological landscape is universal, so it is more prominent. In the natural environment, landform directly affects the general characteristics of the landscape, the distribution system of surface water, climate and biology, or causes some unique weather and biological landscapes. All natural tourism resources have their geological and geomorphic basis, and even many humanistic tourism resources are formed and exist with the help of the foil of the geographical landscape. For example, Mount Tai has become a world-famous tourist attraction, known as "the first of the five mountains", mainly due to its rich historical sites and cultural connotation, but if we continue to explore its deep-seated reasons, it is still because of its unique geological and geomorphic characteristics. Mount Tai is located at the junction of North China Plain and the mountains in central Shandong. Although the altitude is not high (nearly 1,500 meters), the terrain contrast is large, the maximum relative height is 1,400 meters, and the upward viewing angle is large. In addition, the unique shape of Mount Tai complex (mainly gneiss and granite) and fault block mountain makes Mount Tai particularly towering and tall. Therefore, there is the allusion of Confucius that "Climbing Mount Tai and feeling the world is small".

4) Educational Function

Modern tourism has complex social and cultural significance and functions, one of which is education(Piao Song'ai, 2001). Geocultural landscape tourism resources include various typical geological types and geomorphic forms, so they are often important materials for geoscience research and education. For example, the study of strata must be based on the standard stratigraphic section, the study of fold structures must go deep into the mountains, and the study of earthquakes needs the help of seismic traces. Using the scientific education function of geological and geomorphic tourism resources, we can carry out various professional tourism, such as geoscience tourism, fossil museum tourism, karst landform tourism, earthquake relic tourism.

With the improvement of the scientific and cultural quality of contemporary tourists, their desire for knowledge and innovation is becoming stronger and stronger. They are no longer satisfied with the simple consumption of static sightseeing, and they are not satisfied that the guide's explanation only stays on the simple description of the landscape form. They prefer personalized consumption and hope to integrate amusement, aesthetics, learning and experience. They hope to enrich themselves, integrate into nature and surpass themselves through tourism, so as to make their life more positive. Through various forms of professional tourism or ecotourism, tourism activities with amusement nature, exploration spirit and high consumption form are organically combined with popular science education and environmental protection behavior. On the one hand, tourism can give full play to the educational function of geographical landscape resources, integrate education into tourism, and make tourism activities an effective way to cultivate scientific spirit, popularize scientific knowledge and improve people's scientific and cultural quality. On the other hand, science and technology can support and promote the development of local tourism. For example, using science and technology to simulate the occurrence of some geological phenomena can not only enrich the scientific and technological connotation of tourism products, but also increase the interest of tourism, which is conducive to promoting the synchronous development of science education and tourism.

5) Adventure Function

Besides sightseeing, more and more people pay attention to adventure tourism. Adventure tourism can make tourists challenge their physical and mental limits in a difficult environment, so it is very tempting. In particular, modern people are under increasing competitive pressure and highly nervous, they are eager for opportunities to relax their body and mind. For example, in an environment completely isolated from the outside world without telephone and television in the boundless desert, people can release themselves. In addition, in the adventure environment without any entertainment life, family affection and friendship are more precious. Adventure tourism is generally carried out under bad conditions, such as mountain climbing, valley exploration, crossing the desert, etc. In the process of arduous exploration, tourists often break the barriers, help and care for each other. Many people who travel together have finally become unforgettable friends. Mountains are particularly attractive destinations for adventure tourism as they offer a range of activity options in a setting steeped in actual and symbolic representations of adventure: an opportunity to experience what Hamilton Smith (1993) would call "serious leisure"(Paul and Simon, 2003). The geological landscape tourism resources are formed in the long-term geological process, including not only some low and flat landscapes distributed in plain and hilly areas, but also many majestic, strange, steep, desolate mountain and desert landscapes. The latter is a good place for adventure tourism. It can not only enable tourists to appreciate the magic of nature, but also realize tourists' desire to challenge themselves, realize and surpass themselves. In addition, the geological landscape tourism resources also have many functions, such as cultivating sentiment, opening wisdom, improving aesthetic taste.

4.3.2 Geological Landscape Development

The tourism function of geological landscape tourism resources is the basic basis for its rational development and utilization. From the overall trend of the current transformation of tourism consumption, the diversified and comprehensive consumption of tourists gradually occupies a dominant position. Therefore, when positioning the development of tourism products, it is mainly carried out according to the dominant characteristics of resources and combined with their dominant functions, and achieve comprehensive development as far as possible. Accordingly, the tourism products suitable for the development of geological landscape tourism resources mainly include the following.

1) Sightseeing Tourism

The beautiful and unique geological landscape can be used for sightseeing activities. Sightseeing tourism is the main way of mass tourism. Therefore, in order to promote the local landscape tourism resources to the public, we must organize and carry out sightseeing tourism activities. Three aspects should be paid attention to in carrying out tourism. First, we should maintain the original appearance of the local cultural landscape and avoid artificial modification and modification as far as possible. Second, we should provide tourists with all-round supporting services to meet the various tourism needs of tourists. Third, we should pay attention to the protection of resources and environment, because the non-renewable nature of geological landscape tourism resources is more obvious. Once destroyed, it can not be recovered, and the consequences will be permanent.

2) Educational Tourism

Traveling in search of either academic qualifications or broad general learning and observation predates our times by several centuries. And educational tourism can be independently or formally organized and can be undertaken in a variety of natural or humanmade settings (Ritchie, 2003). The geological landscape tourism resources have very prominent scientific significance and value, so they have important scientific education functions. Using these functions, we can carry out a variety of educational tourism, such as scientific investigation, scientific conference, teaching practice, popular science education, museum exhibition and so on. The development of these resources must be based on social benefits and supplemented by economic benefits. The main purpose is to provide a practice place for geoscience research and teaching. Educational tourism activities can be comprehensive, such as visiting and investigating various geological landscapes along the way. It can also be specialized, focusing on a certain kind of geological landscape, and comparing and investigating different aspects of this geological landscape. In order to ensure the economic benefits of development and utilization, the development of educational tourism activities should be combined with the development of other tourism activities. An example is Mount Emei, it has 6,000 meters thick sedimentary rock stratum, which records the development history of this area of the earth for nearly 800 million years and the formation history of Emei fault rock for 70 million years. It is known as the natural geological museum. At the same time, Mount Emei is also known as the plant kingdom because of its wide variety of vegetation. Therefore, Mount Emei is not only suitable for educational tourism, but also for sightseeing, leisure and holiday-making tourism.

3) Sport Tourism

Sports tourism products refer to the tourism activities that tourists mainly aim at participating in some sports activities (Wang Degen ea tl., 2002). Geological landscape tourism resources have incomparable advantages over other natural tourism resources in carrying out sports fitness tourism activities. This kind of activity mainly makes use of the ups and downs of the earth's surface and other necessary natural elements to achieve the purpose of physical fitness through tourists' own sports. There are many kinds of activities, mainly including mountaineering, skiing, rock climbing, hiking, cross-country, exploration and so on. To carry out sports fitness tourism, we should pay attention to the selection and design of routes, eliminate various risk factors as far as possible, and ensure the safety of tourists to the greatest extent.

4) Health Tourism

Although there is no single definition for health tourism, it could be broadly defined as people traveling from their place of residence for health reasons (Ross, 2001). In some areas where the geological landscape is peculiar and beautiful, and the natural elements are suitable, health tourism can be developed. From the perspective of geological landscape, suitable for the development of health tourism is mainly located in mountainous areas. Because mountainous areas are not only geologically and geomorphologically colorful, but also often have beautiful environment, fresh air, and more nature's original appearance, which helps recovery of spirit and energy. At the same time, the mountains generally have lower temperatures, more clouds, weaker solar radiation, higher air humidity and more precipitation, so the climate in mountainous areas is cool and comfortable, which is ideal for summer vacation. However, the requirement of geological landscape for health tourism is only one of the conditions, other conditions such as climate, hydrology and biological conditions are also very important.

5) Leisure and Holiday-making Tourism

After building a moderately prosperous society in all respects, the people's tourism consumption demand will change from low-level to high-quality and diversification, and from focusing on sightseeing to giving both consideration to sightseeing and leisure vacation. Leisure and holiday-making tourism has gradually become an important tourism product. Leisure and holiday‐making tourism is a comprehensive tourism product integrating sightseeing, leisure, holiday-making, experience, entertainment and sports, which is developed by using resources, places and facilities and driven by leisure culture. The geological landscape tourism resources have the unique advantages of developing leisure and holiday-making tourism. The development of such products need to combine and integrate with other product types, enrich the content of tourism activities and realize the diversification of tourism functions.

Chapter Review

This chapter introduced the geological landscape systematically. Firstly, we explained the formation of geographical landscapes and the detailed knowledge about the values of the geographical landscapes, as well as the geographical process. Secondly, the typology and examples of geological landscapes were presented. The geocultural landscape is divided into four sub‐categories and seventeen basic types. The four typologies are natural landscape complex, geological and tectonic traces, surface morphology, natural markers and natural phenomena. Finally, this chapter mainly introduced five functions of geological landscape tourism resources and five kinds of tourism activities suitable for development.

Case 4-1

Case 4-2

Chapter 4 Geological Landscape

 Questions for Discussion

1. What is the definition of geological landscape?

2. How can geological landscape form?

3. What's the geographical process according to this passage?

4. Can you explain the specific values of geographical landscapes when other students ask you?

5. Could you introduce a geological landscape destination in China?

6. What other tourism activities can the landscape tourism resources be developed into ?

7. What are values of geological landscape? (Aesthetic value, educational value, sports value, and cultural and tourism value.)

8. How can geological landscape form? (The formation of the landscape is closely related to geological processes.)

Reading time

Exercises

Chapter 5
Water Tourism-Ocean Tourism

Learning Objectives

(1) Understand the definition of water tourism.
(2) Describe the difference between different types of water tourism.
(3) List the typologies of water tourism.
(4) Be familiar with the main activities for different tour types.
(5) Understand and articulate the impacts of water tourism on the environment.

Technical Words

English Words	中文翻译
flag of convenience	方便旗
eutrophication	富营养化
hypoxia	水体低氧
natural purification mechanism	自然净化机制
dynamic geomorphology	动力地貌学
geomorphological systems	地貌系统

Knowledge Graph

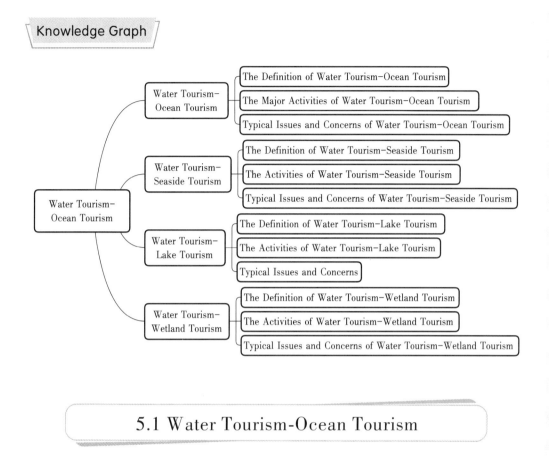

5.1 Water Tourism-Ocean Tourism

5.1.1 The Definition of Water Tourism-Ocean Tourism

There are many ways to define ocean tourism. It is commonly accepted that ocean tourism should integrate tourism and marine space organically. Ocean tourism refers to the sum of the phenomena and relationships caused by the travel and temporary residence of non-settlers in the marine space area.

5.1.2 The Major Activities of Water Tourism-Ocean Tourism

The main activities of ocean tourism include cruise tourism, ocean fishing, sailing and yachting, scuba diving and snorkeling.

Cruise tourism is one of the largest business categories in ocean tourism. It received about 29.7 million passengers in 2019, created jobs for 1.8 million people around the world and contributed over 154 billion dollars to the global economy. Cruise tourism is popular in Caribbean, Mediterranean and Arctic areas as well as other destinations around the world.

Although cruise tourism generates considerable amounts of profits, destinations and ports are not benefited much from this industry. About 40 percent of the bed days sold by the cruise industry are in Caribbean countries, but according to the World Travel and Tourism Council (WTTC), the economic contribution of cruise tourism to Caribbean countries is almost negligible. Most cruise line companies are registered in countries such as Bahamas, Panama, or Liberia, which offer "flag of convenience" to avoid taxation, labor laws, environmental standards, etc. Flag of convenience also favor foreign corporations by restricting the rights of workers and are used to pay low wages.

Fishing is an important recreational activity for ocean tourism. It brings considerable amounts of economic benefits with millions of consumers every year. Recreational fishing can bring multiple benefits to participants, such as relaxing and relieving pressure of work, enhancing family bonding, and promoting interpersonal communications. It is also an activity that integrates entertainment and physical exercise. Through recreational fishing, people's awareness of marine ecology and environment are increased.

Sailing and yachting are special forms of ocean tourism, which comprises of a lucrative market segment with high-income tourists (Diakomihalis, 2007). Scuba diving and snorkeling are popular ocean tourism activities in tropical areas. Scuba diving requires more complicated equipment and specialized training to dive deeper into the ocean. Snorkeling is more popular due to the no-skill requirements.

5.1.3 Typical Issues and Concerns of Water Tourism - Ocean Tourism

Although land-based pollution discharge is an important cause of ocean pollution, ships are also a major source of marine pollution. The United Nations Environment Programme (UNEP) has identified cruise ships as one of the main causes of pollution of marine ecosystems. The waste generated by cruise travel ranges from 2.6 to 3.5 kilograms per person per day. If there is no reasonable disposal method for the cruise garbage, dumping the garbage directly into the ocean will cause problems such as eutrophication, hypoxia, and accumulation of harmful substances in living organisms.

In addition to environmental pollution caused by garbage discharge, cruise ships also cause direct harm to marine life, including dolphins, sea turtles and whales. It is reported that about one-third of whale deaths are caused by collisions to cruise ship propellers; not mentioning a large number of serious injuries caused by collisions. Furthermore, the amount of collision incidents gradually rises as the quality and number of cruise ships increase.

Moreover, it has been noted that activities such as diving can greatly damage corals and the marine ecosystem. For example, corals die once people touch them. A lot of marine lives, such as sea turtles, get sick or even die due to the chemicals in people's sunscreens. The construction of marine tourism infrastructures, such as docks, pontoons and mooring facilities, change the marine habitat environment and affect marine lives.

5.2 Water Tourism-Seaside Tourism

5.2.1 The Definition of Water Tourism-Seaside Tourism

Seaside tourism is based on the unique resource combination at the border of land and sea environments: sun, water, beaches, outstanding scenic views, rich biological diversity (birds, whales, corals, etc.), and sea food. Seaside tourism traditionally runs as the 3S model: sea, sand and sun.

5.2.2 The Activities of Water Tourism-Seaside Tourism

Massive urbanization of coastal areas accommodates the fast-growing tourism needs, leading to many seaside tourism activities, such as boat tours, bird watching tours, beach volleyballs.

The coastal area has coastal landscapes and aquatic features which provide necessary conditions for sightseeing and other leisure activities. Moreover, coastal areas usually have advanced local catering industry. Tasting nutritious and delicious seafood has become one of the primary and popular coastal tourism activities of tourists.

In recent years, coastal sport activities have become popular among young tourists. Surfing as a water sport that combines the two core values of sports: fitness and outdoor entertainment, has recently become a new popular activity among seaside tourists in China. It is reported that in the first half of 2022, surfboard is one of the most fast-growing categories of sport equipment, with an increase of 465.45 percent compared to the same period of 2021. The popular surfing destinations include Wanning, Zhangzhou, Sanya, and Huizhou. Significant growth in surfing tourism consumption is observed in these destinations with increasing rates of 46.46 percent, 99.71 percent, 130.52 percent, and 195.15 percent respectively.

5.2.3 Typical Issues and Concerns of Water Tourism - Seaside Tourism

The development of seaside tourism inevitably has significant impacts on the natural environment including water bodies, coastlines, surface hydrological creatures, soil and vegetation in coastal areas. It is common to see the environmental problems such as water pollution, vegetation destruction, and imbalance of marine ecosystems in coastal tourism destinations all over the world.

Let's use Bali, Indonesia as the example to look into environmental problems caused by seaside tourism activities. Over the past few decades, tourism in Bali has grown exponentially, transforming Bali from a quiet village in the 1960s to an international tourist destination with around 4,300 hotels and 100,000 hotel rooms. In Bali, about 80 percent of the economic activities are related to tourism. Due to the rapid development of tourism, unreasonable planning of municipal facilities, construction waste caused by newly built hotels and restaurants, and the weak environmental protection awareness of tourists and local residents, the environmental problem has become a major threat to the sustainable development of Bali tourism.

In 2020, the pandemic led Indonesia to its first economic recession since the Asian financial crisis in 1998, and Bali's received a huge hit. By the second quarter of 2021, there were only a few travel agencies, restaurants, spas and other tourism-related businesses operating on the island. Many businesses were suspended or permanently closed. More than 105,000 jobs were lost.

However, the declining number of tourism arrivals didn't improve the beach environment. On the contrary, several iconic and famous beaches, such as Kuta and Jimbaran, are covered by garbage. Regular cleaning and waste disposal cannot be maintained during the pandemic. It has been found that before the pandemic, coastal resorts and hotels paid for special "beach cleaning services" to clean up the garbage on the beach regularly. The tourism department also sends garbage trucks and clean-up teams. Thus, the beaches are kept clean, beautiful and attractive to tourists. However, due to the impact of the pandemic, the fast-decreasing number of tourists result in less income of local tourism businesses and government sectors. The budget to maintain the beach environment has to be cut. Now, volunteers from local residents formulated garbage disposal teams take this job and clean beaches time by time.

5.3 Water Tourism-Lake Tourism

5.3.1 The Definition of Water Tourism-Lake Tourism

Lakes are often considered as a separate type of tourism resource because of their special environmental characteristics. Lake tourism allows tourists to enjoy special landscape environment of lakes and carry out various activities based on lakes. It occurs not only on the lake, but also in the surrounding area of the lake, including the lakeshore and facilities in the surrounding region that support the lake as a tourist attraction.

5.3.2 The Activities of Water Tourism-Lake Tourism

Lake tourism (as Figure5-1 shown) includes three levels of activities: the core layer is that tourism activities carry out on the water, including sightseeing on islands in the lake, recreational sports activities on the water (yacht, windsurfing, etc.) and water agriculture related activities. The surrounding layer is lakeside sightseeing and leisure sports, including bird watching, aquarium, etc. The diffusion layer is the sightseeing belt around the lake, including the larger area which relies on the lake for sightseeing, leisure, wellness, conferences and study tours.

Figure5-1　Lake leisure activities
Source: nationalgeographic.com

5.3.3 Typical Issues and Concerns

Lake tourism has the following four features: cultural appraisals; perishable and vulnerable to change; used by multiple users or stakeholders; complex management.

1) Cultural Appraisals

Many lakes are not only natural tourism resources, but also have the attributes of cultural tourism resources as they have close relationships with local communities. It is noted that local communities often serve as tourism attractions in lake areas. Local people also gain economic benefits from tourism related businesses.

2) Perishable and Vulnerable to Change

The lake ecosystem is fragile. Compared with the ocean, the lake has no natural purification mechanism and is easily affected (Hall and Härkönen, 2006). The development of lake tourism leads to constructions of local infrastructure, which might destroy the lake ecological environment, including degraded quality of water, soil, animal habitats, and so on. Damages of water and soil quality can cause negative chain effects, such as eutrophication of water bodies, reduction of oxygen content, cyanobacteria blooms, changes in zooplankton and benthic animal species, simplification of species structure, replacement of dominant aquatic plants by algae, formation of swamps, and eventually lakes disappeared (Müllner and Wikelski, 2004).

3) Used by Multiple Users or Stakeholders

Usually tourism is not the primary function of lakes. They serve other public functions, such as water supply, irrigation, transportation and power supply. Therefore, lakes can be used by multiple stakeholders whose interests may conflict with each other. For example, tourism businesses want to develop motorboating programs on lakes, but local environmental activists and government authorities may reject this proposal if the lake serves as the origin of drinking water for the surrounding areas, or it is included in the wildlife conservation area.

4) Complex Management

Given that lakes serve multiple functions and involve many stakeholders, management of lake tourism is always complex. Tourism business related issues, environmental conservation issues, ecological issues, community related issues, etc. are intertwined and lead to management of lake tourism more complicated.

5.4 Water Tourism-Wetland Tourism

5.4.1 The Definition of Water Tourism-Wetland Tourism

From the perspective of dynamic geomorphology, wetlands are different from other geomorphological systems, and are submerged geomorphological systems with slow currents and undulating water levels (Mitsch, 1994). Wetland tourism is based on wetland resources. Given the fragile ecological environment, wetland tourism enhances public awareness of wetland environment conservation. Wetland tourism activities allow tourists to gain more ecological knowledge of wetlands. It is also an important category of ecotourism due to wildlife, plants, and landscapes in wetlands, which offer unique tourism experiences to visitors.

5.4.2 The Activities of Water Tourism-Wetland Tourism

Many wetland tourism activities are designed to provide ecotourism and sustainable tourism experiences. They include boat tours, board walk, wildlife watching, bicycling, nature trails and so on. All the activities tend to follow sustainable development principles to minimize the impacts of tourism activities on wetland environment. For example, boat tours are strictly limited within a specific area in the wetland, so the oil residuals and noises of the boats do not widely spread.

5.4.3 Typical Issues and Concerns of Water Tourism - Wetland Tourism

To build scenic spots and tourism routes in wetlands, necessary facilities and infrastructure are needed, such as viewing decks, tourist service centers, ticket booths, garbage bins, water plank roads and water, electricity, and communication facilities. Such construction might destroy the soil matrix materials, ruin the vegetation patterns, change the water direction, and ultimately damage the wetland ecological environment.

Damages on wetland ecological environment can also be caused by tourist behavior. Wetland tourism activities largely increase the amount of domestic sewage and domestic garbage. A specific management program is needed to dispose the waste and minimize the damages of tourism activities to the wetland environment. Moreover, the inappropriate tourist behavior, such as littering, trespassing, voluntarily feeding animals, intrusive interaction with wildlife, can cause more damages to wetlands and the inhabitants.

While bringing damages to a limited area of wetlands, tourism activities to a large degree help conserve the whole wetlands. First, tourism brings economic benefits, which raise funds for strategies and programs to protect the wetland ecological system, improve living environment of wildlife, and avoid the environmental degradation. Second, through participating in wetland tourism activities and enjoying beautiful landscapes, tourists can gain more knowledge about the ecological environment of wetlands and enhance people's sense of responsibility in environmental conservation (Tavares, Máquina and Henriques, 2012). Third, from the perspective of local residents, wetland tourism not only drives the development of the local economy, but also improves the living conditions of local residents, including more job opportunities and income. People from other places, including tourism businessmen and tourists, can bring new ideas, thoughts and lifestyles to inspire local people (Lamsal, Atreya, Pant and Kumar, 2016).

Chapter Review

This chapter mainly introduces four types of water tourism, including ocean tourism, coastal tourism, lake tourism and wetland tourism.

Firstly, this chapter introduces the definition of ocean tourism and the basic activities, including cruise tourism, ocean fishing, sailing and yachting, scuba diving

Case 5-1

Case 5-2

Reading time

and snorkeling. At the same time, the positive effect of marine tourism on regional economic development and the existing problems are introduced. This subsection focuses on the possible pollution of the marine environment caused by marine tourism. In addition to the physical damage directly caused by cruise ships to marine organisms, the discharge of pollutants will also cause problems such as eutrophication, hypoxia, accumulation of harmful substances in living organisms.

Secondly, this chapter introduces the basic definition of coastal tourism and the included activities: boat tours, bird watching tours, beach volleyballs. At the same time, the elements included in the 3S model of coastal tourism are introduced: sea, sand and sun. This section introduces the example of Bali to illustrate the possible destructive impact of coastal tourism on the local ecological environment.

Thirdly, this chapter introduces the basic definition of lake tourism and the activities involved, as well as the basic lake types that lakes are considered as tourism resources: crater lakes, underground lakes, rift lakes, oxbow lakes, and artificial lakes. This section also describes four basic characteristics of lake tourism including cultural appraisals, perishable and vulnerable to change, used by multiple users or stakeholders, and complex management.

Fourthly, this chapter introduces the definition of wetland tourism and the activities of wetland tourism. As a kind of eco-friendly tourism, wetland tourism may still cause damage to the environment, but it will also promote the economic development of local communities.

 Questions for Discussion

1. What types of tours are included in water tourism?

2. What activities are included in ocean tourism? What are its possible impacts on the marine environment?

3. What activities are included in the coastal tourism? What does the case of Bali teach you?

4. How to understand the four characteristics of lake tourism?

5. What are the possible impacts of wetland tourism as an eco-friendly tourism on the environment and local communities?

Exercises

Chapter 6
Biological and Climate Landscape

Learning Objectives

(1) Learn the definition and characteristics of biological landscape as tourism resources.

(2) Understand the major types of biological landscape as tourism resources.

(3) Understand the global conservation framework of biological resources with respect to tourism.

(4) Learn the definition and characteristics of climate landscape as tourism resources.

(5) Understand the major categories of climate landscape.

Technical Words

English Words	中文翻译
biological landscape	生物景观
landscape species	景观物种
biological landscape tourism resources	生物景观旅游资源
natural ecosystem	自然生态系统
fauna and flora	动植物
national parks system	国家公园体系
biosphere	生物圈
categories of biological landscape	生物景观分类
climate landscape	气候景观
meteorological landscape	气象景观
categories of climatic and meteorological landscape	气候气象景观分类

Knowledge Graph

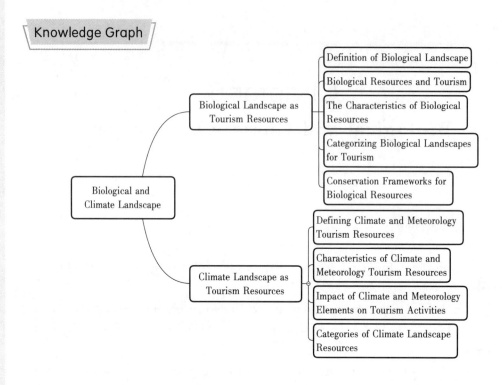

6.1 Biological Landscape as Tourism Resources

In the long historical evolution process of life on the earth, life evolves and develops from simple to complex and low to high level in form and from ocean to land in habitat. Eventually life occupies every corner of the ocean, land, and lower atmosphere, and eventually the earth's biosphere takes shape. Currently, life on the earth generally entails three categories: plants, animals and microorganisms. As resources for tourism development purpose, it mainly includes plant resources, animal resources and the natural and human environment in which the two types of biological resources inhabit. Biological landscape is the most vital, dynamic, and typical type of tourism resources on the planet we live in(Zheng Qunming, 2008).

6.1.1 Definition of Biological Landscape

Bio-life is an integral part of the natural geographical environment and the subject of the natural living environment.

By definition, according to USAID (2008), biological landscape can be a process for mapping the spatial distribution of landscape species. The resulting biological landscape reflects the information on abundance and density of each species and the habitat quality.

Biological landscape tourism resources refer to resources with high aesthetic value which can beatify the environment and can be used for tourism development (Gao Zengwei and Lu Xiao, 2010).

6.1.2 Biological Resources and Tourism

With the development of modern tourism, a considerable part of bio-life has become the object of tourist visitation and enjoyment. Biological resources are the most distinctive category of natural landscape tourism resources with the most vigor and vitality. They constitute an entity of the natural landscape with the periodic activities of their own life rhythms and the ever-changing morphological characteristics. In almost all tourism activities, the biological landscape has played a significant tourism resources function.

Animals and plants are widely distributed in most areas of the earth's surface. During their long-term adaptation and development, they have formed regular and diverse types of fauna and flora under different environmental conditions, and have become the most distinctive and attractive existence on the earth's surface. Plants have the functions of beautifying the environment, decorating the landscape, and cultivating the artistic sense of aesthetics; while the appearance, shape, color, movement, sound, and living habits and environment of animals are attractive and lively tourism landscape resources. They can enrich the natural landscape, conserve the ecological sustainability, beautify the tourist attractions, enhance the visitors' interest and visiting experience, and nurture the visitors' aesthetic appreciation on nature as well as their environmental awareness(Wu Yijing, 2009).

6.1.3 The Characteristics of Biological Resources

Compared with other natural tourism resources, biological tourism resources have distinctive characteristics.

1) Vitality

The biggest difference between biological tourism resources and other natural tourism resources is that they are full of vigor and vitality. Bio-organisms have life characteristics such as growth and reproduction, aging and death, flowering and falling leaves, migration and predation. Their existence adds vitality to the natural world, and can make the tourist landscape a lively landscape complex. The integration of flora and fauna with other natural landscape is the most harmonious expression of nature. Typical examples can be cited, such as various birds with the vast wetland landscape at the mouth of the Yellow River; the tropical rainforest vegetation with the Amazon River; and the migrating wildlife on the African savannah(Bi Bi and You Changjiang, 2013).

2) Diversity

Diversity refers to the state of being diverse or variety, while the term "bio-diversity" or "biological diversity" refers to the heterogeneity present in the world or a habitat, ranging from macromolecules within the cells to biomes. Biodiversity comprises:

(1) species diversity: variety of species and abundance of species;

(2) genetic diversity: genetic variability present within the species;

(3) ecological diversity: the diversity of ecosystems within a geographical area.

The diversity of biological tourism landscapes is more or less created by the diversity of biological species. In addition, due to the diversity of the natural environment, the morphology of some species will change, and the phenomenon of varied morphologies of the same species will appear.

In the lower layer of the atmosphere, the entire hydrosphere and the upper part of the lithosphere, with a thickness of about 20 kilometers, biological life forms a special circle called the biosphere. It can be said that bio-life exists in any place on the earth, regardless of land or sea, or sky or underground. The biological species and the natural ecosystem are rich and diverse, and of high tourism value as well. Coupled with the unique biological landscapes artificially interfered by human being (in the positive way, such as afforestation and artificial breeding) in various regions, there are extensive and rich biological tourism resources on the earth's surface.

The vast territory and complex and diverse natural conditions enable China to have possessed all types of ecosystems in the northern hemisphere, forming a complex biota composition, making China one of the eight countries which have the richest biodiversity in the world and also one of the countries with the most abundant bio-tourism resources.

3) Seasonality

Seasonality refers to the characteristics of seasonal landscape formed by the transformation of biological forms and spatial positions with seasonal change. As the seasons change, the fauna and flora also undergo periodic change, with flora being more prominent. For example, different plants bloom in different seasons, such as camellias and cherries in early spring; water lily in summer, chrysanthemums in autumn; and snowdrops and daffodils in winter. The leaves' colors of many plants also change with the change of seasons. For example, the red and orange leaves of maple trees in eastern Canada make magnificent landscape of the region. Some birds migrate from north to south on a regular basis with the seasons change, for example, flocks of swans migrate from Siberia, Russia, every year to the wetland of the Yellow River in Dongying, China, and stay there for the whole winter, which attracts a lot of people to go visiting and watching them.

Another example is the Great Migration in East Africa as one of the most sought-after experiences for wildlife and nature enthusiasts. The Great Migration is the ever-moving circular migration of over a million wild animals across the Serengeti-Mara ecosystem. The constant movement of columns of wildebeest, joined by a host of companions, follow an age-old route in search of grazing and water. After calving in the southern part of Tanzania's Serengeti near the Ngorongoro Conservation Area, the animals journey through the Serengeti up and around in a clockwise direction towards the Masai Mara in Kenya, and returning again near the end of the year. Along the way, high drama is always present, as thousands of animals are taken by predators, and thousands more are born, replenishing the numbers and sustaining the circle of life(Asilia, 2022).

4) Aesthetic Value

By definition, aesthetics is a branch of philosophy that questions the beauty in art and aesthetic valuation of artworks, and it has different and complementary meanings depending on the field in which it is defined(Tribot et al., 2018).

Landscape aesthetics is defined as the enjoyment and pleasure felt through the observation (and experience) of environmental scenery (Swaffield and McWilliam, 2013). The aesthetic value of fauna and flora is usually expressed and perceived through their colors, shapes, sounds, habits, movements, scales, and other features.

Indonesia has a high potential for the diversity of flora and fauna species together with their ecosystem. Henri et al. (2017) argued in their research that the abundance of the plant and animal species in the Pelawan Biodiversity Park at Central Bangka, Indonesia indicated the park had high competitiveness for tourism attraction supported by the presence of key species, flagship species, and rich bird species for bird watching, and that preservation of natural resources can be done through using the concept of ecotourism.

China is one of the countries with the richest animal and plant resources in the world, and there are a large number of plants that can attract tourists with their flowers, leaves, shapes and fruits. For example, Luoyang's peony, Yunnan's camellias, and Inner-Mongolia's populus euphratica forest are all popular tourism attractions. Different animals show different physical characteristics and colors due to different geographical locations, climatic zones and differences in living habits, and together with their habitats, they all constitute tourism landscape resources. The peacock and elephant in Xishuangbanna, the Manchurian tiger in Northeast China, and the giant panda in Sichuan Province are all typical examples.

5) Reproducibility

The high reproductive ability of bio-life determines the regeneration and sustainable utilization of biological tourism resources. On the basis of biological reproduction, people use the characteristics of biological domestication and spatial mobility to locally change the ecological environment conditions, and use artificial intervention to domesticate, transplant, raise, and cultivate many species of animals and plants, and thus forming many artificial biological landscapes. For example, China has protected the endangered giant panda and its living habitat through human intervention, i.e., artificial reproduction, so that more people can visit and appreciate the giant panda which is also taken as "living fossil". However, the reproduction of bio-life is relative. For those vulnerable biological species that are on the verge of extinction, once they are destroyed and exhausted, they will become irrecoverable. Therefore, they need to be cherished and protected by human beings.

Designated as a World and National Heritage Site, the Great Barrier Reef Marine Park sprawls out for 2,300 kilometers along the Australian coastline, and brings an eclectic mix of coral and marine life together. Coral reefs are vitally important for a number of reasons. Not only are they incredibly diverse, providing ideal living environments for both endangered and non-endangered creatures, but they also act as protection against the damaging effects of waves and storms on coastlines. In addition, their beautiful colors and special habitat make an incredibly popular tourist hotspot. However, threats such as overfishing, pollution, outbreaks of predatory species, and ocean warming resulting from climate change are serious issues affecting the coral reef reproduction.

6) Vulnerability

Although biological tourism resources are reproducible and renewable resources, they are fragile to resist external disturbance. The emergence of catastrophic environments, changes in the earth's environment, and excessive human interference will cause a large number of bio-species reduction or even extinction. For example, the catastrophic environment of the Cretaceous Time in the geological period made the dinosaurs that dominated the earth then become extinct. Human beings over-exploit and utilize resources, leading to the destruction of ecosystem, the deterioration of the ecological environment, and the danger of extinction of many species of fauna and flora, such as the giant panda, the white-flag dolphin, the South China Tiger, and the red-crowned cranes, etc. in the case of China. According to statistics, since 2000, more than 110 kinds of mammals and more than 130 kinds of birds have disappeared from the earth, and now the speed of species extinction is accelerating(Bi Bi,2013). It can be seen that the biological tourism landscapes are extremely fragile, and therefore, ecotourism with equal emphasis on protection and development of the natural resources should be promoted.

According to IUCN(2022), more than 41,000 species are threatened with extinction, and that is still 28 percent of all assessed species. The IUCN Red List of Threatened Species is the world's most comprehensive information source on the global extinction risk status of animals, fungus and plant species. Open to all, it is used by government organs, non-profit organizations, businesses and individuals. According to the IUCN Red List, species are classified as: extinct, extinct in the wild, critically endangered, endangered, vulnerable, near threatened, least threatened, data deficient and not assessed. Among them, "endangered" refers to condition when a taxon or a species does not meet the "critically endangered" standard, but its wild population is likely to face extinction in the near future, such as blue whales, elk; "vulnerable" refers to the condition that, over a period of time, its wild populations face a higher chance of extinction, such as great white sharks, polar bears. In addition, there are quantitative criteria. The giant panda, for instance, was once categorized as "endangered", but now, thanks to the effective effort of conservation by Chinese government and professional organizations, it has been re-categorized as "vulnerable" in 2021(Xinhua net, 2021).

7) Cultural and Education Attributes

Biological tourism resources have special cultural value. Certain characteristics of animals and plants can enlighten people's minds and cultivate people's sentiments. For example, the pine, bamboo and plum, known as the "three friends of the cold season", have become the symbols of not being afraid of adversity; the orchid symbolizes the noble character; the peacock and the elephant are the symbols of the beauty and the power of the Dai minority group in China. Many animals and plants are also used as representation of a country, a nation, and a city, and they entrust people with certain spiritual pursuits. For instance, the bald eagle has been the national bird of the United States since 1782, when it was placed with outspread wings on the Great Seal of the country. It appears in many government institutions and on official documents, making it the most famous bird in all of America. Besides, the polar bear has the association of Russian nation, and koala has the association of Australia.

Conserving the biological resources is conserving our environment and human living habitat. The biological tourism resources also have high research and education value for environment and resource conservation. The evolution of human civilization also represents the changes of human-nature relation as well as the evolving cognition of human beings towards nature and biological resources. Industrial revolution advanced dramatically the human technology of developing and exploiting resources including the biological resources. As a result, the species of fauna and flora have been reducing and disappearing, and in turn the ecological balance has been threatened as a result, bringing about consequences such as global warming and climate change. Therefore, research and education based on the natural resources, and biological resources in particular, is of high necessity and significance to prevent further deterioration of the environment and ensure a balanced and sustainable system of the ecological world which is related to the living environment and life quality of the human beings closely.

Established in 1872, the Yellowstone National Park is the earliest and the largest among the almost 400 national parks in the United States. The American people take the Yellowstone National Park not merely a natural attraction, but more of a national monument that reminds the beauty their nature holds and that attests the American history they take pride in, and that they take as the soul of the American West (National Park Service, 2022).

National Parks are taken as the largest classroom where people can learn about human-nature relations through experiencing nature including fauna and flora(Thompson and Houseal, 2020). The National Park Service of the United States provides wildness classroom, field trips, or even multi-media distance learning with the abundant biological resources that the Yellowstone National Park holds.

6.1.4 Categorizing Biological Landscapes for Tourism

Biological tourism landscapes mainly include flora resources and fauna resources. Flora resources include dense and lush vegetation, precious exotic flowers and plants, and ancient and famous trees, etc.; fauna resources mainly include rare species of wild animals which constitute attraction for tourists. Biological tourism resources provide the natural backdrop for the cultural landscape, protect the ecological environment, beautify tourist attractions, and cultivate tourists' sentiments. Also, they play a very important role in popular science education and investigations as well as eco-tourism activities.

1) Flora Tourism Resources

The varied striking characteristics made flora tourism resources one of the most attractive scenes. Many plants have high aesthetic ornamental value and become ornamental plants. Some are flowering plants attracting visitors with color, shape, scent and long-lasting blooms; some are foliage plants attracting visitors with their unique leaves. Some plants are held as precious due to their very rare species and numbers over the process of biological evolution. Some plants develop in human society with their inherent characteristics and become a symbol of a certain spirit. Also, there are ancient and famous trees, large-scale forest vegetation, grasslands, shrubs, aquatic plants, perennial and annual plants, and other plant landscape resources with comprehensive charming features.

(1) Forest landscape.

For the continental ecosystem of the earth, the total forest area is 5 billion hectares, accounting for 32.6 percent of the land area. Forest is the largest and most complicated ecosystem on land. Forests have various functions such as purifying air, raising water sources, maintaining water and soil, and regulating climate. They are the key factors of protecting the environment and maintaining the ecological balance of the land. Forests can carry out a variety of tourism projects, which are important places for people to conduct scientific investigations, adventure, health and wellness, ecological tourism as well as other activities. Forest landscapes can be divided into two categories: virgin forest landscape and artificial forest landscape.

China's virgin forests are mainly distributed in Daxing'an Mountain range,

Xiaoxing'an Mountain range, Changbai Mountains in the northeast, the southeast of Hengduan Mountains, and the southwest of Tibet. Artificial forests are mainly distributed in hilly areas in the south of the Yangtze River. Due to different natural conditions in various places, different forest landscapes have been formed. Xishuangbanna has a lush tropical virgin forest landscape with a wide variety of plants and is known as the plant kingdom. The mangrove landscape is distributed in the coastal area in the south of China. In Sichuan, Hunan, Zhejiang, Jiangxi, Jiangsu and other places, there are many varieties of bamboo forests, forming a large "bamboo sea" landscape.

① Tropical rainforest landscape.

The largest and most typical tropical rainforests are distributed near the equator, including the Amazon River in South America, the Congo River in Africa, and the tropical area of the Southeast Asia. Rainforest in China is mainly distributed in Hainan Island, Xishuangbanna, and other tropical places.

The tropical rainforest vegetation demonstrates extremely rich and diversified species, for example, there are more than 300 species of arbor trees alone in Brazil's rainforest per square mile, and many arbor species also have tall plate-like roots and stem flowers. Furthermore, the species community structure is very complex and there are as many as three or four layers of arbor plants, and there are also very rich vines and epiphytes, which is a plant community with rich species and complex structure too. Abundant plant resources and suitable living environment also support a wide variety of fauna species, especially insects, reptiles and amphibians with the largest variety and number, and primates often appear.

② Mangrove forest landscape.

Mangrove forests are mainly distributed in the tidal flats and shoals in the junction of land and sea in the tropical and some subtropical area. Mangroves are one of the most biologically diverse ecosystems in the world. They are very rich in biological resources. They are places for many marine animals to forage, inhabit and reproduce. They are also wintering sites and transfer stations for migrating birds. The dense pillar roots and breathing roots of mangroves can play the functions of preventing wind and waves, promoting siltation and protecting stalls, consolidating banks and berms, and purifying air and seawater.

China's mangrove forests are mainly distributed in Hainan, Guangdong, Guangxi, Fujian and Zhejiang. At present, mangrove national nature reserves have been established in Futian of Zhuhai, and Zhanjiang of Guangdong, Dongzhaigang of Hainan, Shankou in Guangxi, and other places as well in China.

③ Subtropical forests with evergreen leaves.

Subtropical evergreen broad-leaved forests are mainly distributed on the east coast of the subtropical continent and belong to the forest vegetation type under humid monsoon climate. Geographically, they are specially distributed in the Yangtze River Basin in China,

Southern Japan, and the Southeastern United States. Most of the tree species are evergreen broad-leaved trees such as lauraceae, fagaceae, magnoliaceae, orchidaceae and camellia.

The abundant natural food and agreeable climate environment in these areas have given birth to abundant animal resources, such as insects, birds, monkeys, reptiles.

The area of evergreen and leafy forests in China is vast, starting from near the Tropic of Cancer in the south, to the Qinling-Huaihe line in the north, and basically extending along the eastern margin of the Tibetan Plateau in the west, with many subspecies rare species distributed in these regions, such as ginkgo biloba, metasequoia, silver fir, golden pine, and goose palm; and also there are rare animals such as giant panda, golden monkey, pangolin, and South China tiger. Taking Dinghushan Mountain in Guangdong Province as a specific case, it is a complete subtropical monsoon evergreen broad-leaved forest landscape. There are more than 2,400 plant species here, among which there are quite a few endemic species too. The national key protected plants here include wild lychee, feather pine, etc. There are also descendant plants that appeared on the earth more than 200 million years ago—cycad. It provides habitat for more than 100 species of wild animals, and the national key protected animals including leopards and pythons can be seen here(Bi Bi and You Changjiang, 2013).

④ Landscape of temperate deciduous broad-leaved forests.

Temperate deciduous broad-leaved forest is a typical forest ecosystem under humid climate conditions in the middle and southern temperate zone of the earth, and is mainly distributed in Western Europe, eastern North America and East Asia. In China, it is mainly distributed in the north and the Northeast China. The tree species of this kind of forest mainly include oak, maple, poplar, birch, etc., and the wild animals in habit in the forest include deer, squirrel, rat, fox, wolf, hare, and bear. For example, Changbai Mountain National Nature Reserve is one of the areas with the most abundant animal and plant species at the same latitude. The main protection objects are temperate forest ecosystems and rare animals and plants species. There are more than 1,600 species of higher plants and more than 3,500 kinds of wild animals and plants. The first-class protected animals include Siberian tiger, sika deer, sable, etc. What's more, there are more than 800 kinds of herbal plants, and precious herbal materials such as ginseng and gastrodia.

⑤ Northern coniferous forests landscape.

Also known as taiga, the northern coniferous forests landscape is formed by pine and fir plants, and it is a cold temperate zone vegetation and its distribution is quite wide, mainly distributed in Eurasia and northern North America. In China, it is mainly distributed in Daxing'an Mountain range and the Altai Mountains. The community structure is simple, the canopy is neat and the layers are distinct, and the arbor is dominated by pine, spruce, fir, hemlock and larch, mostly mono-dominant forests. The typical wild animals in the forest are moose, reindeer, lynx, snow hare, squirrel, grouse, etc. Half of the world's wood production comes from such forests.

The virgin forests of Changbai Mountain are dominated by large areas of temperate coniferous forest landscapes, and there are many expensive Korean pines, and the vertical distribution of natural landscapes is relatively obvious.

(2) Exotic and rare plants.

Exotic plants are something special, and unlike the common plants, these plants are often known for a characteristic that is unique on the earth, such as the baobab—the monkey bread tree; the apricot leaf eucalyptus—the tallest tree on the Australian grassland which is generally about 100 meters high, and the highest is 156 meters; the Baiqi chestnut tree—the thickest tree in Sicily, the Mediterranean, which has a trunk diameter of 17.5 meters and a circumference of 55 meters; the largest flower—rafflesia in Indonesia in the tropical rain forest of Java and Sumatra, with a diameter of about 1.4 meters and a weight of more than 50 kilograms; the banyan tree—the tree with the largest canopy, being famous all over the world for the "one tree forming a forest". The canopy shade of a banyan tree in Bangladesh is as much as 10,000 square meters, which can accommodate thousands of people to enjoy the shade.

The emergence, development and extinction of plant species have always been continuing since life began on the earth 3 billion years ago. New species have been continuously produced, and old species have been continuously oriented to extinction. Only a few plant species have survived in the history of biological evolution. These rare and endangered plants are the main objects of human protection, and these plants have extremely high landscape value. Examples of memorable rare plants in the world are rich, such as the royal water lily, which grows in the Amazon River Basin of South America, with the diameter of its largest round leaf up to 4 meters; cycad, the oldest seed plant in the world, once dominating the earth with dinosaurs, and known as " the living fossil" plants; the dove tree, also known as handkerchief tree or davidia involucrate, which is the only species in the genus and a medium sized tree native to altitudes of 3,600 to 8,500 feet (1,097 to 2,591 meters) in western China with its common name of dove tree in reference to its distinct pairs of white bracts dangling from the tree like large white handkerchiefs and in fact, sometimes referred to as the handkerchief tree. All these exotic and rare plants constitute strong attraction to go to visit and observe them.

(3) Grassland landscape.

Grasslands are an important part of the plant landscape. The vast grassland is not only a nutritious pasture for grazing, but also an ideal tourism landscape. The grassland is large and open, and the unique culture and customs that grassland bears attract tourists greatly. People can ride horses, camels, and participate other activities of the local life on the grasslands, and experience the special customs of ethnic minorities in home of the local people.

① Tropical savanna.

Tropical savanna is mainly distributed in the tropical region with obvious dry and wet seasons, mainly found in the Brazilian Plateau, East Africa, India and other places, where are dominated by xerophyte and high temperature perennial herbs of about 1 meter tall, and are secondly occupied by some drought-tolerant shrubs and scattered shrub communities. Due to the high growth capacity of grass and the feature of sparse and open vegetation on the grassland, ungulate herbivorous mammals such as zebras and giraffes, and some large carnivores, such as African lions and African leopard, are mostly distributed here, forming a unique natural landscape of tropical savanna. The tropical savanna in Africa is the most typical and most widely distributed among the same species in the world.

② Temperate grassland.

Temperate grasslands are mainly composed of xerophytic perennial herbs, distributed in arid inland to semi-humid areas, mainly including Eurasian grasslands, North American grasslands, and South American grasslands. Its plant species are mainly composed of tufted grass stipa, fescue, and awn grass, as well as scattered small shrubs and a variety of dicotyledonous weeds, such as legumes and compositae. The open temperate grassland is suitable for large herbivores that are good at running, such as bison, yellow sheep, wild ass and camels.

The grasslands in China are an important part of the temperate grasslands of the Eurasian continent. They start from the Songnen Plain in the north, passing through the northern and central parts of the Inner Mongolia Plateau, the northern and western parts of the Loess Plateau, extending to the vast Qinghai-Tibet Plateau hinterland. Hulunbuir grassland and Xilin Gol grassland in Inner Mongolia are the most typical and beautiful temperate grasslands in China. The grassland landscape there attracts millions of tourists to visit and experience the natural and cultural charms on the grassland. There are many rare species unique to the alpine meadows distributed on the Qinghai-Tibet Plateau, such as Tibetan antelope, yak, wild ass, marmot, and together with hundreds of species of flowers which fully bloom amid the abundant water and grass in midsummer, they form a unique and vivid grassland landscape attracting tourists.

(4) Tourism landscape of botanical gardens and eco-agri parks.

① Botanical gardens.

A botanical garden is a garden dedicated to the collection, cultivation, preservation and display of an especially wide range of plants, which are typically labelled with their botanical names. It may contain specialist plant collections such as cacti and other succulent plants, herb gardens, plants from particular parts of the world; there may be greenhouses, shade-houses, again with special collections such as tropical plants, alpine plants, or other exotic plants. Most are at least partly open to the public, and may offer guided tours, educational displays, art exhibitions, book rooms, open-air theatrical and musical performances, and other entertainment for visitors. Worldwide, there are now about 1,800 botanical gardens and arboreta in about 150 countries (mostly in temperate regions) of which about 550 are in Europe (150 of which are in Russia), 200 in North America, and an increasing number in East Asia. These gardens attract about 300 million visitors a year (Wikipedia, 2022).

China is currently fostering a natural reserve system for the in-situ conservation of wildlife, while the National Botanical Garden System is a key part of ex-situ conversation. According to the National Forestry and Grassland Administration, the national botanical garden system will consist of botanical gardens of various scales spreading across the country. It will provide an integrated conservation network for wild plants, and play a vital role in China's biodiversity protection efforts. China's plant diversity is among the highest in the world, providing habitats for over 36,000 types of higher plants. To protect rare and endangered plant species, China has so far built nearly 200 botanical gardens, where 60 percent of its native plant types are under in-situ conservation, i.e., the core function of botanical gardens. However, the existing gardens are scattered and lack of systematic management. National botanical gardens system is expected to provide overall guidelines and sci-tech support for in-situ plant conservation in China, thereby reducing the extinction risks from natural disasters and extreme weather conditions, and meanwhile, these gardens serve as important carriers of national and regional cultures and resources for environmental and patriotic education (Xinhuanet, 2022).

Wikipedia (2022) cited a list of botanical gardens and arboretums in China, the majority of which consist entirely of China native and endemic species while a few have a collection of plants from around the world. These botanical gardens and arboreta are in both national and provincial-level administration of China, with a few are privately owned:

China National Botanical Garden, Haidian District, Beijing;
South China National Botanical Garden, Guangzhou, Guangdong;
Qinling National Botanical Garden, Zhouzhi County, Xi'an, Shaanxi;
Xi'an Botanical Garden, Qujiang New District, Xi'an, Shaanxi;
Hong Kong Zoological and Botanical Gardens, Hong Kong;
Shenyang Botanical Garden, Liaoning;
Nanjing Botanical Garden, Memorial Sun Yat-Sen, Jiangsu;
Xishuangbanna Tropical Botanical Garden, Yunnan;
Lijiang High-Alpine Botanical Garden, Yunnan;
Wuhan Botanical Garden, Hubei;
Mount Lushan Botanical Garden, Mountain Lushan, Jiujiang, Jiangxi;
Chenshan Botanical Garden, Shanghai;
Lanzhou Botanical Garden, Lanzhou, Gansu.

② Eco-agri parks.

Eco-agricultural tourism resources refer to the ecological agricultural resources that can be viewed and enjoyed by tourists. From the perspective of landscape ecology, it mainly includes economic forest areas, various fruit parks, famous and special aquatic product areas in various waters and agricultural sightseeing parks (Bi Bi and You Changjiang, 2013). According to the Niogata-Japan practice, Agri-park is a facility for agricultural education, and as a learning center, it promotes local agriculture towards the younger generations and visitors looking for a lifestyle closer to the nature. This pleasant farm life experience allows the discovery of organic farming and cultivation (Kanpai, Japan, 2022).

Another case to cite for understanding eco-agri park is China Ecological Agriculture Tourism Park which is located in Shouguang, Shandong, China with a total area of 370 hectares, including 121 hectares of rivers and 249 hectares of river beaches. It is a comprehensive open garden that integrates leisure, entertainment, eco-agriculture tourism and popular science education. The ecological agriculture park connects four major themed scenic spots with the natural water body of the Mi River, i.e., the vegetable expo area, the flower city style area, the forest fruit oasis area, and the landscape pattern of the water sightseeing area, which greatly improve the ecological tourism environment of the local place. Its main planning objectives are: taking the hometown of "the Nongsheng" Jia Sixie as the connotation, featuring the ecological agricultural culture of Shouguang, "the hometown of vegetables in China", and creating a splendid appearance of "green plants, blue water, and colorful vegetables"(Shouguang Municipal Government, 2012).

2) Fauna Tourism Resources

There are many kinds of fauna species in the world, and they are the most dynamic wildlife forms in nature. The color, posture and vocalization of some wild life are of great aesthetic value. All kinds of wildlife exhibit the variety and vitality of natural beauty. Fauna landscape tourism resources can be divided into ornamental animals, rare animals, migrating animals and performing animals (Bi Bi and You Changjiang 2013).

(1) Ornamental animals.

An ornamental animal is an animal kept for display or curiosity, and can be either in a park or in the wildness. A wide range of mammals, birds and fish have been kept as ornamental animals. In many cases ornamental animals have often formed the basis of introduced populations, sometimes with negative ecological effects, but a history of being kept as ornamental animals has also preserved breeds, types and even species which have become rare or extinct elsewhere. From the tourism perspective, ornamental animals refer to those animals with aesthetic characteristics such as shape, color, posture and sound, that constitute tourism attractions(Bi Bi and You Changjiang, 2013).

Animals have different shapes, especially some rare birds and beasts, which are amazingly strange in shape. Typical examples are the tigers and lions. They are majestic and tall, with bright and noble fur. They are born with the spirit of kings; cranes are known for their slender and elegant figure; the four legs of the elephant are like pillars, compatible with its strange long nose. The moose has a donkey's tail, two deer's horns, four cow's hooves, and a camel's neck, all of which are of great ornamental value.

The richness of animal colors is comparable to that of plants. Most of them are generally not affected by seasons and climates, such as golden monkeys, red-crowned cranes, zebras, and flamingos. There are also a few that change with seasons or the environment, such as chameleons, thunder birds, and snow rabbits.

Animals are moving scenes. People enjoy their various movements and postures such as dexterity, lightness, vigor, and quaintness. The mighty power of a tiger going down the mountain, the freedom of a fish swimming in the water, the vigor of the horse galloping, the dexterity of apes climbing, the power of elephants moving out of the forest, and the beauty of peacocks spreading their tails. Smart animals such as monkeys, dogs and dolphins can be trained to do acrobatic performances, providing entertainment for visitors of all ages.

The animal calls are also varied. Some are gentle and sweet, some are loud and rough, and some are peculiar and weird. For example, there is the special bird in the Huangshan Mountain, China, which can tweet in eight tones; and the laughing bird in the Australian forest can make a hearty and loud laughter like a human. The calls of various animals are of special interest to visitors.

① Migrating animals.

Animal migration is the relatively long-distance movement of individual animals, usually on a seasonal basis. It is the most common form of migration in ecology. It is found in all major animal groups, including birds, mammals, fish, reptiles, amphibians, insects, and crustaceans. The cause of migration may be local climate, local availability of food, the season of the year or for mating. Large-scale animal migrations have formed great tourist attractions. According to the spatial location and migration model, such migration with tourism resource values can be further divided into three categories: bird migration, mammal migration, and fish migration.

Many species of birds migrate long distances in the air with seasonal changes, which constitutes popular tourism attraction. Birds migrate with the change of temperature. In the northern hemisphere, they generally live in the cool north in summer, migrate to the south in autumn, spend the winter in the warm south, and fly back to its habitat in the north again in spring. For a specific area, those who come to spend summer are called summer migratory birds, those who come to spend winter are called winter migratory birds, and those who pass through the area are called passing birds. The spring swallows are a type of a summer migratory bird in China. Every spring, they fly thousands of miles from India and other places to all parts of China for summer and then fly back to spend winter in India. Swans are winter migratory birds for the cities of Dongying and Weihai,

China. Each year they fly from their habitat in Siberia to the two cities for winter and make wonderful tourism scenes for the local people. The red-coated blue-tailed robin is a summer migratory bird for the northeastern region of China, a winter migratory bird for the southern China, and a passing bird for the northern China.

The most spectacular scene of migrating mammals is found on the African tropical savanna. When the rainy season begins, xerophytes grow fast and grasslands are quickly covered with green grass and colorful flowers. At this season, herbivores such as antelopes and zebras leave the mountains and move towards the recovered grasslands, followed by carnivorous beasts such as lions and leopards, as well as hyenas and jackals. When the rainy season ends, the grassland dries up and dies in the sunlight, and the animals begin to migrate reversely again.

The periodic migration of fish is often called fish migration. Fish, like other animals, require different environmental conditions at different stages of their life process. For example, the salmon migration is considered the most magnificent fish migration in the world. The salmon migration is the time of the year when salmon, which have migrated from the ocean to fresh water, swim against the stream to the upper reaches of rivers, where they spawn on gravel beds. After spawning, all species of Pacific salmon and most Atlantic salmon die, and the salmon life cycle starts over again with the new generation of hatchlings. The annual migration can be a major event for predators such as grizzly bears, bald eagles and sport fishermen, and meanwhile watching the salmon swimming against the stream becomes a major tourism event in autumn. Such magnificent scene can also be found in China at the same season at the joint of the Heilongjiang and Ussuri River where the salmon is also called Damaha fish.

② Rare animals and zoo animals.

Rare animals refer to the rare and precious wild animal species with high scientific research and tourism development values. Some rare animals grow in the wild, while others are maintained by artificial breeding, more often found in zoos or breeding centers that are open to the public. For example, a small number of giant pandas, China's national treasure, live in the wild in the Giant Panda National Park. However, if tourists want to watch and learn about giant pandas, they usually need to go to the Chengdu Research Base of Giant Panda Breeding in the suburb of Chengdu, China.

With over 10,000 zoos estimated worldwide, holding millions of wild and rare animals in captivity, the scale of the zoo resources and industry is huge. Capitals and major cities across the world often have zoos, as well as a great many other captive wild animal facilities that have developed over the years. The justifications for the existence of zoos include species conservation, education and research, and amusement for the visitors as well(Bornfree, 2022). Henry Doorly Zoo in Nebraska, USA is ranked No.1 among the largest zoos in the world while Beijing Zoo in China raked No.3.

6.1.5 Conservation Frameworks for Biological Resources

National parks have now been a hot spot for discussion as a balancing effort between conservation and development of the natural biological resources. In fact, national park system is only one of the conservation efforts that have been practiced so far in the world (Fennell, 2008), drawing from Nelson, who summarized the most practiced conservation frameworks as follows.

1) Scientific Reserve/Strict Nature Reserve

Areas with some outstanding ecosystem features and/or species of flora and fauna of national scientific importance, representative of particular natural areas, fragile life forms or ecosystems, important biological or geological diversity, or areas of particular importance to the conservation of genetic resources. Concern is for continuance of natural processes and strict control of human interference.

2) National Park

A relatively large area where one or several ecosystems are not materially altered by human use, the highest competent government authority has taken steps to prevent or control, and visitors are allowed to enter under special conditions for inspirational, educative, cultural, and recreative uses.

3) Natural Monument/Natural Landmark

Area normally contains one or more specific natural features of outstanding national significance, which should be protected because of uniqueness or rarity. Ideally little or no sign of human activity.

4) Nature Conservation Reserve/Managed Nature Reserve/Wildlife Sanctuary

A variety of areas fall into this category. Although each has as its primary purpose of protection of nature, the production of harvestable renewable resources may play a secondary role in management. Habitat manipulation may be required to provide optimum conditions for species, communities, or features of special interest.

5) Protected Landscape or Seascape

A broad category includes a wide variety of semi-natural and cultural landscapes within various nations. In general, two types of areas, those where landscapes possess special aesthetic qualities resulting from human – land interaction and those that are primarily natural areas managed intensively for recreational and tourist uses.

6) Resource Reserve (Interim Conservation Unit)

Normally extensive, relatively isolated, and lightly inhabited areas under considerable pressure for colonization and greater exploration. Often not well understood in natural, land use, or cultural terms. Maintenance of existing conditions to allow for studies of potential uses and their effects as a basis for decisions.

7) Natural Biotic Area/Anthropological Reserve

Natural areas are the places where the influence or technology of modern humans has not significantly interfered with or been absorbed by the traditional ways of life of inhabitants. Management is oriented to maintenance of habitat for traditional societies.

8) Multiple Use Management Area/Managed Resource Area

Large areas are suitable for production of wood products, water, pasture, wildlife, marine products, and outdoor recreation, which may contain nationally unique or exceptional natural features. The areas can be planned and managed on a sustained-yield basis with protection through zoning or other means for special features or processes.

9) Biosphere Reserve

They are intended to conserve representative natural areas throughout the world through creation of global and national networks of reserves, which can include representative natural biomes, or communities, species of unique interest, examples of harmonious landscapes resulting from traditional uses, and modified or degraded landscapes capable of restoration to more natural conditions. Biosphere reserves provide benchmarks for monitoring environmental change and areas for science, education, and training.

10) World Heritage Site

To protect natural and also cultural features considered to be of world heritage quality; examples include outstanding illustrations of the major stages of earth's evolutionary history, habitats where populations of rare or endangered species of plants and animals still survive, and also outstanding archaeological or architectural sites. Stress on maintenance of heritage values for worldwide public enlightenment, and to provide for research and environmental monitoring.

11) Wetlands of International Importance (Ramsar)

Marshes, swamps, and other wetlands of value for flood control, nutrient production, wildlife habitat, and related purposes. Management procedures designed to prevent destruction and deterioration through national agreement to an international convention known as Ramsar after the site in Iran where the convention was initially agreed to by a number of founding countries.

Fennell further pointed out that key issue for balance between environmental and resource conservation and development is to better understand the place and role of human beings with regard to the human-nature relation. Conservation and protection should be the prerequisite for developing all the biological resources into tourism landscapes and products for entertaining tourists.

6.2 Climate Landscape as Tourism Resources

A pleasant climate is one of the necessary conditions for the development of tourism activities. Varied climate and meteorological phenomena are an important part of tourism resources. They have characteristics of being regional, temporal and seasonal, variable, rapid changing, backgrounding and scene borrowing, rhythmic and orienting, and reproducing as well. The various elements such as cold, heat, moisture, wind, cloud, rain, thunder, fog, etc. that make up the meteorological climate resources not only have the function of directly creating climate landscapes, but also have a profound impact on tourism activities, mainly manifested in following aspects as: affecting the seasonal changes of the landscape; affecting the formation of regional landscapes; affecting the spatial and temporal distribution of tourism flows; affecting tourists' experience and comfort; and affecting the layout of tourist areas.

6.2.1 Defining Climate and Meteorology Tourism Resources

China National Tourism Administration (CNTA) issued the national standard of *Classification, Investigation and Evaluation of Tourism Resources* in 2003, which clearly identified climatic landscapes as one of the types of tourism resources and belonged to the category of natural tourism resources. The main manifestations of climate landscapes include ice and snow landscapes, and meteorological landscapes. The former entails ice, snow, and rime wonders. While the latter entails Buddha light, sunrise, sunset, moonscape, cloud sea, cloud waterfall, aurora, polar night, and mirages.

Climate is the long-term weather pattern in an area. Climate resources usually refer to light, heat, water, wind, atmospheric components, etc. As the main natural resources indispensable to human production and life, they can be directly or indirectly used by human beings, or provide material and energy to human beings under certain technical and economic conditions. Climate resources can also be developed for tourism purpose.

Meteorology is the general term for various physical phenomena and physical processes in the atmosphere, such as cold and heat, drought and moisture, wind, clouds, rain, snow, frost, fog, lightning, and thunder. Meteorological resources refer to the part of meteorological conditions that human beings can develop and utilize to create social and economic benefits, for instance, to utilize tourism development to create employment, economic revenue, and social welfare. In other word, this part of resources is also called meteorological landscape.

6.2.2 Characteristics of Climate and Meteorology Tourism Resources

1) Being Regional

Geographical latitude, distribution of coast and land, and topographic fluctuations play a decisive role in the formation of large-scale climate landscape. The zoning distribution of climate makes the meteorology and climate tourism resources in various places, demonstrating distinctive regional characteristics. Some special sights only appear in certain occasions and places. For example, soft rime appears along the Songhua River; Hainan Island of China becomes the best place to spend winter because it is located in the tropical area with an annual average temperature of 23 to 25 degrees.

2) Being Temporal and Seasonal

The formation and changes of various meteorological elements such as temperature and humidity have certain regularity. Different meteorological landscape elements appear at different times in a year, with obvious seasonal changes, and similarly weather phenomena appear at different times in a day. For example, many tourists visiting Mount Huangshan hope to appreciate the sea of clouds but not many have the opportunity to see it because there are only 40 days in a year to see the sea of clouds at Mount Huangshan. Similarly, snow and ice landscapes are only active in winter, while mirage and Buddha lights are generally seen only at noon or afternoon time.

3) Being Variable

Physical phenomena and processes in the atmosphere tend to change rapidly. Typical changes such as cold, warm, cloudy and sunny time in a day often affect the color, light, and shade of the landscape, giving passengers a varied sense of beauty.

4) Being Rapid in Change (Transient)

The meteorological elements such as fog, rain, lightening, light change very rapidly. Typical scenes such as Buddha light, mirage, sunrise, and sunset light are all meteorological landscapes that may appear and disappear in an instant. For example, the Buddha light of Emei Mountain only appears in a short period of time after sunrise or before sunset, so that tourists can enjoy the magnificent scenery only if they can seize the opportunity.

5) Being Backgrounding and Scene Borrowing

Meteorology and climate landscapes generally do not have stable entities. If they are developed as tourism products, such landscapes often have to be coordinated with other tourism resources, with the help of other landscapes as the background. For example, clouds, fog, rain are always combined with elements such as mountains, forests, and water to form beautiful integrated landscapes. The reason why Hainan Island can become a paradise for spending winter lies in that, in addition to the advantages of tropical marine monsoon climate with agreeable temperature in winter, the background elements such as blue sky, clear water, beach, Li ethnic culture, and Wuzhi Mountain scenery are also attracting factors for tourists.

6) Being Rhythmic and Orienting

Given the invariability of tourists transportation means, travel motivation, and affordability for travel, the main factor affecting tourism flow is the regional differences of tourism destinations. These regional differences are often influenced by climate factors. The climate has regular changes between years and months, so the tourism flow will change rhythmically in the low season, the normal season and the high season with the change of the climate.

7) Being Reproducing

Meteorological landscapes appear regularly and can be reused and reproduced by nature or by human interference. Climate resources are abundant in various places, the use of which usually does not cause conflicts in contrast with some scarce resources which are often the focus of conflicts in the high seasons.

6.2.3 Impact of Climate and Meteorology Elements on Tourism Activities

1) Regional Differences in Climate Form Different Natural Tourism Landscapes

Differences in climate conditions of different places form different natural tourism landscapes. For example, the monsoon region in eastern China has abundant precipitation and sufficient sunshine, and is an area for abundant tourism resources such as forests, lakes, rivers, seas, waterfalls, and beaches. The non-monsoon area in the northwest China has less precipitation and has an arid and semi-arid climate, where is mainly distributed with tourism resources such as deserts, gravel beaches, cold deserts, grasslands, and saltwater lakes, and other tourism resources. The southern China region is rich in precipitation with long humid rainy season and lush vegetation, forming the beautiful scenery of southern Chinese landscape. Regional differences in climate will also affect human landscape and regional culture such as architecture and ethnic costumes.

2) Seasonal Changes Affecting the Natural Landscape

Due to the seasonal changes of climate, other landscapes also have corresponding seasonal changes, so that the same scenic area presents varied landscapes in different seasons. Taking Mount Taishan as an example, in spring, you can enjoy winter jasmine flowers all over and taste the early spring tea in the mountains. In summer, you can escape the burning heat in the mountain where the temperature is 8 to 12 degrees Celsius lower than in the city. You can see colorful leaves in autumn and snow on the green pines in winter.

3) Climate Affecting Spatial Distribution of Tourism Flow

The seasonal changes of climate lead to the change rhythm of low season, normal season and peak season in the tourism industry. The mild climate in spring and autumn is often the peak tourist season; the hot summer and freezing winter are usually the flat and low seasons when motivation for travel is relatively low.

6.2.4 Categories of Climate Landscape Resources

The climate landscapes in general are mainly categorized as meteorological tourism resources and climatic tourism resources.

1) Meteorological Resource

Meteorological resources refer to the part of meteorological conditions that can be developed and utilized for tourism development to entertain tourist and meanwhile create employment, economic revenue, and social welfare.

(1) Cloud and mist.

The visible aggregates, composed of tiny water droplets or ice crystals formed by the condensation of water vapor in the air due to the drop in atmospheric temperature, are called clouds. When they float close to the ground, composed of tiny water droplets, often appearing in white, and the horizontal visibility is less than 1 kilometer, so they are called called fog.

Due to the strong fluidity of the air, the clouds and mists are either thick or light, and they are changeable in shape. In mountain scenic areas, clouds and fog often constitute wonderful landscapes and become an important part of mountain scenery. The sea of clouds in Mount Huangshan is an amazing case. Mist may also constitute some unique local landscape features. For example, London in the United Kingdom and Chongqing in China are both famous as cities of mist.

(2) Rain.

Rain is the condensation of water vapor in clouds that falls to the ground. Rainfall is not only the main source of water supply for rivers, lakes and other water bodies, and an important source of water that nourishes all things in the world, but also the source of natural beauty that can be admired. Every spring, the southern part of China often has long-lasting rainy weather, forming a unique rain landscape. The rain scene has a touch of dim and hazy beauty like an artistic work of impressionism.

(3) Snow.

Snow is solid water that falls from the atmosphere to the ground. When the temperature is at or below freezing point, the water vapor directly condenses into a solid state, i.e., ice crystals. Because the molecules of ice crystals are based on hexagons, the basic shape of snowflakes is hexagonal.

Snow scene is a special precipitation phenomenon that occurs in winter in mid-latitude regions, high latitude regions and mountainous areas above the snow line. Combined with other natural conditions, such as mountains, forests, glaciers, etc., the snow constitutes a special scene. Snow scene has great ornamental value and is an important part of meteorological tourism resources, which has a strong attraction to tourists. China and the middle and high latitude countries have many scenic spots known for snow, such as "the Linhai Snowfield" in northeastern China, the snow cap of the Mount Fuji in Japan, and the snow mountain landscape in Switzerland. In addition, snow also provides conditions and possibilities for winter ice and snow sports tourism activities, such as skiing, skating, snow and sculpture. The 2022 Winter Olympic Games in China definitely promotes the development of ice and snow sports and tourism in China.

(4) Rime.

Rime is a needle-shaped, granular milky white condensation that gathers on the surface of objects on the ground, forming a fluffy white ice layer on the tree branches and other objects. The pine branches and the bushes may look like huge white corals when they are covered with fluffy rime. The Songhua River in Jilin Province has the most famous rime landscape in China. The rime phenomenon often occurs in winter in the high latitude Great Lakes regions of Canada and the United States. The rime may create a breath-taking wonderland out of usually ordinary settings in grey winter days, making a strong tourism attraction.

(5) Mirage.

A mirage is a kind of natural scene, and it is a naturally-occurring optical phenomenon in which light rays bend via refraction to produce a displaced image of distant objects or the sky, usually appearing in the open terrain such as the sea surface and desert in the middle and high latitude areas. Mirage attracts many tourists with its rarity and peculiarity. Its appearance has two characteristics: first, it appears repeatedly in the same place, for example, fantastic mirages often appear over Alaska in the United States; second, the time of mirage appearance is relatively fixed. For example, the mirage at Penglai, Shandong Province mostly appears in May and June every year, while in Alaska, the United States, the mirage usually appears within 20 days after June 20. These characteristics and rules allow people to follow them and use them as resources to design and develop tourism products.

(6) Buddha light.

Buddha light is a unique beautiful and fantastic scene in the mountains. Its magic lies in the appearance of a colorful halos in the sky opposite the viewer, with a human figure in the center of the halos, as if the Buddha had come to the world. Buddha light is actually an atmospheric optical phenomenon produced by the diffraction of sunlight through fine water droplets suspended in the air. In China, Buddha light can be viewed in quite a few famous mountains such as Mount Huangshan, Mount Lushan, Mount Taishan, and Mount Emei. The appearance of the Buddha light spectacle requires the combination of many natural factors such as sunlight, terrain and sea of clouds, and so it is relatively rare to see. It is often considered good luck and blessing for tourists to have the opportunity to view Buddha light.

2) Climatic Resources

Climate tourism resources generally refer to the climatic conditions that can make people feel comfortable and are conducive to tourism activities. The availability of pleasant climatic conditions and the length of its duration are the prerequisites for the development of those tourist destinations which are not so rich in tourism resources, and meanwhile, agreeable climate is also a determining condition for the length of the tourist season of a destination. Restricted by many factors that affect the formation of climate, the spatial distribution of pleasant climate also has obvious zonal and non‐zonal patterns. In the horizontal zone structure, the pleasant climate is mainly distributed in the humid and semi-humid climate zones in the middle and low latitudes, especially in the coast and island areas. Climate tourism resources not only directly participate in landscaping, but also are one of the basic external conditions for human activities, and are an important factor for tourists to choose their destination and length of stay. According to the characteristics of tourism destinations, climatic tourism resources can be divided into the following categories.

(1) Climate landscape to beat summer heat.

The climate to avoid summer heat refers to the climate in certain area that is suitable for spending the summer. Such places are usually called summer resorts which refer to areas with excellent climatic conditions, either near the sea, the lake, or near the mountains, etc., where people can come to stay away from the summer heat. Usually the average daily temperature of these summer resorts maintains a certain stability over the summer time and is of course much lower than other places. For example, the four most famous summer resorts in China are known as Beidaihe in Qinhuangdao City, Hebei Province, Jigong Mountain in Xinyang City, Henan Province, Mogan Mountain in Huzhou City, Zhejiang Province, and Lushan Mountain in Jiujiang City, Jiangxi Province, and they all benefit from their climatic advantages. Another case is Qingdao, Shandong Province, as a coastal city, with its agreeable temperature of around 25 to 30 degrees Celsius in summer time, Qingdao is an ideal place to beat the summer heat and hence attracts millions of visitors from all over the country every year.

(2) Climate landscape to beat the winter cold.

The climate to avoid winter cold refers to the climate in certain area that is suitable for spending the winter. In the case of China, Guangdong, Guangxi, Hainan and southern

Yunnan are all desirable places to spend the winter time and beat the winter cold. Hainan Island, in particular, has a tropical monsoon climate, with an annual average temperature of 22 to 27 degrees, fresh air, varied birds, and fragrant flowers, making the first choice for most tourists to go for winter to avoid extreme cold in their place of residence.

(3) Sunny climate landscape.

Sunlight is an important climatic tourism resources, and countries along the Mediterranean coast fully employ the subtropical Mediterranean characteristics of the climate to develop tourism. They have long hours of warm sunshine there at the beach, strongly attracting tourists from other parts of the Europe where they cannot have enough sunshine and warm temperature in winter season, such as the UK and Northern European countries.

(4) Phenological landscape.

Phenological landscape refers to the climatic landscapes with seasonal changes of various plants, animals, hydrology and meteorology, or the landscapes formed by all the above mentioned factors, such as the tourist landscapes made by the seasonal flowers, or reproduction and migration of animals. The Great Wildlife Migration in East Africa is a typical phenological landscape, attracting a large number of tourist with wildlife interest from all over the world.

(5) Landscape of extreme and special climates.

Extreme and special climatic tourism resources are those landscapes formed by extreme climatic conditions, such as usually extremely cold. For example, the cold ice and snow climate is an important tourism resource for winter tourism with appropriate topographical conditions, such as ice caving in Iceland, experiencing Sweden's Ice-hotel, sleeping in an authentic snow igloo in Finland, ice fishing in Alaska, etc.(Olander, 2019).

Case 6-2

Chapter Review

This chapter mainly introduces the concept, characteristic, categories of biological tourism landscapes, and climate landscape as tourism resources.

The definition of biological landscape and biological landscape tourism resource are given. As one of the most important tourism resources in nature, the biological resource is discussed in relation to tourism. Then the characteristics and categories of biological landscapes are presented, and the global frameworks for conservation of biological resources are introduced. The conservation principles in tourism development based on fauna and flora resources are stressed.

The definition of climate landscape is introduced, and the values of climate landscape as tourism resources are identified, and the global framework for conservation

Case 6-3

Case 6-4

of biological resources is introduced. The characteristics and categories of climatic and meteorological resources are presented in details. Also the impact of climate and meteorology elements on tourism is discussed.

Questions for Discussion

1. What is the definition of biological tourism landscape?
2. What are the characteristics of biological tourism resources?
3. How biological resources are categorized?
4. What are global frameworks for biological resource conservation introduced in this chapter?
5. What's the definition of climate tourism landscape?
6. What are the characteristics of climate tourism resources?
7. How climate resources are categorized?
8. How do the climate and meteorology elements impact tourism?

Chapter 7
Heritage Tourism Resources

Learning Objectives

(1) Describe the definition of heritage attractions.

(2) Explain the typology of heritage tourism resources.

(3) Apply the relevant theories and forms of heritage tourism resources to the tourism development.

(4) Analyze the measures of heritage tourism resources protection.

Technical Words

English Words	中文翻译
heritage tourism resources	遗产旅游资源
natural heritage	自然遗产
forest parks	森林公园
tangible cultural heritage	物质文化遗产
movable cultural relics	可移动文物
immovable cultural relics	不可移动文物
lineal or serial cultural heritages	线性文化遗产
intangible cultural heritage	非物质文化遗产
mixed heritage	混合遗产
a special theme of the comprehensive museum	综合博物馆
thematic site museum	专题性遗址博物馆
relic parks	遗址公园

Knowledge Graph

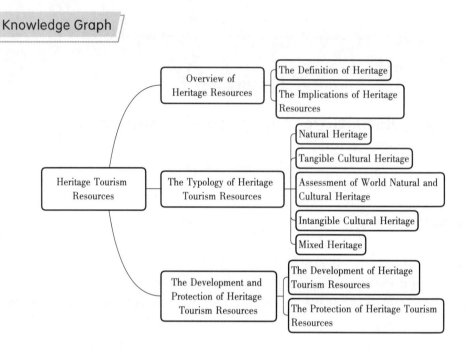

Heritage, with historical, artistic and scientific values, is the wealth left by history and nature to mankind. Some of them are considered as the representatives of local culture and the symbol of the community or country. China with a long history is rich in natural and cultural heritage. These heritages represent the wisdom and spirit of Chinese and reflect the vitality and creativity of China. With the trend of cultural and tourism integration, heritage because of its innate cultural and emotional connections with people has become one of the most important tourism resources with increasing attraction to tourists.

7.1 Overview of Heritage Resources

7.1.1 The Definition of Heritage

In the West, the word "heritage" was usually used in the private domain before the middle of the 20th century, specifically referring to that "which is or may be inherited by individuals or communities and passed on to successors" (Aird, 1994). Until the 1960s, there was international concern over the flooding of the Abu Simbel Temples, a treasure of ancient Egyptian civilization, to build the Aswan High Dam in Egypt. With the rise of international protection movement and environmental protection movement, the term of heritage began to spread to the social domain gradually, and its definition began to include the conscious inheritance and promotion of the past natural or culture resources (Shi Chenxuan, 2008).

In the *Convention Concerning the Protection of the World Cultural and Natural Heritage* released on November 16, 1972, natural heritage and cultural heritage were defined as follows.

1) Natural Heritage

For the purposes of this Convention, the following shall be considered as "natural heritage".

(1) Natural features consisting of physical and biological formations or groups of such formations, which are of outstanding universal value from the aesthetic or scientific point of view;

(2) Geological and physiographical formations and precisely delineated areas which constitute the habitat of threatened species of animals and plants of outstanding universal value from the point of view of science or conservation;

(3) Natural sites or precisely delineated natural areas of outstanding universal value from the point of view of science, conservation or natural beauty (UNESCO, 1972).

2) Cultural Heritage

For the purpose of this Convention, the following shall be considered as "cultural heritage".

(1) Monuments: architectural works, works of monumental sculpture and painting, elements or structures of an archaeological nature, inscriptions, cave dwellings and combinations of features, which are of outstanding universal value from the point of view of history, art or science;

(2) Groups of buildings: groups of separate or connected buildings which, because of their architecture, their homogeneity or their place in the landscape, are of outstanding universal value from the point of view of history, art or science;

(3) Sites: works of man or the combined works of nature and man, and areas including archaeological sites which are of outstanding universal value from the historical, aesthetic, ethnological or anthropological point of view(UNESCO, 1972);

(4) In the provisions of the Convention, special emphasis is placed on "outstanding universal values", which is also the standard and basis for the world heritage selection activities that have attracted much attention. Although the focus is on having "outstanding universal value", each country should promise not only to conserve the World Heritage Sites situated in its country, but also to protect and conserve its cultural and intangible heritage.

This chapter adopts the definition of scholars Tunbridge and Ashworth (1996), heritage is here defined as "artefacts, remembered personalities, symbols and associations". They believed that apart from the material things such as objects,

Case 7-1

buildings, sites and places, the intangible features that can represent the meaning of the "past" can also be called heritage, such as collective memory and habits caused by some historical reasons. Heritage includes both material "buildings and relics" and intangible "folk customs and memories". According to their definition, the scope of heritage is quite wide, whether it is material or non-material, cultural or natural, ranging from historical sites to living habits. As long as it has outstanding universal value and is historical, it can be considered as a heritage. For example, after thousands of years of changes, Henan has formed not only the natural heritage represented by Longmen Grottoes and Yin Ruins in Anyang, but also the cultural heritage represented by Yan-huang Culture, Yin-shang Culture and Yellow River Culture.

Since China joined the Convention in 1985 and began to apply for items of world heritage, the concept of heritage and related concepts have increasingly attracted the public's attention. The concept of heritage evolved with the social development. In the future, in order to meet the needs of reality and adapt to social development, its meaning will be further developed and expanded.

7.1.2 The Implications of Heritage Resources

The value of heritage is self-evident. Generally speaking, its value is mainly reflected in three aspects: history, aesthetics and technology. As for the development of tourism resources, the emphasis is on its historical value and practical significance.

1) Cultural Symbolism

In the 21st century, heritage resources have become an important part of many areas. They are the cultural representatives or symbols of a region or a city. According to the Australian ICOMOS, cultural significance means "aesthetic, historic, scientific or social value for past, present or future generations"(*Burra Charter*, 1999). Cultural significance is a notion that helps in assessing the value of heritage. A heritage with cultural significance can provide cultural knowledge for individuals, and further can be appreciated by future generations. The aesthetic, historic, scientific and social values need to be understood carefully in establishing the cultural significance of the place.

For example, artists, architects and literati from the middle ages, the Renaissance, modernism and other times have left a large number of tangible and intangible cultural heritages in Paris. Paris attaches great importance to the protection and reuse of human history, so as to create a distinctive brand effect with urban characteristics, making Paris and even the whole France a synonym for romance, fashion and art. The cultural policy of Paris puts forward that the theme of the cultural planning of Paris is "heritage, creation and education". At present, Paris is recognized as one of the world's great creative culture centers and cultural life centers famous for its "art of life".

2) Historical Significance

Heritage is produced and inherited under certain historical conditions. As a product of history, it must be a memorial of the times and reflect the natural, economic, scientific, technological, military and cultural conditions at that time. It contains huge historical information. Heritage enables people to "travel" into the past and forget the stress of the present while learning something of the history and culture of society. The combination of various heritages has accumulated profound and long-standing cultural heritage and condensed huge information in the political, economic, cultural and social fields of the region within a period of time. In this vein, the heritage can reflect history, confirm history, complete history and inherit history.

Heritage is a visualized textbook for learning ancient history, although we can understand the history of human development comprehensively and systematically by reading history textbooks. One of the best ways to make up for this deficiency is to visit the heritage site directly.

For example, China's historical changes could be reflected by Tianjin's rich and splendid cultural heritage. Tianjin is a prosperous city by water transportation. In the Ming dynasty, Tianjin built a city at Sanchakou to protect the capital and develop trade. After the Opium War, Tianjin became a trading port. During the period of the Republic of China, Hebei New Area became the political and cultural center of modern Chinese in Tianjin. After the founding of the People's Republic of China, Tianjin became the second largest city in the north. As a world-famous ancient city, Tianjin's splendid canal cultural heritage has witnessed national unity, cultural integration, social development and national progress.

Another example is the Terra Cotta Warriors. Known as the eighth wonder of the world, the Terra Cotta Warriors mausoleum of the First Emperor of Qin has been introduced from various angles and sides in various types of books, with pictures and texts. But only by turning over the books and reading books, we can only imagine how spectacular it is. Only when you visit the site of the Terra Cotta Warriors Museum, can you really feel its grandeur and admire its artistic charm. On the one hand, you can have a sense of national pride; on the other hand, you can also truly appreciate the majestic style of the First Emperor of Qin who unified China.

3) The Tourism Value

First of all, the rich historical and cultural connotation of the heritage will attract a large number of tourists to take advantage of various opportunities to visit, in order to increase historical knowledge. In this regard, Xi'an is still an excellent model. Banpo village tells tourists that primitive people settled here; the Terra Cotta Warriors show the army formation of Qin State.

Secondly, due to the unique characteristics of some sites and relics, coupled with the publicity of the mass media, they are often shrouded in a layer of mystery, attracting some people with strong curiosity to explore the ancient world, such as the Terra Cotta Warriors in the mausoleum of the First Emperor of Qin dynasty. After reading various introductions or hearing the descriptions of people around them, many people have the idea of having a look. They should have a face-to-face experience of the style of the Terra Cotta Warriors of the Qin dynasty, see its invincible military array, appreciate its overall artistic effect, and examine its artistic characteristics. They can also imagine and conceive beautiful pictures and beautiful literary works.

Thirdly, the transformation of heritage resources into tourism resources can drive the development of regional economy. Shandong provincial government gives full play to the advantages of the Grand Canal tourism resources and makes every effort to build " the Lufeng Canal" cultural tourism brand. In 2016, the five cities along the canal received a total of 150 million tourists and earned a tourism revenue of 140 billion yuan (Hu Mengfei, 2021). The development of cultural heritage tourism in Shandong Province not only promoted the economic development of the areas along the canal but also injected funds into heritage protection, realizing the benign interaction between protection and development.

7.2 The Typology of Heritage Tourism Resources

Over the long course of history, human beings, blessed with the gifts of nature, created brilliant civilizations and left behind an invaluable treasure-cultural and natural world heritage. These irreplaceable cultural and natural assets with outstanding universal value represent a magnificent genetic map of human civilizations and the most beautiful chapters of nature(UNESCO, 2022).

The classification and evolution of heritage resources are the product of the continuous expansion and development of heritage connotations. At present, the internationally recognized classification of heritage is the Classification of the United Nations Educational, Scientific and Cultural Organization (UNESCO, 2005), namely natural heritage, cultural heritage, mixed heritage, cultural landscape and intangible cultural heritage. The type of heritage and the relationship between each heritage can be represented in Figure 7-1.

Figure 7-1 UNESCO heritage classification system

7.2.1 Natural Heritage

1) Definitions of Natural Heritage

Natural heritage is nature's miraculous creation within hundreds of millions of years, carrying the spiritual and cultural values of human beings, and is related to the ecological security of the earth. According to the *Convention Concerning the Protection of the World Cultural and Natural Heritage* (1972), as mentioned in 7.1.1, it is not difficult to find that natural heritage is a prominent example of an important stage in the evolutionary history of the earth, is a prominent example of important ongoing geological processes, biological evolutionary processes, and the interrelationship between people and the natural environment, and a unique, rare or wonderful natural phenomenon, landform or area of rare natural beauty.

2) Characteristics of Natural Heritage

The natural heritage not only has outstanding universal value but also keeps integrity. In summary, it has the following characteristics.

(1) Containing all the necessary elements to reflect the outstanding universal value of the heritage site;

(2) The area is large enough to ensure that the characteristics and processes that embody the universal value of the heritage site are highlighted;

(3) Well protected.

3) Types of Natural Heritage Resources

There are numerous amazing natural heritage resources in China, which can be divided into world natural heritage, scenic and historic interest areas (which may be mixed natural and cultural heritage), nature reserves, geoparks, forest parks, wetland parks and water conservancy scenic spots(Guo Jinaying and Qin Rong, 2014). Its connotations and characteristics are as follows.

(1) Scenic and historic interest areas.

Scenic and historic interest areas are national legal natural heritage or natural and cultural dual heritage protection sites, and their natural and cultural landscapes can reflect important natural changes and major historical development processes. They are usually in a natural state or maintain the original appearance, and are nationally representative, known as "natural museums". For example, Huanglong scenic and historic interest area in northwestern Sichuan Province, Wulingyuan scenic and historic interest area in Hunan Province are well-known scenic and historic interest areas.

(2) Nature reserves.

The nature reserve is a national statutory natural heritage protection site. The nature reserves refer to representative natural ecosystems, natural concentrated distribution areas of rare and endangered species of wild animals and plants, and the land, water bodies or sea areas where natural monuments of special significance and other protected objects are located. They are home to many rare species and are endowed with unique natural beauty, fascinating landscapes, rare ecological processes and exceptional biodiversity. At present, China has initially formed a network of nature reserves with a more reasonable layout, complete types and functions, which has played a huge role in protecting wild animals and plants and biodiversity, maintaining ecological balance and improving the ecological environment.

(3) Geoparks.

Case 7-2

The geopark is a unique natural area composed of geological relics landscape with special geological scientific significance, rare natural attributes, high aesthetic ornamental value, a certain scale and distribution range, and the integration of other natural landscapes and cultural landscapes. The geopark is not only a key protected area for geological relics landscape and ecological environment, but also a base for geological scientific research. For example, Dali-Cangshan, Sanqingshan, Huangshan, Jiuhuashan, etc. are classic geoparks.

(4) Forest parks.

The forest park is a park established in an area with a large area with one or more ecosystems and a unique natural landscape of the forest. The definition of forest park according to the *China Forest Park Landscape Resources Grade Evaluation* (1999) promulgated by the State Bureau of Quality and Technical Supervision is: with a certain scale and quality of forest landscape resources and environmental conditions, forest tourism can be carried out and in accordance with the statutory procedures to declare the approval of the forest region.

The purpose of establishing a forest park is to protect all the natural environment and natural resources within its boundaries and to provide a better environment for recreation, retreat, summer vacation, cultural entertainment and scientific research. In 1982, China established the first national forest park in Zhangjiajie, Hunan Province. As of 2019, a total of 897 national forest parks have been established in mainland China.

(5) Wetland parks.

The wetland park is a specific wetland area with significant or unique ecological, cultural, aesthetic and biodiversity values as the main body, with a certain scale and scope, its functions are to protect the integrity of the wetland ecosystem and maintain the ecological process and services of the wetland, and can be used for public visits, leisure or scientific, cultural and educational activities.

At present, China has begun to form a wetland protection network system with wetland protection areas as the main body and a combination of wetland protection communities, wetland parks, marine function special protection areas, wetland multi-purpose control areas and other management forms.

(6) Water conservancy scenic spots.

Water conservancy scenic spots refer to the water or water conservancy projects as the basis, water conservancy scenic resources, that is, water areas (water bodies) and related shoreland, islands, forests, grasses, buildings and other natural landscapes and cultural landscapes that can be attractive to people, which belong to the natural heritage resources jointly created by man and nature. The types of water conservancy scenic spots include reservoirs, wetland, natural rivers and lakes, urban rivers and lakes, tank farms, soil and water conservations, etc. Different types have different resource characteristics and theme-positioning.

7.2.2 Tangible Cultural Heritage

1) Definition of Tangible Cultural Heritage

In the long history of human development, human has created a rich and colorful material and spiritual civilization, leaving a vast sea of cultural heritage for future generations(Wang Degang and Wang Wei, 2010). Tangible cultural heritage is a cultural relic with important cultural, artistic, historical and scientific value, as well as a historical legacy after the end of a cultural form or the continuation of a cultural tradition to this day (Sun Hua, 2020).

2) Characteristics of Tangible Cultural Heritage

(1) Spiritual characteristics.

Tangible cultural heritage is the accumulation of spiritual wealth created by human beings, essentially the creation of spiritual labor. Tangible cultural heritage can be used as a resource mainly due to the development and utilization of its spiritual contents. Although modern technology can replicate ancient buildings and artifacts, replicas can never create new spiritual content and cultural value(Wang Chen and Wang Yuan, 2016).

(2) Derivable characteristics.

The spiritual content of tangible cultural heritage can be combined with other material carriers to form new products. This derivative feature allows people to develop and utilize the spiritual content of cultural heritage without destroying its original state. For example, historical and cultural sites are immovable tangible cultural heritage, and usually the common way to use them is through the development of historical and cultural attractions to create cultural tourism products.

(3) Tradable characteristics.

Tangible cultural heritage can be traded in the market as an economic resource. The purchaser acquires the right to invest and develop tangible cultural heritage resources by purchasing property rights or operating rights(Wang Chen and Wang Yuan, 2016). For example, some ancient streets, ancient towns, celebrity former residences and other ancient buildings can sell their management rights to private individuals under the premise of complying with the *Law of the People's Republic of China on the Protection of Cultural Relics* to encourage individuals to repair, replace and purchase ancient buildings.

(4) Depletion characteristics.

Resource depletion is usually the tendency for a resource to be progressively depleted, to no longer be of resource use, or can't be used sustainably. The depletion of tangible cultural heritage may be due to various reasons, such as the erosion of the natural environment, changes in the social environment, and man-made destruction. The depletion of tangible cultural heritage is usually manifested as: the material carrier of the inheritance is depleted by long-term exhaustion, for example, ancient buildings and open-air sculptures are eroded due to natural environmental factors, cultural relics are invaded by the humid air; depletion of resource usage value, for example, due to the excessive development of cultural and historical sites, although their material carriers are there, their spiritual content has been lost.

3) Types of Tangible Cultural Heritage Resources

According to different standards, tangible cultural heritage can be divided into different types. The typology of *the Convention Concering for the Protection of the World Cultural and Natural Heritage* released by the UNESCO in 1972 is widely cited. Based on it, tangible cultural heritage could be classified into three typologies.

(1) Monuments.

Monuments are specific material dependencies, which are human relics and vestiges left behind in the process of historical development, with historical, artistic and scientific value. Its basic features are: first, it must be created by human beings or related to human activities; second, it must be a past that has become history and cannot be recreated. Monuments can be classified according to different criteria. For instance, according to the different materials of production, monuments can be divided into stone, jade, bone, wood, bronze, porcelain, textiles, paper items and so on. While according to the different functional attributes, it can be divided into religious monuments, folk cultural monuments and so on.

(2) Groups of buildings.

The groups of buildings are the carrier of culture and art, and an important part of tangible cultural heritage resources. The building has distinct cultural and regional characteristics. For example, the Imperial Palace of the Ming and Qing dynasties in Beijing, also known as the Forbidden City, was the largest palace in the world. The Forbidden City complex is solemn and magnificent, showing the supreme majesty of the feudal emperor. In addition to the Forbidden City, Temple and Cemetery of Confucius and the Kong Family Mansion in Qufu have become the largest places to worship Confucius in China because of their large scale, majestic and magnificent buildings. In addition, the pyramid born from the ancient Egyptian culture, the historical building complex of Hue in Vietnam, and other ancient architectural complexes representing the Chinese historical culture, such as the classic garden composed of various pavilions, terraces, galleries and pavilions, and the ancient city of Lijiang, are all important groups of buildings.

Case 7-3

(3) Sites.

The site is the remnant of human activities, the features of the site are incomplete remnants, with a certain regional scope. The site can be divided into prehistoric human activity sites and socio-economic and cultural sites(Wang Degang and Wang Wei, 2010).

① Prehistoric human activity sites.

It refers to the sites left by various human activities in the pre-historic era, including human activity sites, primitive settlements, etc. Peking Man Site at Zhoukoudian, Archaeological Ruins of Liangzhu City and Dawenkou Culture Site are all prehistoric human activity sites(Song Shu and Liu Bin, 2020). The houses, cave dwellings and crypts that lived in prehistory, such as the Site of the Original Settlement in Xi'an Banpo, belong to the primitive settlement.

② Socio-economic and cultural sites.

Socio-economic and cultural sites can be specifically divided into place of historical events, military sites and ancient battlefields, traffic sites and temples, such as the Great Wall of China, Angkor Wat in Cambodia, the Maritime Silk Road, Borobudur temple complex in India(Wang Degang and Wang Wei, 2010).

In addition to the above-mentioned classification of tangible cultural heritage by UNESCO, according to the *Law of the People's Republic of China on the Protection of Cultural Relics* (1982) promulgated by the National People's Congress (NPC) and *the Opinions on Strengthening the Protection of Intangible Cultural Heritage* (2005) promulgated by the CPC Central Committee and the State Council, tangible cultural heritage also can be divided into immovable cultural relics and movable cultural relics. Among them, immovable cultural relics cannot be moved by external force and their value and performance will be affected after moving, including ancient ruins, tombs, buildings, cave temples and stone carvings; important historical sites and representative buildings of modern times; as well as historical and cultural cities, neighborhoods, villages and towns that have outstanding universal value in terms of architectural style, distribution or combination with environmental scenery. Movable cultural relics are relics that can be moved by external force without changing their value and performance after moving, including important objects, works of art, documents, manuscripts, books, etc.

Some other classification systems of tangible heritage are constructed with different classification criteria(Sun Hua, 2020). One is to classify according to the geometric form of tangible cultural heritage, including point heritage, linear heritage and plane heritage. Among them, point heritage includes cultural relic sites or the main body of cultural relic protection units; linear heritage refers to the dot-like heritage formed by the series of artificially created linear remains, or arranged in chains along naturally formed linear boundaries, such as the Silk Road(Ren Huanlin and Liu Mei, 2016). As for the plane heritage, it is the concentrated area of heritage. The other is classified according to the functional use of tangible cultural heritage, which can be divided into agricultural heritage, industrial heritage, military heritage and so on.

In short, tangible cultural heritage is a material, tangible, and palpable culture(Peng Zhaorong, 2008). China became a party to the *Convention Concerning the Protection of the World Cultural and Natural Heritage* on December 12, 1985. On October 29, 1999, China was elected as a member of the World Heritage Committee. Since its inception with UNESCO in 1986, about 37 China's cultural heritage sites were inscribed on the World Heritage List. China has a large number, diverse types and rich connotations of cultural heritage, involving archaeological sites, cave temples, ancient buildings, cultural landscapes, historical towns and town centers, heritage canals, heritage routes and other types, the time spans nearly 100 years, and the space spans nearly 5,000 kilometers, covering the representative achievements of all stages and development fields of the history of Chinese civilization of "pluralism and integration", showing the long-standing cultural inheritance, unique spiritual pursuit and ecological wisdom of Chinese.

7.2.3 Assessment of World Natural and Cultural Heritage

Natural and cultural heritage is the common wealth of all mankind, and world heritage aims to jointly protect natural areas and cultural heritage of outstanding value around the world. Whether a natural heritage can be inscribed on the World Heritage List depends primarily on whether it has outstanding universal value. To be included on the World Heritage List, sites must be of outstanding universal value and meet at least one out of ten selection criteria set out in *the Convention Concering for the Protection of the World Cultural and Natural Heritage* (1972). Criteria (① to ⑥) relate to cultural properties, and the remaining criteria (⑦ to ⑩) relate to natural properties. While many properties may only meet some natural or cultural criteria, mixed properties will meet some natural as well as some cultural criteria.

① to represent a masterpiece of human creative genius;

② to exhibit an important interchange of human values, over a span of time or within a cultural area of the world, on developments in architecture or technology, monumental arts, town-planning or landscape design;

③ to bear a unique or at least exceptional testimony to a cultural tradition or to a civilization which is living or which has disappeared;

④ to be an outstanding example of a type of building, architectural or technological ensemble or landscape which illustrates (a) significant stage(s) in human history;

⑤ to be an outstanding example of a traditional human settlement, land-use, or sea-use which is representative of a culture (or cultures), or human interaction with the environment especially when it has become vulnerable under the impact of irreversible change;

⑥ to be directly or tangibly associated with events or living traditions, with ideas, or with beliefs, with artistic and literary works of outstanding universal significance. (The Committee considers that this criterion should preferably be used in conjunction with other criteria);

⑦ to contain superlative natural phenomena or areas of exceptional natural beauty and aesthetic importance;

⑧ to be outstanding examples representing major stages of earth's history, including the record of life, significant ongoing geological processes in the development of landforms, or significant geomorphic or physiographic features;

⑨ to be outstanding examples representing significant ongoing ecological and biological processes in the evolution and development of terrestrial, fresh water, coastal and marine ecosystems and communities of plants and animals;

⑩ to contain the most important and significant natural habitats for in‐situ conservation of biological diversity, including those containing threatened species of outstanding universal value from the point of view of science or conservation.

7.2.4 Intangible Cultural Heritage

1) The Definition of Intangible Cultural Heritage

UNESCO's *Convention for the Safeguarding of the Intangible Cultural Heritage* defines the concept of intangible cultural heritage, which means the practices, representations, expressions, knowledge, skills, as well as the instruments, objects, artefacts and cultural spaces associated therewith, that communities, groups and, in some cases, individuals recognize as part of their cultural heritage. This intangible cultural heritage, transmitted from generations to generations, is constantly recreated by communities and groups in response to their environment, their interaction with nature and their history, and provides them with a sense of identity and continuity, thus promoting respect for cultural diversity and human creativity (UNESCO, 2003). Under *Convention for the Safeguarding of the Intangible Cultural Heritage*, intangible cultural heritage includes items in five areas: oral traditions and expressions, including language as a vehicle of the intangible cultural heritage; performing arts; social practices, rituals and festive events; knowledge and practices concerning nature and the universe; traditional craftsmanship.

In 2005's *Opinions of the General Office of the State Council on Strengthening the Safeguarding of China's Intangible Cultural Heritage*, General Office of the State Council of China defined it as inherited by each ethnic group from generations to generations, referring to various traditional cultural manifestations (such as folk activities, performing arts, traditional knowledge and skills, as well as related utensils, objects, handicrafts, etc.) and cultural spaces closely related with the lives of the populace. *The Law of the People's Republic of China on Intangible Cultural Heritage*, adopted on February 25, 2011, defines intangible cultural heritage as various traditional cultural manifestations which are handed down by the people of all ethnicities from generation to generation and regarded as a constituent part of their cultural heritage, and physical objects and premises related to the traditional cultural manifestations. Intangible cultural heritage includes traditional oral literature and the language as a carrier thereof, traditional fine arts, calligraphy, music, dance, drama, folk art and acrobatics, traditional artistry, medicine and calendar, traditional rituals, festivals and other folk customs, traditional sports and entertainment, and so on. China's definition of intangible cultural heritage is basically the same as UNESCO's definition.

2) The Nature of Intangible Cultural Heritage

The most essential nature of intangible cultural heritage is its cultural nature. Intangible cultural heritage was originally called oral and intangible cultural heritage, folk creation, traditional culture and folk creation, etc., these names also highlight their immateriality, which is a condensation of the wisdom and ability formed by people in the process of long-term practice (Xu Xiaomeng, 2022). Intangible cultural heritage is the cultural creation of the ancestors in their unique social environment, and has been circulated for a long time in the social life, reflecting the social customs and people's etiquettes at that time, and reflecting people's outlook on life and values at a deep level. There are many intangible cultural heritages that are passed on orally, representing the national cultural memory of these groups, which has a strong vitality, and are passed down from generations to generations (Luo Rong, 2012).

3) Characteristics of Intangible Cultural Heritage

(1) Inheritance.

Intangible cultural heritage is passed down from generations to generations and is constantly recreated in adaptation to its surroundings and interaction with nature and history. Inheritance is manifested in the fact that intangible cultural heritage is generally only passed on to familiar and close people, with distinct national and family characteristics. Its basic transmission method is oral transmission, these skills and techniques are passed from predecessors to the next generation. It is this inheritance that makes it possible to preserve and continue the intangible cultural heritage, once the inheritance activities are stopped, it means extinction(Li Shitao, 2007). For example, Manas, a local traditional folk literature in Kizilsu Kirghiz Autonomous Prefecture, Xinjiang, is one of the world's intangible cultural heritages. It depicts the heroic Manas and his seven generations of descendants who led the Kirgiz people in their struggle against foreign invaders and various evil forces. In the course of thousands of years of word-of-mouth communitcation, the Kirgiz people have integrated their knowledge and understanding of the things around them and their spiritual and cultural heritage into Manas for generations. It is an encyclopedia of Kirgiz national folk culture, with multidisciplinary values such as literature, history, language, folklore.

(2) Variability.

Variability is also known as transmissibility, portability, or loanability. Intangible cultural heritage can be transmitted among people through teaching, which in turn may lead to its spread to other people, regions and countries. In this process, intangible cultural heritage will develop and change with the local history and culture, but its core content has not changed. If it is completely changed, it will not be a cultural heritage of this kind(Li Shitao, 2007). For example, many traditional festivals in China have spread to surrounding countries and regions, such as South Korea and Japan, but the customs and habits of these traditional festivals may change to a certain extent, and these changes are caused by the cultural and social environment of the region. Intangible cultural heritage is not fixed, it is flexible, and it will constantly mutate in the process of transmission, thus developing new content.

(3) Viability.

Specifically, viability refers to the existence of intangible cultural heritage. Viability is evident in traditional oral literature, music, acrobatics, festival customs and traditional craft skills in intangible cultural heritage. The creators of intangible cultural heritage are the performers and implementers of various arts, who are at the core of "living" culture. Without the actual participation and creation of these people, intangible cultural heritage will not exist. At the same time, the viability also shows that intangible cultural heritage is changing. The culture in society is not static, and the intangible cultural inheritance will also be affected by the surrounding environment, constantly interacting with nature, reality and history, constantly changing, innovating and developing. Specific values, forms of existence, and changing characters create the living characteristics of intangible culture(He Xuejun, 2005).

(4) Regional characteristics.

Intangible cultural heritage is produced in specific regions and is influenced by unique regional environment. The culture, religion, standard of production and living of the region, and daily life customs determine the characteristics and inheritance of intangible cultural heritage. Intangible cultural heritage is a product of the region and represents the characteristics of the region; its development, protection and inheritance depend on the settings and conditions of its existence, and without the region, it loses its soul(Li Shitao, 2007). The Peruvian "Scissor Dance", the Chinese Tibetan "Tibetan Opera", "Regong Art", "Gesar", the Kirgiz "Manas", and the Mongolian "Long Tune" have distinct regional characteristics. The regional nature reflects and strengthens the national nature of intangible cultural heritage.

(5) Nationality.

Nationality refers to being unique to a certain nation, deeply branded by the nation, and reflecting the unique way of thinking, wisdom, world outlook, values, aesthetic consciousness, emotional expression and other factors of a specific nation. It is the dynamic cultural gene of a nation and a reflection of the social life of the nation for thousands of years, showing the unique cultural form and cultural personality of a nation, and promoting unity and cohesion among ethnic groups(Li Shitao, 2007). For example, the Qiang New Year Festival, which is the traditional annual festival of the Qiang people, is called "Rimeiji" in Qiang, which means an auspicious and joyful festival, with the theme of offering blessings to the heaven and making thanksgiving. The celebration is held every year on the first day of the tenth month of the lunar calendar, usually for three to five days. During the New Year Festival, the Qiang people of various villages jointly hold ceremonies and wish to worship the gods of heaven, mountains and villages; men, women, and children dressed in costumes celebrate the festival collectively. It is a concentrated display of Qiang culture and Qiang New Year Festival, which integrates literature, history, religion, architecture, ethics, philosophy, folklore, singing, dancing, food and other cultures, and it is also a multi-angle presentation of the personality characteristics of Qiang culture.

4) Types of Intangible Cultural Heritage Resources

The national, historical, cultural and even national conditions of each country are different, and the items included in the intangible cultural heritage are not exactly the same. With a long history and many ethnic groups, China has diverse types of intangible cultural heritage. China's classification of intangible cultural heritage mainly includes traditional oral literature and the language as a carrier, traditional fine arts, calligraphy, music, dance, drama, folk art and acrobatics, traditional artistry, medicine and calendar, traditional rituals, festivals and other folk customs, traditional sports and entertainment and other intangible cultural heritage.

(1) Traditional oral literature and the language that serves as its carrier.

China has many literary works of word of mouth, most of which are taught orally, and their contents involve in poems, stories, etc. The folk oral cultural heritage in China is rich and colorful as a result of a long history and a splendid culture, such as the four major Chinese folklore stories—*Cowherd Weaver Girl*, *Lady Mengjiang Crying on the Great Wall*, *Liang Shanbo and Zhu Yingtai*, and *White Snake Biography*. *Gesar King Biography* in Tibet, Mongolian folk epic *Jianger*, *Manas* in Xinjiang, etc., all have unique artistic charm, providing us with great aesthetic enjoyment and diversified inheritance methods. It has become an important part of the overall content of Chinese national culture.

(2) Traditional fine arts, calligraphy, music, dance, drama, folk art forms and acrobatics.

These are traditional performing arts. Traditional fine arts include projects such as sculpture, paper-cutting, embroidery, wooden board paintings, etc. Traditional calligraphy is divided into Chinese calligraphy and minority calligraphy, such as Manchu calligraphy. Traditional music, includes folk songs and string music, string and bamboo flute music, wind music, drum music and blowing music and other instrumental music, as well as rap music, opera music, such as Hakka music in Guangdong, Mongolian horse-head fiddle music, Hakka mountain song in Meizhou. Traditional dances are mostly used in various ceremonial occasions, from national sacrifices, pilgrimages, wars, celebrations, royal succession, to the people's weddings and funerals, sowing and harvesting, etc., such as stilts, Yangko, the farmers' dance of China's Korean ethnic group.

Case 7-4

Traditional drama is a comprehensive stage style that uses songs and dances to perform stories. There are many kinds of Chinese drama, and many types of opera are included in the list of intangible cultural heritage, such as Peking opera, Cantonese opera, Shadow Puppet opera, Tibetan opera. Traditional folk-art forms are based on folk rap literature, which integrates rap literature, music and performance, including cross-talk, storytelling, big drums, etc., and listed in the intangible cultural heritage of cross-talk, Suzhou Pingtan, Xinjiang Song, Shandong Drum, etc.

Case 7-5

Traditional acrobatics refers to the collective name of various extraordinary skills which were also called miscellaneous tricks and acrobatic music in ancient times. The art of acrobatics originated in the Qin dynasty and was called Jiao-Di Opera. After thousands of years of inheritance and development, it has developed from simple skill performance to a comprehensive performing art with bands, dance, lighting and so on.

Case 7-6

(3) Traditional technology and arts, medicine and calendars.

Traditional technology and arts, mainly referring to traditional handicrafts, are the skills of people to make natural materials into products with a unique artistic style through manual labor. It conveys a unique cultural connotation that combines aesthetic and practical functions. The traditional handicrafts inscribed on the National Intangible Cultural Heritage List include movable type in China, the traditional handicrafts of making Xuan paper, the traditional firing technology of Longquan celadon, etc.

Traditional medicine refers to the natural medicine traditionally used for prevention, treatment and health care of all ethnic groups in China, as well as systematic theoretical or empirical knowledge of processing and applying these drugs for disease prevention and treatment, including traditional Chinese medicine and other ethnic medicine. Ethnic medicine is the traditional medicine of ethnic minorities, of which Tibetan medicine, Mongolian medicine, Uyghur medicine, Dai medicine are the four major ethnic medicines in China, they have a large number of historical documents, monographs, complete medical theory system and rich clinical practice experience.

Traditional calendar is divided into the lunar calendar and the calendar of some ethnic minorities. The lunar calendar, known in ancient times as the summer calendar, orbits the moon around the earth as a month, dividing the year into 24 solar terms, the appearance of which is related to ancient agricultural production.

(4) Traditional etiquettes, festivals and other folk customs.

Folk custom is a way of life created, used and passed down from generations to generations by the people in a country or nation, and it is a true reflection of the history, culture and society of a specific region. Folklore generally includes traditional etiquette, festivals, religious beliefs, food, ethnic costumes, etc. China has a vast territory, many nationalities, and a rich variety of folk customs, such as the Dragon Boat Festival, the Dai Songkran Festival, the Yi Torch Festival, the Mazu belief and custom, the Qinhuai Lantern Festival.

(5) Traditional sports and entertainment.

Case 7-7

Traditional sports refer to the sports activities handed down from ancient times to the present day by various ethnic groups in China, including sports with military attributes, such as martial arts, archery, wrestling; sports with fitness attributes, such as Shaolin Kung Fu, Tai Chi, Wing Chun. Traditional entertainment refers to a variety of folk games with an entertainment nature, such as dragon boat race, swing.

Except for above five intangible cultural heritage items, there is also some room for the discovery of new intangible cultural heritage in the future.

7.2.5 Mixed Heritage

1) The Definition of Mixed Heritage

The dual heritage, also known as composite heritage or mixed heritage, is a heritage that has both natural heritage and cultural heritage. Under the World Heritage Convention, mixed heritage is representative of both natural and cultural beauty, and it does not have separate evaluation criteria, but rather evaluates them on the basis of the criteria of cultural heritage and natural heritage. It is not a simple superposition of cultural and natural heritage, but contains a deeper meaning, and is a masterpiece of human understanding and transformation of nature to live in harmony with nature(Cong Shasha, 2008).

2) Characteristics of Mixed Heritage

(1) Having different natural factors.

Mixed heritages around the world are mostly related to mountains, lakes, plateaus, cliffs and other aspects in terms of natural factors, such as the Willandra Lakes Region in Australia, the Rock Islands Southern Lagoon of Palau, and the Mount Taishan in China. In terms of cultural factors, most of these mixed heritage sites have a certain religious and historical culture, such as the Ahwar of Southern Iraq, China's Mount Huangshan, Emei scenic area including Leshan Giant Buddha scenic area.

(2) Covering a wide geographical areas.

These mixed heritages usually have sufficient space as a support in order to meet "the integrity" required by the World Heritage Convention and to provide sufficient conditions for their natural and cultural development. Most of them are dough-like distribution, and cover a wide area, such as Mount Taishan and Mount Huangshan.

(3) Located in a culturally prosperous place suitable for human life.

These mixed heritages have unique and profound cultural connotations, and the places where they are located are also areas with superior natural environment and unique culture, which are suitable for human survival. Good geographical conditions allow people to thrive in these places, while creating a unique culture that makes this natural place rich in culture. For example, Mount Taishan is one of the birthplaces of ancient culture in the Yellow River Basin, while Buddhism and Taoism are also thriving here, and the culture is all-encompassing, which is the symbol of the Chinese nation and the epitome of Oriental culture.

3) The Number of World Mixed Heritages

As of July 6, 2019, there are 39 mixed heritage sites in the world, with 4 in China. Mixed heritage abroad includes the Wadi Rum protected area in Jordan, the Tasmanian Wilderness in Australia, the Mount Athos in Greece, and the Laponian area in Sweden. The four mixed heritage sites in China are: Mount Taishan, Mount Huangshan, Mount Emei scenic area and Leshan Giant Buddha scenic area, Mount Wuyi.

Mixed heritage is the basis and embodiment of the harmonious coexistence of human beings and nature. Recognizing and protecting mixed heritage is not only the inheritance of human culture, but also the cherishing and protection of the natural environment.

Case 7-8

7.3 The Development and Protection of Heritage Tourism Resources

7.3.1 The Development of Heritage Tourism Resources

1) Theories of Heritage Tourism Resources Development

(1) Motivation-process-aim model of experience tourism.

The motivation-process-aim model was proposed to design the experience tourism (Sun Gennian, 2006). As shown in Figure 7-2, the experience process includes three dimensions, namely perceptible, understandable, and participatory, which are the key points of tourism experience management. The three dimensions of "experience aims" are novelty, affability, and satisfaction, which are the final purposes of the tourism experience. Three dimensions of tourism motivation are equalization, disengagement, and stimulation, which are the key drivers of the tourism experience. According to the theory of tourism experience, heritage tourism development should also pay more attention to enhancing the perceptible, understandable, and participatory sense, and promote the activation and visualization of tourism resources.

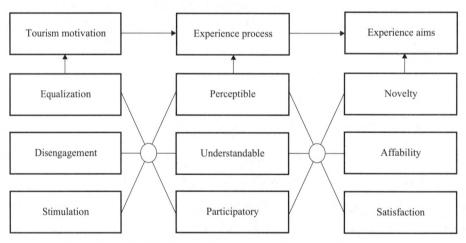

Figure 7-2　Model of motivation-process-aim of experience tourism

The design of heritage tourism products in destinations should aim to create conditions for tourists to obtain authentic experience. No matter the scenery environment is real, historical, or artificial, the authenticity of the experience is reflected in the perceptions of tourists' sensory(Song Yongmei and Sun Gennian, 2006). In the development of heritage tourism resources, planners should try to restore the original nature according to history, and create an authentic natural or historical atmosphere for tourists(Zhang Jianzhong and Sun Gennian, 2012).

(2) Theory of heritage activation via tourism.

The concept of heritage activation was first proposed by Taiwan scholars. In the 20th century, Taiwan was facing the problems of closing factories, severing personnel, and selling machinery and equipment in the process of industrial transformation and privatization, scholars in Taiwan created the idea of "heritage activation" to preserve the industrial heritage as well as properly solve a series of livelihood problems left under the special historical background of modernization development(Yu Xuecai, 2010).

Yu Xuecai introduced it into heritage tourism, which means the process of transforming heritage resources into tourism products without affecting the protection of heritage. He indicated that there were five levels of heritage: well-preserved heritage, basically well-preserved heritage, complete destroyed heritage, heritage only with sites left, and heritage only recorded in the historical documents. For those heritages with only sites and documents, he suggested restoring them.

Based on this finding, scholars further proposed the pattern of heritage preservation and tourism development corresponding relationship (as shown in Figure 7-3).

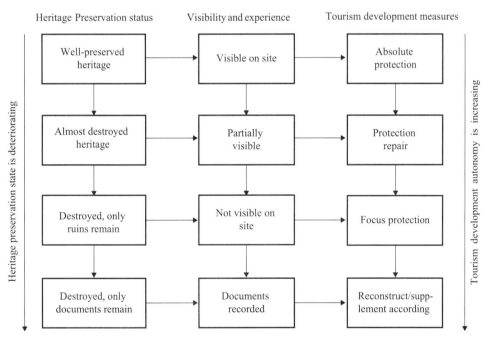

Figure 7-3　The pattern of heritage preservation and tourism development corresponding relationship

According to them, heritage preservation state and the corresponding measures can be divided into four levels. The first level is well-preserved heritage, which is visible on-site and visitors' experience is complete, and it should be developed under absolute protection and being made best use for tourism. The second level is almost destroyed heritage, which is partially visible on-site and imaginable for tourists, planners should take measures to protect or repair the heritage, as well as employ resources by developing tourism products. The third level is the destroyed heritage with only ruins remained, which is not visible on-site and hard to identify for tourists, planners should give special stress on protecting and focus on typical reconstruction. The fourth level is the destroyed heritage with only documents remained, which is completely invisible, planners should take measures to reconstruct the heritage according to the literature.

(3) Other theories.

In the study of Rios et al. (2020), a strategy for socio-economic and sustainable development through geoeducation, geotourism, and geoconservation was proposed (as Figure 7-4 shown). The project emphasizes that the construction of geopark should be based on strong support from the community, involving authorities, educational institutions, and local businesses.

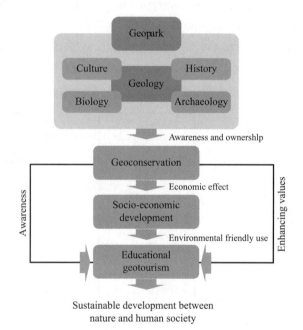

Figure 7-4   Schematic diagram showing the functions and requirements of geoparks

UNESCO has advocated for intangible cultural heritage tourism (ICHT) for its dual-fold benefits, i.e., to gear up the economy and encourage sustainable development. Whereas well-established geotourism combining with ICHT may further boost up not only the conservation of geoheritage legacy, but also complement each other and may also reopen an fresh avenue of tourism-economy. Therefore, to achieve the sustainable development of the community, Halder and Sarda (2021) developed a promotional strategy relevant to the development of ICHT, based on geotourism. This strategy makes the concept clearer of combining the two sub-branches of modern tourism (as Figure 7-5 shown).

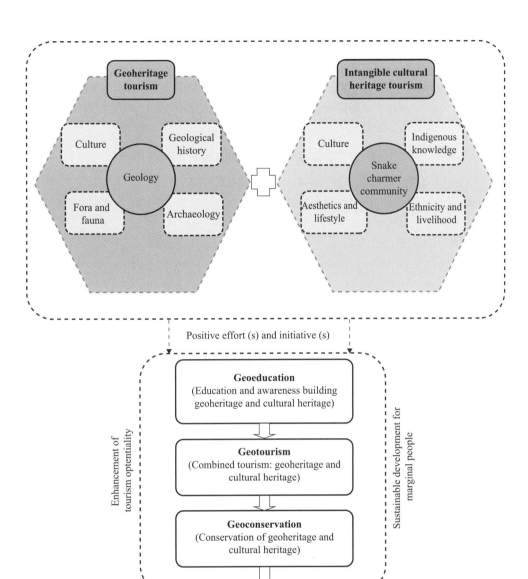

Figure 7-5 Schematic layout for combining geoheritage and cultural heritage

Hence, this concept (combining the mentioned two sub-branches) would offer a desired result after making constructive efforts and initiatives. On the one hand, it will boost up existed tourism economy; on the other hand, it will help the sustainable development of a marginal group (snake charmer) in an eco-friendly way.

The prime goal is to highlight the geoeducation, geotourism and geoconservation potentials of the community people and geoheritage sites. Geoeducation provides the platform for education and awareness exclusively of geological history, past geo-climatic environment, lithology and overall physical landscape of the selected geo-sites or (underdeveloped) geoparks. Large-scale geotourism makes the promotional establishment and costing become easier and cheaper, which attracts more tourists and helps to adds more bonuses of the community locals. Geoconservation is beneficial to protect and restore the over-exploitation heritage site, and also provides an alternative way of livelihood of inheritor of intangible cultural heritage.

2) Development Forms of Heritage Tourism Resources

The development of heritage tourism resources is mostly in the form of museums, relic parks, and theme parks, while the development of intangible heritage tourism resources is in the form of tourism performance.

(1) Museums.

Tourism and museum industry mutually infiltrate, promote each other, and develop together. The tourism industry promotes the function of museums to develop towards diversification, popularization, and humanization, and the museum industry makes tourism more knowledgeable. There are two main types of tourism development of heritage resources in the form of museums: a special theme of the comprehensive museum and a thematic site museum.

① Special theme of the comprehensive museum.

Ruins and relics are one of the key exhibition objects of comprehensive museums, and most of them are presented in the form of relics, pictures, miniature models, texts, etc. The famous special theme heritage site in China is the Changsha Mawangdui Tombs in Han dynasty, which exhibits more than 1000 historical items, including lacquer, textile garments, bamboo slips, and silk manuscripts. It was built in four units: Preface Hall, World-shattering Excavations, Life and Art, Collection of Bamboos and Silk, and Dream of Immortality, showing the life of upper-class people of the Han dynasty. In order to deepen visitors' understanding of Han history, the exhibition not only relies on rich display forms such as sound, light, and electricity, but also pays attention to improving visitors' participation by using the experience activities such as "archaeological tour".

② Thematic site museum.

Thematic site museum refers to the museum on or beside the site to collect, study and display the unearthed cultural relics such as houses, tombs, cellars, ash pits. This type of museum is quite attractive for tourists due to its originality and regionality. The well-known thematic site museums in China include the Yandu Site Museum of Western Zhou dynasty, the Sanxingdui Museum in Sichuan, ect.

(2) Parks.

① Relic parks.

According to *Cihai*, the relic parks are public gardens for people to leisure or carry out recreational and sports activities, and are an important part of the urban public space and green space system (Wang Degang and Wang Wei, 2011). The relic parks usually integrate historical and cultural elements with touristic economic activities, which have high sightseeing, cultural and educational value (Tao Xiaoli et al., 2013). The popular relic parks in China include Tang Paradise, Site of the Epang Palace, Daming Palace in Xi'an, Yuanmingyuan Site Park ,ect.

② Theme parks.

The theme park, an activity space with the functions of sightseeing, leisure, entertainment, and education, is artificially designed and constructed with the theme of the relics (Wang Degang and Wang Wei,2011). The Gold Reef City Theme Park in South Africa is a relics theme park built on a gold mining site, which attracts lots of tourists from the world.

(3) Tourism performance.

Performance refers to the art of shaping images and conveying emotions through singing, body movements and facial expressions. Thus, tourism performance is a kind of commercial performance that serves for tourists, which is designed according to the cultural background of tourist attractions and aims to attract tourists to watch and participate(Li Leilei,2005; Bie Jinhua, 2009).These cultural performances are all designed and adapted based on the local tangible cultural heritage or intangible cultural heritage resources (Li Jianmei,2016).

Case 7-9

For example, Yang Liping's *Dynamic Yunnan* is a well‐known tourism performance, showing the ethnic customs of the Yi, Miao, Bai and other ethnic minorities in Yunnan Province. It not only inherits and spreads traditional culture and art, but also enriches the visitors' cultural life and cultural experience, and improves the visitors' artistic experience and impression.

7.3.2 The Protection of Heritage Tourism Resources

Heritage tourism resources generally have high historical, cultural, aesthetic, archaeological and other values, but at the same time, they are fragile and vulnerable to damage. Therefore, protection takes priority over tourism. The following measures usually are taken to protect heritage tourism resources.

1) Establishing Conservation Protocols

The United Nations' *Transforming Our World:The 2030 Agenda for Sustainable Development* clearly states that "further efforts should be made to protect and safeguard the world's cultural and natural heritage". As the only international cultural cooperation agency of the United Nations system, the United Nations Educational, Scientific and Cultural Organization (UNESCO) has identified the protection of heritage as one of its main business since its inception. There are several relevant international regulations of heritage protection, for example, *Declaration on the Rights of Indigenous People* (2007); *Transforming Our World: The 2030 Agenda for Sustainable Development* (2015) promulgated by the UN; *Convention Concerning the Protection of the World Cultural and Natural Heritage*(1972), and *Convention on the Protection and Promotion of the Diversity of Cultural Expressions*(2005) promulgated by UNESCO. These documents focus on agreeing on basic rules in the declaration, recognition, protection, assistance, and financing of the world heritage, and based on which they have successively announced the world heritage list(Liang Bao'er and Ma Bo, 2008).

In *Convention Concerning the Protection of the World Cultural and Natural Heritage*(1972), five protection measures were proposed for World Heritage.

(1) to adopt a general policy which aims to give the cultural and natural heritage a function in the life of the community and to integrate the protection of that heritage into comprehensive planning programs;

(2) to set up within its territories, where such services do not exist, one or more services for the protection, conservation and presentation of the cultural and natural heritage with an appropriate staff and possessing the means to discharge their functions;

(3) to develop scientific and technical research and to develop operational methods that enable countries to respond to threats to their cultural or natural heritage;

(4) to take the appropriate legal, scientific, technical, administrative and financial measures necessary for the identification, protection, conservation, presentation and rehabilitation of this heritage;

(5) to foster the establishment or development of national or regional centres for training in the protection, conservation and presentation of the cultural and natural heritage and to encourage scientific research in this field.

Additionally, government departments at all levels in China have issued several documents to establish sound supervision and safeguard mechanisms of heritage protection. For example, *Regulations for the Implementation of the Cultural Relics Protection Law of the People's Republic of China* (2003) promulgated by the State Council, and *Administrative Measures for the Protection of World Cultural Heritage* (2006) promulgated by the Ministry of Culture and Tourism of the People's Republic of China(as Table 7-1 shown).

Table 7-1 Relevant standard-setting texts and documents of heritage

Level	Policy in English	Policy in Chinese	Time	Department
World Level	Globally Important Agricultural Heritage Systems	全球重要农业文化遗产系统	2002	UN
	Declaration on the Rights of Indigenous People	土著人民权利宣言	2007	UN

Continue

Level	Policy in English	Policy in Chinese	Time	Department
	Transforming Our World: The 2030 Agenda for Sustainable Development	2030年可持续发展议程	2015	UN
	Convention for the Protection of Cultural Property in the Event of Armed Conflict	关于发生武装冲突时保护文化财产的公约	1954	UNESCO
	Convention on the Means of Prohibiting and Preventing the Illicit Import, Export, and Transfer of Ownership of Cultural Property	关于禁止和防止非法进出口文化财产和非法转让其所有权的方法的公约	1970	UNESCO
	Convention Concerning the Protection of the World Cultural and Natural Heritage	保护世界文化和自然遗产公约	1972	UNESCO
	Convention on the Protection of the Underwater Cultural Heritage	水下文化遗产保护公约	2001	UNESCO
	Convention for the Safeguarding of the Intangible Cultural Heritage	保护非物质文化遗产公约	2003	UNESCO
	Convention on the Protection and Promotion of the Diversity of Cultural Expressions	保护和促进文化表达多样性公约	2005	UNESCO
	Policy on Engaging with Indigenous Peoples	与土著人民接触的政策	2018	UNESCO
	The Operational Guidelines for the Implementation of the World Heritage Convention	实施保护世界文化与自然遗产公约的操作指南	2008	UNESCO
	Xi'an Declaration on the Conservation of the Setting of Heritage Structures, Sites and Areas	西安宣言(2005)——关于古建筑、古遗址和历史区域周边环境的保护	2005	ICOMOS
National Level	Regulations for the Implementation of the Cultural Relics Protection Law of the People's Republic of China	中华人民共和国文物保护法实施条例	2003	the State Council
	Administrative Measures for the Protection of World Cultural Heritage	世界文化遗产保护管理办法	2006	Ministry of Culture

Continue

Level	Policy in English	Policy in Chinese	Time	Department
	Measures for the Administration of Monitoring and Inspection of World Cultural Heritage in China	中国世界文化遗产监测巡视管理办法	2006	State Administration of Cultural Heritage
	Law of the People's Republic of China on the Protection of Cultural Relics	中华人民共和国文物保护法	1982/2017	National People's Congress
	Intangible Cultural Heritage Law of the People's Republic of China	中华人民共和国非物质文化遗产法	2011	National People's Congress
	Opinions on Further Strengthening the Protection of Intangible Cultural Heritage	关于进一步加强非物质文化遗产保护工作的意见	2021	CPC Central Committee and the State Council
Provincial Level	Regulations on the Protection of Wulingyuan World Natural Heritage in Hunan Province	湖南省武陵源世界自然遗产保护条例	2000	Hunan People's Congress
	Sichuan Province World Heritage Protection Regulations	四川省世界遗产保护条例	2002/2015	Sichuan People's Congress
	Regulations of Zhejiang Province on the Protection of the World Cultural Heritage of the Grand Canal	浙江省大运河世界文化遗产保护条例	2020	Zhejiang People's Congress
	Beijing Central Axis Cultural Heritage Protection Regulations	北京中轴线文化遗产保护条例	2022	Beijing People's Congress

2) Applying Protection Technology

Modern science and technology are becoming more and more extensively applied in the protection of tourism resources (Li Tianyuan, 2013). In the protection of heritage tourism resources, the commonly used scientific technology includes mathematical methods, physical methods, chemical methods, biological methods, engineering methods, satellite and remote sensing technology, information technology protection, etc.

Physical methods are often employed in the protection cultural heritage.For example, using ultraviolet lamps to irradiate paper cultural relics and copper utensils can effectively kill pests and microorganisms. In the protection of animals, scientists put on GPS positioning collars for giant pandas released into the wild, which can monitor the movements of giant pandas and provide timely rescue in case of their abnormal behavior.

Chemical methods are mainly applied to protect bronzes, city walls, murals, etc. For example, bronze wares will react with chemical substances in the air after they are unearthed, forming corrosive white spots on the surface of bronze ware, which can be completely removed by chemical methods.

3) Social Education

Nowadays, many intangible cultural heritages have been integrated into modern life, and social education is helpful to protect heritage tourism resources. For example, wheat straw paintings in Harbin have been innovated over years and turned into works of art that have become popular in the shops of tourism destinations. At the same time, some primary schools in Yunnan Province have set classes to teach intangible cultural heritage such as the embroidery and dance sticks of Yi. In addition, a national-level portal website "China Intangible Cultural Heritage Digital Museum" was opened by China Intangible Cultural Heritage Protection Center, as a discourse platform for the public to learn and participate in protection of the intangible cultural heritage.

Case 7-10

Case 7-11

Case 7-12

Reading time

Chapter Review

This chapter mainly introduces the heritage tourism resources and their development and protection.

Firstly, the definition of heritage tourism resources is heritage resources developed by tourism including artefacts, remembered personalities, symbols and associations.

Secondly, there are four typologies of heritage tourism resources, namely natural heritage, tangible cultural heritage, intangible cultural heritage and mixed heritage.

Finally, the development of heritage tourism resources is mostly in the form of museums, relic parks, and theme parks, while the development of intangible heritage tourism resources is in the form of tourism performance. The global authorities and organizations usually take the following measures to protect heritage tourism resources, such as establishing conservation protocols, applying protection technology and social education.

Questions for Discussion

1. What is tangible cultural heritage? What are the types of tangible cultural heritage resources? Please find more examples to illustrate.

Exercises

2. Please find out more examples of world natural and tangible cultural heritage resources, and understand their connotations and characteristics.

3. Please consider the relationship between intangible cultural heritage and traditional culture.

4. Do you have personally experienced intangible cultural heritage or mixed heritage? Please talk about your feelings.

5. Please refer to the latest literature, share with your classmates the latest theories you found about the tourism development of heritage resources, and make comments.

6. Please choose a kind of heritage tourism resources that you are interested in and talk about how to balance the tourism development and protection of these resources.

Chapter 8
Humanistic Activities

Learning Objectives

(1) Describe the definitions of humanistic activities.
(2) Recognize the basic types of humanistic activities.
(3) Understand the relationship between humanistic activities and tourism.
(4) Understand the related issues and concerns of humanistic activities in tourism development.

Technical Words

English Words	中文翻译
humanistic activities	人文活动
personnel records	个人记录
art	艺术
folk customs	民俗
modern festivals	现代节日
festivals and events	节事
hometown/residence of celebrities	名人家乡/名人故居
performance	表演

Knowledge Graph

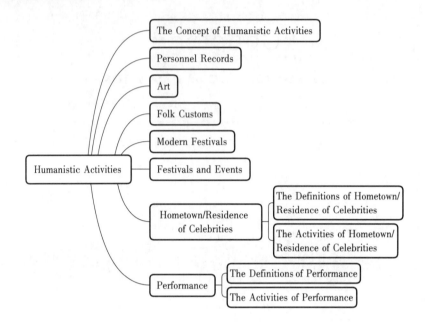

8.1 The Concept of Humanistic Activities

Humanistic activities refer to all the cultural activities in human society, and they are mirrors of society and history. Researchers have developed multiple definitions of humanistic tourism resources in previous studies. Humanistic tourism resources refer to objects and factors that can reflect history, politics, economy, culture, social customs and other aspects in human society. They should be man-made resources that are attractive to tourists and can contribute to tourism development and create social, economic and environmental benefits(Tien et al., 2019).

As a branch of the humanistic tourism resources, humanistic activities have a key feature which differentiates themselves from other humanistic tourism resources: it should be dynamic. Humanistic activities are developed, inherited, innovated and obliterated continuously along with the development of the human society. As a result, their attractiveness dose not rely on the solidified collection of objects or monuments, but on the evolution process behind it.

To summarize, humanistic activity tourism resources refer to the human-involved dynamic process or the witnesses and production of such dynamic process, which are valuable and usable for tourism purposes. The intangible cultural heritages, such as oral traditions, performing arts, social practices, rituals, festive events, knowledge and practices concerning nature and the universe or the knowledge and skills to produce traditional crafts, are the most common and well-known forms of humanistic activities(as shown in Figure 8-1). Meanwhile, the modern culture activities are also humanistic activities, such as music festivals, food festivals, sports events.

Figure8-1　Dragon boat race in Foshan, China
Source:nanhaitoday.com

Nowadays, humanistic activity is getting prominent in tourism development. It becomes more important for humanistic activities to satisfy tourist needs due to the increasing competitions. After the rapid growth of mass tourism, tourists are gradually not satisfied with the rushing sightseeing through the tourist spots. As a result, numerous of tourists are seeking for special and in-depth experience, which are more cultural related. At the same time, cultural activities are suitable for the elegant and popular taste of cultural tourists, as well as traditional or classical resources with a long history or modern activities with entertainment.

The humanistic activity has great influence on tourism development of a destination. Humanistic activities contribute to the destination by attracting tourists during slow periods or slack season. In addition, destinations benefit from humanistic activities as they attract attentions from visitor and media. It would also provide a great opportunity for building and broadcasting the destination brand. Moreover, the humanistic activity can enhance tourists' experience by adding extra elements to the tourism product, so visitors can engage into the activities and have embodied experience. However, humanistic activities also bring issues and problems to destinations. For example, environmental problems come with many modern festivals.

8.2 Personnel Records

Technically, personnel record means a file containing the employment history and actions relevant to individual personnel and volunteer activities within an organization. It usually includes general information, hiring documents, job performance, post-employment information, etc. While in a boarder sense, personnel records can be considered as the footprints of individuals, including the places they lived in or traveled to, or the spots which have significant meaning to them.

In tourism, the personnel records of the celebrities or film characters are tourism resources that have a great potential to attract visitors. Tourists may follow the footsteps of the celebrities to visit the place that they have been to, or travel to the filming locations in order to be immersed into the scenery that the fictional characters have been in. Thus, the celebrity fandom tourism and film induced tourism are the most common forms of tourism which are based on the personnel records.

Celebrity fandom tourism refers to the tourism behaviors taken by the fans of the celebrities. Those tourism activities usually take place in destinations that are related to celebrities. Generally speaking, celebrity fandom tourists tend to have high participation into such activities. Tourists or fans have affection for the celebrities, so the spots they may go are related to their idols. In addition, interactions between fans during the trip enhance their sense of belonging and personal identity within the fan's community. Celebrity fandom tourists like to take photos about the trip and post them on social media.

Film induced tourism, also called the media-induced tourism or screen tourism, refers to the visit to the filming location due to the appearance of a certain destination on the media such as movies, televisions, online videos. As a personnel record related tourism behavior, it is promoted by experience of the characters and movie plots, rather than by the fandom to the actors or actress. The *Roman Holiday* by Wyler in 1953 is a classic example that induced tourism by movie. Since the film was released, countless of audiences have been obsessed by the princess Ann's unforgettable day around Rome. Even after over a half of a century, tourists still like to follow the princess Ann's footprints while visiting Rome, such as visiting the Piazza di Spagna, or putting hands into Mouth of Truth to satisfy curiosity raised by the movie(as shown in Figure 8-2).

Figure 8-2　Tourist touches the Mouth of Truth as Princess Ann did in the *Roman Holiday*.
Source:oddviser.com

　　Destinations benefit from personnel records related to tourism activities, such as celebrity fandom tourism and film induced tourism. First, the personnel records can be great attractions to the tourists. The fans of celebrities may transmit their affection on the celebrities to the tourism destinations. Therefore, fans tend to consume irrationally, which offers an opportunity of promoting local businesses of the destination. In addition, the personnel record of celebrities can attract the media's attention which helps promote the destination image.

　　But there are also a few concerns about the personnel records related tourism. First, tourists may just attach to the celebrity but are not very interested in the destination. In addition, it can also be a concern that revisits become less and less after the pilgrimage for the footprints of celebrities. Second, the relationship between a destination and the celebrities or characters in the films can be a threat to sustainable development of a destination. Two primary forms of personnel records related to tourism are strongly attached to some popular culture presented in music, movie, etc. However, fashion often changes unpredictably and rapidly. The trend of an idol or a movie won't last long in most cases. Even worse, the negative news of the celebrities may reduce the visits to a destination sharply. As a result, destination should be cautious when investing the tourism programs only related to the celebrities or characters, or establishing a destination brand only based on the personnel record.

8.3　Art

　　Art, as a subdivision of culture, comprises of many creative endeavors and disciplines. It is a diverse range of human activities in creating visual, auditory or performing artifacts, expressing the author's imaginative, conceptual ideas or technical skill, intended to be appreciated for their beauty or emotional power. In the narrow sense, the art normally refers to its three classical branches: painting, sculpture and architecture. While in a boarder definition, music, theater, film, dance, and other performing arts, literature, and other media are also included in arts. People often go to museums to experience these excellent art works(as Figure shown in 8-3).

Figure 8-3 Visitor'experience in an immersive art installation
Source: ilovetheBurg.com

Arts and tourism have been tightly connected since the ancient times. At that time, artists used arts to record the places around them during the travel and express their view of the world (Alexander, 2022). Nowadays, art tourism denotes that people travel, explore and engage in activities related to art. Generally speaking, art tourism refers to seeing art in tourism (Franklin, 2018), including such activities as traveling to art festivals, concerts, wine and cuisine events, visiting famous museums, and so on.

People attend art tourism for classic art and modern art. Art tourism for classic art refers to the visit for master pieces of the ancient times. For example, Louvre Museum owns a rich collection of oil paintings, sculptures and cultural relics. Over 10 million visitors visit Louvre Museum each year to watch the world's greatest works of art such as *Mona Lisa* by Leonardo da Vinci and *Venus de Milo* sculpture. The art tourism for modern art refers to the journey chasing for modern art which is different from works of art in the classical period and is created in a new style, such as the modern visual art, blues music, jazz music.

The Mississippi Delta Blues Road Trip is a typical example of modern art tourism. Highway 61, also known as the Blues Trail, is one of the first stops many blues fans choose. It begins in Memphis, Tennessee and crosses the border south into Mississippi, connecting the footprints of famous blues artists. The Mississippi Blues Trail Road Trip tells stories about blues artists by images, texts, music, etc. Stories are about the places they lived, the times in which they existed, and how those influenced their music. The marker sites run from city streets to cotton fields, train depots, cemeteries, clubs, and churches. By visiting murals, museums, historic inns and clubs regarding blue jazz, participating in some music events and enjoying the cuisines which exudes southern charm, tourists receive immersive art tour experiences.

In addition, depending on the meanings and degree of involvement in the art, the art tourists are divided in to two primary groups: primary art-related tourists and multi-primary arts-related tourists. Primary art-related tourists' main purpose is to see art. In general, this group of art tourists tends to be the kind of people who regularly visit art attractions or venues. Multi-primary arts-related tourists, for them, art is equally important with some other reasons for the visit. These tourists may travel for some non-art purposes, but they also experience art in the destination. Though some differences exist between the two primary groups, there are a few shared key features of the art tourists. Usually, they are better educated, and willing to spend more time and more money at a destination. Furthermore, they are more likely to stay in hotels rather than with family or friends.

Art tourism promotes both art and tourism. Art attracts tourists with more activities, such as festivals and events, museums, and also bring styles, culture, beauty and a sense of continuity of living to tourism. Meanwhile, tourism creates a channel whereby arts can be presented to the broad audiences and gain more support and appreciation. It also boosts tickets sales and museum gift shop sales, and brings more event and festival attendees.

There are some concerns with the art tourism. First, art may not be attractive for the general public. Appreciating art requires some expertise, which sets boundary to the tourists. As a result, it is challenging to attract new consumers to the art tourism products, despite the increasing resources of art tourism exits. To improve this situation, it is recommended for destinations to organize approachable exhibitions and interpretation service to the public, in order to attract more people to take part in art tourism and improve artistic accomplishment of the public. Second, given specific characteristics of art tourists, the market segment of art tourists is viable. It is a challenge for destinations to design appropriate tourism products, satisfy this viable market segment, at the same time maintain other groups of tourists.

8.4 Folk Customs

Folk customs are developed and practiced primarily by small, homogeneous groups living in far and isolated areas. Folk customs such as the provision of clothing, shelter, transportation and food have evolved differently in different areas of the world, because natural resources vary widely from place to place. Normally, folk customs pass along informally from one to another through verbal instruction or demonstration. There are three basic forms of folk customs: oral tradition, material culture, and customary lore.

First of all, oral tradition refers to the words both written and oral, which are spoken or sung in the traditional utterance in repetitive patterns. Those words and phrases usually conform to a traditional configuration recognized by both the speaker and the audiences. In particular, tales, proverbs, songs, jokes, sayings, folk music are the most common forms.

Second, material culture which includes all artifacts that you can touch, hold, live in or eat, is another form of the folk customs. They are tangible objects, with a physical presence for use either permanently or temporarily. This kind of culture transmits across generations and means a lot to those who make and use these objects. Food presentation is one example of the material culture. Taking dim sum served morning in Guangdong as an example, it is a typical symbol of Cantonese cuisine, which can be traced back to 150 years ago. Not only the food itself, but also the social interactive culture and lifestyle of the locals related to it makes it an attraction to tourists. Moreover, handicraft is another kind of the material culture. These works are usually made in traditional methods. Their styles and patterns are transmitted across generations, which often convey special meanings. It is noteworthy that handicrafts are important sources of the souvenirs. Architecture is also a crucial component of the material culture. The architectural techniques and styles are deeply influenced by the local natural environment and culture, reflecting the living habits and aesthetic tendency of the local people. It often serves as a tourism attraction itself.

The third major type of folk customs is customary lore. It can be a single gesture such as handshake, or it can be a complex interaction of multiple folk customs and artifacts, which can be seen in special events, celebrations, weddings, birthday parties, rituals, etc. Traditions of Christmas celebrations, such as decorating the Christmas tree, singing the carol, and having Christmas meal, or the customs in Chinese New Year like pasting spring couplets, having reunion dinner on New Year's Eve, visiting to relatives and friends and giving and receiving luck money are all customary lore.

Folk customs are important tourism resources that can be extensively developed into cultural tourism products, such as traditional performances(as shown in Figure 8-4), rituals, events and festivals, souvenir, food. Some tourism suppliers combine all these elements and create cultural theme parks in order to provide tourists with a comprehensive cultural experience.

With the increasing engagement between the folk custom and tourism, authenticity has become an issue. Researchers have identified multiple dimensions of authenticity in tourism, like the staged authenticity, constructed authenticity and existential authenticity. Some scholars argue that tourists always hold a consistent value orientation towards "the authenticity", regarding "being authentic" as a good thing (Silverman, 2015). However, in tourism practice, especially in the tourism performing products, "the pure authenticity" or "the real truth" might not exist. Folk customs in these products are staged and particularly designed for tourists, while the real and authentic culture is not shown.

Figure 8-4　Playing the tradition instrument of the Tujia ethnic
Source: Zhangjiajie Tour Club

The ethnic theme parks, such as the Tujia Ethnic Folk Garden, located in the central area of Zhangjiajie City in Hunan Province, are typical cases. This theme park is a tourist attraction that displays the classic buildings, folk customs, food, dance of Tujia ethnic minority. It is converted from the previous palace of Tusi (appointing national minority leader in the Yuan, Ming and Qing dynasties) of Tujia ethnic minority. Tourists can see the tradition of Tujia Maogusi Dance, and watch their wedding performance. Tangible presentations of Tu culture including the jewelries, clothing, batik craft, tapestry, silverwares, tree root carvings, etc. are also demonstrated in the performances. However, all the performances are created for tourists. Acting personnel in the performances are workers who might not know much about ethnic culture and do not have close relationship with local community. Therefore, it is criticized by scholars that folk custom performance in tourism attractions is manifestation of commercialization. Such phenomenon can exert negative impacts on local culture and cultural identity of local people.

Interestingly, it is noted by some scholars that the tourism performances of folk customs are not responsible for providing tourists with "real reality", but to meet tourist needs for entertainment activities during the travel. Tourist experience of authenticity involved in folk custom performances is an existential reality. As long as tourists themselves believe that their experience of tourism performance is authentic, it is authentic. Such commercialized presentation of folk customs is the threat to sustainable development of local culture.

8.5 Modern Festivals

Modern festivals can reflect a particular locale history, traditional culture, contemporary life, entertainment and recreation. Festivals often take place in tourism destinations as supplement products of tourism products.

Modern festivals are organized with two major themes: entertainment and social causes. Festivals for entertainment are set up to provide entertaining experiences to attendants. Typical examples can be music festivals, food festivals, film festivals, etc. Festivals for social causes usually aim to raise public attention or public support for a typical social issue or disadvantaged groups. They are usually charity activities, regarding issues such as environmental conversation, healthy concern, climate change.

Modern festivals offer multiple benefits to destinations. First, they are attractions that lure tourists to experience such human-interactive feelings and engage with music, local culture, food, etc. Second, festivals can enrich tourists' activities and experiences in destinations, if their primary travel purpose is not for the festival. Being in a crowd of people with shared interest or preference, individuals would be able to gain a sense of belonging (J. Wang et al., 2020), and fosters communal identity(Gannon et al., 2019). Third, festivals help destinations go through the low seasons and maintain tourism-related businesses profitable.For examples, ski destinations in Colorado host Summer Festivals, Apple Harvest Festivals, etc. during summer and autumn, when ski business is off and destinations are not busy.

Modern festivals have three types of impacts on the host communities: the economic impact, socio-cultural impact, and environmental impact. From the economic perspective, festivals can bring financial income and employment. Moreover, modern festivals can be an effective way to enhance the destination image regionally, nationally or internationally through the marketing of festivals. Thus, promotion opportunities are extended to local business and their sales are boosted up. For example, Taste of Chicago is one of the largest outdoor food festivals in the world, it lasts about five days every summer since 1980 and locates in Chicago's beautiful Grant Park on the city's magnificent lakefront. The major theme of this festival is to show the diversity of Chicago's dining community. In addition to delicious food served at the festival, music and exciting activities are provided for family attendees. In 2017, this festival attracted 1.6 million attendees and 66 restaurants and food trucks, resulting in sales around 1.9 million dollars. This festival also brings considerable opportunities to related tourism businesses including hotels, local transportation such as taxi and Uber, restaurants, facility renting, entertainment company, shopping and parking. Other attractions such as museums, zoos, Wills Tower are also benefited from this festival which brings more visitors.

Modern festivals bring positive and negative socio-cultural impacts to host communities. On the positive side, modern festivals offer a chance for community development. For example, local infrastructure can be improved due to the growing tourism demand; local residents may form a new identity and place attachment. In addition, modern festivals provide good opportunities to increase awareness, gain support, and raise founding for some social issues. For example, the Pink Run started in 2010 is aimed at raising public awareness of breast cancer and raising funds for treatment of patients suffering from this disease. Modern festivals can also promote civic pride, the Xitang Hanfu Culture Week is a case in point. Hanfu is the traditional clothing of Han people, which is considered as a symbol of Han culture. The purpose of this festival is to inherit and promote Chinese traditional Han culture. Attendees of this festival are recommended to dress in Hanfu. The festival offers Hanfu shows and multiple workshops that tourists can attend.

However, it has been well recognized that modern festivals bring negative socio-cultural and environmental impacts to host communities. It might cause disruptions to local residents' daily life. For example, they may suffer from crowds, huge noises and heavy traffic due to huge amounts of attendees of the festival visiting the destination in a short period of time. Many local residents show negative attitudes and even conflict with visitors verbally or physically. Moreover, modern festivals are hotspots for crime activities. People are under threats of pickpocketing, drugs, or massive shooting during the festival, which also put enormous pressure on public administration. Negative environmental impacts caused by modern festivals can be sanitation maintenance, litter and trash management, and pollution to the natural environment.

8.6 Festivals and Events

Festivals and events refer to happenings at a given place and time, usually of some importance and meanings, to celebrate or commemorate special occasions (Westcott et al., 2014). It usually has a consistent and unified design, event theme, and purpose.

According to the size of the events, events include mega events, special events, hallmark events, festivals, and local community events. Mega events are usually international events with over one million attendees, and are considered as "must see" events. Such events are recurring for a period of time. For example, the Olympic Games are held every four years. Mega events are able to bring high levels of media coverage, prestige, and economic benefits to the host community (Westcott et al., 2014). Hallmark events, particularly the hallmark tourism events are one-time or recurring events, which are developed with the primary purpose of increasing awareness and attractiveness of a tourism destination in the short and/or long term. Through uniqueness, status, and significance, hallmark events create interests and draw attentions of potential attendees and tourists, and ultimately bring economic benefits to the host destination.

Based on the theme, events can be grouped into three categories: sport events, music events, and cultural events, all of which can serve as tourism resources. The sport events are staged for recreational or professional sport races. Sport events can always draw tourism related activities to host destinations (Mallen and Adams, 2008). The Olympics Games, the FIFA World Cup, and the Super Bowl, are all the world-class famous sport events, drawing attendees and tourists to the host destination from all over the world. Music events not only appeal to music fans, but also attract ordinary tourists who would like to immerse into the atmosphere. Some large music events, such as the Mawazine in Rabat, Morocco, and Summerfest in Wisconsin, USA are among the largest music festivals in the world, attracting attendees internationally. In addition to sport events and music events, many events' theme is related to culture, such as food expo, ethnic festivals, local cultural fairs. They are valuable tourism resources that provide attendees and tourists all kinds of cultural experiences. It is worth of noting that all these categories of events are not rigidly differentiated. They often overlap or combine. For example, a sport event can include some music elements; and people can also find music and even sport activities in ethnic cultural festivals.

Festivals and events are important tourism attractions. Take the Carnival of Brazil as an example, in 2019, about 1.5 million tourists visited Rio de Janeiro for this event. Many destinations' MICE industry have to deal with the off-seasons. For example, tourism in Las Vegas is very seasonal. The city has determined to take advantage of famous hotels, resorts and convention centers to develop MICE industry. Now, Las Vegas is one of the largest MICE destinations in the world, receiving missions of attendees to the city during the tourism off-seasons.

Famous events help destinations to rebuild or enhance the destination brand by media. The London 2012 Summer Olympics sets a good example. More than 20,000 journalists, camera crew and other media people gathered in London. Websites and social media also played significant roles in drawing attention of the public, London 2012's social media sites have attracted 4.7 million followers and LOCOG reported that there were 150 million tweets about the Games. The destination brand image of London was enriched and became well-known across the world. A brand "Inspired by 2012" was derived from the Olympic Games, which sets an optimistic and positive perception of the city and country.

Events diversify visitors' experiences by adding extra elements to tourism products.

For example, ski tourists normally participate in skiing, ice-skating, snowboarding when they visit ski destinations. Harbin International Ice and Snow Sculpture Festival(as Figure 8-5 shown) in China provide ice-and-snow themed shows to ski tourists, which combine ice dance, ice magic, clown comedy, catwalk models, ice acrobatics, music, local food, etc. Tourists' experiences are greatly enhanced and diversified by this hallmark tourism event.

Figure 8-5　Harbin International Ice and Snow Sculpture Festival
Source: nationalgeographic.com

8.7 Hometown/Residence of Celebrities

8.7.1 The Definitions of Hometown/Residence of Celebrities

The hometown or residence of celebrities refers to the places where celebrities were born, grew up, lived, studied during the period of residence, it is a place that celebrities had a major influence or major events occurred during their residence. Through the visit to the hometown or residence of celebrities, people can see, reflect and understand the growing paths of celebrities, related history and culture, and so on. Hometown or residence of celebrities is a valuable cultural tourism resources. Springfield is famous because President Lincoln has lived and worked there for about 10 years before he moved to Washington D.C. People visited his house and learned about his work and personal life during that period of time, as well as political events, history, civil war, architecture design, etc.

Hometown or residence of celebrities does not always tie to historical characters. Many tourists are curious to visit hometown or residence of celebrities in nowadays. Most tourists to Los Angeles would make a trip to Beverley Hills, taking a look at homes of super stars, even they are not fans of these people.

To sum up, hometown or residence of celebrities, as a kind of cultural tourism resources, provides visitors experiences with multiple elements, including history and nostalgia, architecture, arts, popular culture, etc. Many destinations have included such places as important tourism attractions.

8.7.2 The Activities of Hometown/Residence of Celebrities

1) Sightseeing Tour

Almost all the sightseeing tours are arranged in residence of historical celebrities. Historical celebrities have been recorded in the annals of history with their ingenuity and brilliant achievements. Many of them are admired as role models for future generations. Sightseeing tours operated in such places demonstrate the daily life of these great people, roll out the history and culture in old time with stories, which provide immersive, cultural, historical, and nostalgic experiences to visitors.

2) Visit to Related Memorials

Memorial halls, including cultural halls, museums, art galleries, etc., are cultural venues for collecting and exhibiting material cultural heritage left by celebrities, in order to commemorate celebrities. Through such activities, sightseeing tours are transformed into cultural tours. Museums and various memorial halls with profound cultural heritage have been increasingly recognized by the general public, and have gradually become important tourism attractions.

3) Celebrity Theme Events

As an important cultural heritage, the tourism resources of historical celebrities can show the great features and achievements made by historical celebrities. In addition, cultural heritage can be venues to hold celebrity theme events, offering all kinds of activities involving history, culture, art, food, traditional art crafts, etc.

China (Qufu) International Confucius Cultural Festival was founded in September 1989. The event is mainly based on the theme of commemorating Confucius and promoting the Confucius culture. It integrates history, education, tourism, academic research, scientific and technological activities. The festival attracts millions of Confucian scholars, advocates and tourists to the destination every year.

8.8 Performance

8.8.1 The Definitions of Performance

Tourism performances refer to performances in tourism attractions, with the main content about the history, culture or folk customs of the area, and with tourists as the primary audience. Tourism performances bring a lot of benefits to destinations, such as enriching the cultural demonstrations, enhancing destination image, extending visitors' length of stay, increasing their expenses. For tourists, tourism performances satisfy their needs for a deep understanding of local people and culture. It is also an effective means to keep the declining culture alive.

8.8.2 The Activities of Performance

Performances in destinations include three primary types based on the content: large-scale landscape performance, comprehensive performance, and original folk customs performance.

1) Large-scale Landscape Performance

The large-scale landscape performance breaks through the space limitation of traditional stage. It takes the natural landscape as the stage and background, and integrates the real natural environment into the performance. Generally speaking, the financial cost of this type of the performance is very high. Local folk customs, myths and legends, historical legends and other cultural elements are often displayed in the large-scale landscape performance. High technology on lighting, sound, etc. can be frequently used in such performances which provide immersive and aesthetic experiences to audiences.

2) Comprehensive Performance

Comprehensive performances mainly refer to large-scale tourism performances including singing, dancing, and acrobatics. The content of the performance can be local culture, folk customs, historical allusions, myths and legends, etc.

3) Original Folk Customs Performance

Most performances in this type are staged in areas where ethnic minorities live. These areas are rich in ethnic tourism resources, well preserved original cultural resources and ethnic customs. In such performances, both the content and the artistic form tend to be authentic. Many performers belong to local ethnic people, enhancing the authenticity of the performance.

Case 8-1

Case 8-2

Reading time

Impression Liu Sanjie is staged in Yangshuo, Guilin, Guangxi Province. It is the first large-scale landscape outdoor performance in China, which sets on the Lijiang River. The whole performing area covers two kilometers of water area and twelve small hills. This performance brings a new form of live performance that includes natural scenery as the stage and background.

Impression Liu Sanjie is about the legend singer of Guangxi, Liu Sanjie, but it is not limited to her story. By using the image of traditional Chinese painting and rhythms of local songs, *Impression Liu Sanjie* shows the lifestyle, the folk customs, and natural landscapes of the Lijiang River. The performance demonstrates the lifestyle, traditions and culture of multiple ethnic groups in the area, including Zhuang, Yao, Miao, Dong. As of July 2019, it has performed more than 7,000 times, watched by 18 million domestic and foreign viewers, and made over 2 billion yuan.

Chapter Review

This chapter introduces the humanistic activities, which can be recognized as tourism resources. Humanistic activities refer to all the cultural activities in human society, and they are mirrors of society and its history. In this chapter, humanistic activity tourism resources refer to the human-involved dynamic processes or the witnesses and production of such dynamic process, which are valuable and usable for tourism purposes.

In this chapter, we went through several types of humanistic activities tourism resources, including personnel records, art, folk customs, modern festivals, festivals and events, hometown/residence of celebrities and performances. And we have discussed a few issues and concerns related to the tourism development based on the humanistic activities, including authenticity, environmental impact, etc.

In summary, humanistic activities are vivid parts of the tourists destinations, and they have been still being in a dynamic process.

Questions for Discussion

1. What is the definition of humanistic activities?

2. Please illustrate the relationship between humanistic activities and tourism, using a particular type of humanistic activities as an example.

3. Please discuss the potential negative effects to the culture and environment when developing tourism based on humanistic activities.

4. Please discuss how to integrate the elements of the humanistic activities to build a brand of the distinctive culture in a tourist destination.

Exercises

Note

Chapter 9
Tourism Commodities

Learning Objectives

(1) Learn the definitions and attributes of tourism commodities.
(2) Learn the categories of the tourism commodities.
(3) Understand the meaning of handicrafts and their contemporary development.
(4) Understand the definitions and attributes of souvenirs.
(5) Understand the concepts of specialties.
(6) Understand the characteristics of modern tourism supplies and consumables.

Technical Words

English Words	中文翻译
tourism commodity	旅游商品
commodity attribute	商品属性
souvenir	纪念品
functionality	功能性
symbolic meaning	象征意义
handicraft	手工艺品
traditional craft	传统工艺
specialty	特产
product of geographical indication	地理标识产品
tourism supply and consumable	旅游用品与消耗品
cultural creativity	文化创意
smart travel equipment	旅游智能装备

Knowledge Graph

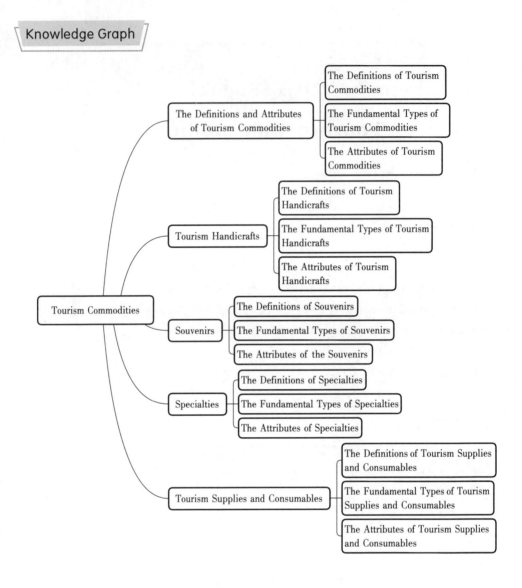

9.1 The Definitions and Attributes of Tourism Commodities

9.1.1 The Definitions of Tourism Commodities

According to Karl Marx, commodities are labor products used for exchange, with natural and social attributes. The former refers to the utility of a thing that satisfies people's needs, that is, the use-value. And the latter refers to the exchange of a commodity for another, which is based on its use value for others, the exchange value. Value is the basis of the exchange value, and the exchange value is the manifestation of value. A commodity is the unity of use-value and value, and value is the most essential feature of a commodity. In a broad sense, commodities include not only material commodities but also intangible services. In a narrow sense, commodities only refer to the tangible goods.

Therefore, in the broad sense, tourism commodities refer to a general term of both tangible commodities and intangible commodities with tourism cultural connotations purchased by tourists for tourism, or before, during, and after the tourism process; while in the narrow sense, tourism commodities refer to the material goods that have commemorative significance and reflect the characteristics of the tourist destination, that are purchased by tourists out of non-commercial purposes (Ma Yaofeng et al., 2010; Huang Jiyuan, 1999; Miao Xueling, 2004; Guo Lufang et al., 2008).

1) International Definitions of Tourism Commodities

Generally, souvenirs are synonymous with tourism commodities. Souvenir, as its original indication that is an action to remember, represents an object through which something is remembered. Therefore, souvenirs refer to objects that are symbolic reminders of an event or experience (Swanson et al., 2012).

However, as a kind of tourist commodity, the souvenir is something that is found in shops and markets. The object includes many things such as arts and crafts, postcards, booklets, T-shirts, natural materials, markers, local products(Litirell et al., 1994; Gordon, 1986).

Moreover, tourist art is always discussed. Tourist art represents a unique expression of place and genuine artistic style that makes especially for the consumption of souvenirs (Hume, 2014). Tourist art is an important factor that has an impact on the designs and production of souvenirs, consumer expectations towards souvenirs, and the successful promotions of products as souvenirs. When tourists come to a place, they may attempt to buy the things of the functional embedded arts. The local people thus begin to mass-produce the objects that are in the traditional forms and designs. These objects satisfy on the one hand the local people's own aesthetic traditions; on the other hand, the buyers' yearning for "authenticity". In the process, the basic motifs and/or forms of the traditional art may persist, but the size and complexity may diminish and the materials and format may change drastically (Graburn, 1984). This always occurs during the process of commoditization in tourism. But commoditization does not necessarily destroy the meaning of the traditional products, neither for the locals nor for the tourists (Cohen, 1988). On the contrary, commoditization may save the disappearing art.

According to the purchasing purposes, souvenirs have use-value, exchange-value, sign-value and spiritual-value (as shown in Table 9-1).

Table 9-1　Values of souvenirs

Values	Purchasing purpose of souvenir
Use-value	To use as a memento of the tourist experience; For utilitarian use of everyday life while being on vacation (and after returning home)
Exchange-value	For the price (cheap—expensive); For investment purposes (expecting to gain a higher price in the future)
Sign-value	For prestigious purposes and social status gaining; For collecting (usually authentic, unique and rare souvenirs)
Spiritual-value	For the empowerment of religious faith; For the belief that certain religious souvenirs have supernatural powers (healing and protecting identities)

What the tourists buy are not only souvenirs but also their necessary personal items such as clothes, jewelry, duty-free goods and electronic goods (Turner et al., 2001). Shopping as a tourist activity can make tourist product attractive because it is a source of pleasure.

According to UNWTO, tourism expenditure refers to the amount paid for the acquisition of consumption goods and services, as well as valuables, for own use or to give away, for and during tourism trips. It includes expenditures by visitors themselves, as well as expenses that are paid for or reimbursed by others (United Nations, 2010).

2) Domestic Definitions of Tourism Commodities

At present, domestic tourism scholars have not reached an agreement on the concept of tourism commodities. On the one hand, the term per se is vague, uncertain and dynamic developing; on the other hand, there are deputes and differences about the concepts of tourism commodities, tourism products, tourism purchases, and souvenirs, as follows:

Tourism commodities are the products or services produced by tourism enterprises that meet the needs of tourists (Wang Kejian, 1991).

Tourism commodity is a comprehensive concept. It does not refer to a certain product or service purchased by tourists in the process of tourism, nor to the simple superposition of those products and services. It refers to a commodity group composed of a series of unit products and services that are only realized in tourism activities (Zhou Daren, 1988).

Tourism commodities are the physical objects that tourists buy in their tourism activities. It can also be called tourism purchases (Tao Hanjun et al., 1994).

Tourism commodities or called tourism purchases refer to the tangible goods purchased by tourists out of non-commercial purpose that are mainly composed of souvenirs (Miao Xueling, 2004).

In a broad sense, tourism commodities include souvenirs, daily tourism necessities, specialties, various arts and crafts, cultural relics, antiques and their replicas, and various tourism supplies. In a narrow sense, tourist commodities refer to crafts and souvenirs (Jiang Binghua, 2005).

Tourism commodities are tourism purchases, including tourism supplies, souvenirs, tourism consumer products, etc. that are part of tourism products (Zhang Yong, 2010).

From the perspective of commodity life cycle, the whole process of commodities includes development, production, circulation, consumption, and abandonment, which also provides three dimensions for understanding tourism commodities: demander, supplier and commodity circulation. This means, tourism commodities have different "roles" that can be those purchased by "tourists", those produced by the "tourism production system" and those circulate in the "tourism commodity market" (Lu Kaixiang et al., 2017). Within the dimension of commodity circulation, tourism commodity refers to physical object that exists in the tourism market and is open to tourists; within the dimension of demander, it includes tangible attachment that is related to tourism activity such as label and packaging; within the dimension of suppliers, it also includes intangible attachment that is related to tourism experience such as cultural elements and symbolic meanings (as shown in Figure 9-1).

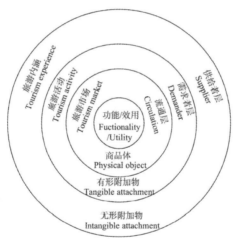

Figure 9-1 Conceptual model of tourism commodity

9.1.2 The Fundamental Types of Tourism Commodities

According to UNWTO, all individual goods and services (those that satisfy the wants and needs of individuals) can potentially be part of tourism expenditure. This includes not only the typical services acquired by visitors like transportation, accommodation, food, and beverage, etc., but also other items such as valuables (paintings, works of art, jewelry, etc.), all food prepared and unprepared, all manufactured items whether locally produced or imported, all personal services (United Nations, 2010).

According to our country's *Basic Terminology in Travel and Tourism*(GB/T 16766-2017), "shopping tourism" refers to tourism with the main purpose of purchasing famous brand commodities, local specialties, and souvenirs.

In the classification of tourism resources in China, tourism commodities are regarded as a single category of tourism resources. According to *Classification, Investigation and Evaluation of Tourism Resources* (GB/T 18972-2017), tourism commodities are seen as "tourism purchases" with three categories of agricultural products, industrial products and handicrafts. Specifically, "tourism purchases" include planting, forestry, animal husbandry, aquatic products, aquaculture industrial products and productions; daily industrial products and tourism equipment products; stationery products, textiles and dyeing, furniture, ceramics, gold and stone carving and sculpture products, gold and stone tools, paper art and lamp art, and paintings.

Some researches argue that tourism commodities include souvenirs, cultural relics, antiques and imitations, practical handicrafts, local specialties, special arts and crafts, and tourist daily necessities (Li Yan, 2001). Or, tourism commodities refer to tourism shopping that can be mainly divided into three categories: souvenirs, tourism supplies and tourism consumables (Liu Dunrong, 2002). However, there is dispute about the necessities of tourism activities because food, beverages, as well as toiletries, and daily necessities consumed by tourists in the process of tourism are always purchased according to their usual preferences. This kind of expenditure is relatively stable and limited (Chen Shengrong, 2006). The current classification of tourism commodities is mainly a mixture of two methods. One is based on tourism activities, including tourism consumables and tourism supplies. The other is based on the characteristics of commodities, including souvenirs, tourism handicrafts, tourism specialties, etc (Lu kaixiang et al., 2017).

To sum up, tourism commodities include souvenirs, handicrafts, specialties, and tourism supplies and consumables.

9.1.3 The Attributes of Tourism Commodities

Analyzing the above definitions, purposes and categories, we can see that although their respective starting points and focuses are different, the basic attributes of tourism commodities are generally the same, mainly in the following two aspects: function and symbol.

All individual goods and services, in particular, those that satisfy the wants and needs of tourists can potentially be part of tourism commodities. Actually, there is a subtle difference between wants and needs. Needs are necessities and wants are desires. Necessities emphasize the use-value of tourism commodities. Desires represent the attraction and value of tourism commodities, which is greatly enhanced by symbolic and cultural elements such as art and craft.

9.2 Tourism Handicrafts

Handicrafts are the art crafts produced by hand labor or through skillful hands. The key words for understanding handicrafts, as the noun shows, are skill and hand. In Chinese, both "Gong" and "Yi" mean skill. Handicraft is the cultural vein of Chinese nation's creation that has continued for thousands of years. It exists between the daily necessities of local people and carries people's aesthetic feelings, the wisdom of creation and ethical thoughts (Pan Lusheng, 2012).

9.2.1 The Definitions of Tourism Handicrafts

According to *the Convention for the Safeguarding of the Intangible Culture Heritage* adopted by UNESCO(2003), handicrafts in particular with the traditional craftsmanship, are classic intangible heritage that refers to "the practices, representations, expressions, knowledge, skills, as well as the instruments, objects, artefacts and cultural spaces associated therewith, which communities, groups and, in some cases, individuals recognize as part of their cultural heritage. This intangible cultural heritage, transmitted from generation to generation, is constantly recreated by communities and groups in response to their environment, their interaction with nature and their history, and provides them with a sense of identity and continuity, thus promoting respect for cultural diversity and human creativity."

As Rousseau argued in *Emile*, "Of all the occupations which can provide subsistence to man, that which brings him closest to the state of nature is manual labor. Of all conditions, the artisan is the most independent of fortune and men." Handicraft is "the craft creation and its production that are created and inherited by the broad public, mainly reflecting the public's lives, thoughts and feelings, and expressing their aesthetic and artistic tastes" (Tian Xiaohang, 2007). Traditional craftsmanship includes "traditional methods, material handling, industry beliefs, teacher-inheritance relationships of handicraftsman, taboo worship of handicrafts, and the folk functions and meanings of handicrafts per se"(Li Hongyan, 2012). Life and production experience is an important basis for the inheritance and development of handicrafts. Being artificial products made by manual techniques, by the means of transformation of natural objects through decoration and carving, handicrafts not only serve people's daily life but also express their spiritual world (Fang Lili, 2004).

Since the early 1970s in China, traditional crafts have had some influence. By the beginning of the 21st century, traditional craft was listed in the National Intangible

Cultural Heritage List and attracted attention of provinces, cities and regions. The handwork and creativity of traditional crafts also pave the way for rural handicrafts and the rural revitalization strategy. In the new era, China actively promotes rural revitalization and traditional crafts and makes the plan for both development by building the pattern of "one township and one industry, one village and one product". Meanwhile being committed to the new development philosophy within the whole process of the revitalization of traditional crafts, China carries out the evaluation of the protection and inheritance of intangible cultural heritage representative projects of traditional crafts via classified policies and scientific management; encourages the enterprises of traditional crafts to use modern production technology and management methods, and distinguish between manual production and mechanical production by setting up the special manual production lines; these are useful to improve the value of manual production, enrich product categories and cultivate high-end brands for meeting the diverse consumer needs (Ministry of Culture and Tourism of the People's Republic of China et al., 2022).

9.2.2 The Fundamental Types of Tourism Handicrafts

In the classification of ancient China such as the *Ritual Works of Zhou · Kao Gong Ji*, the "hundred handicrafts" are divided into six categories: wood crafts, gold crafts, leather crafts, dyeing crafts, pottery crafts and crafts of city planning. This is also the classification system of ancient Chinese handicrafts.

In *Dream Pool Essays*, Shen Kuo listed 20 categories, including Yu Hao wooden construction scriptures (a book about wooden construction method, written by Yu Hao), Wei method (a method for measuring terrain) and Zhui method (a method for measuring astronomy), gap product operation (a method of mathematics) and huiyuan method (an approximate method for calculating the arc length of a circular arch), Curong (one of the chess games), Zaogong (a bow-making handicrafts), the method of chessboard change (a method of calculating the change of go chess), Tan chess (a type of board games), Zengcheng method (an multiplying method), typographic printing, Weipu (a method of measuring astronomical calendars), moxibustion, go chess, divination by sheep (a form of divination practiced by western and northern ethnic groups in ancient China), Wooden pagoda of Brahma Temple (a technique for strengthening the buildings), beard, eyebrows and hair (a technique to identify the function of viscera), leechcraft (Diagnosis should not just follow medical books), Ligusticum wallichii and kuh-seng (leechcraft beyond medical books), Mozi (facsimile of calligraphy copybook), a clerical script written in loose brush (an art of calligraphy), and Fengzhen buddhist doctor (a superb leechcraft).

In modern classification, there are two common methods. One depends on the function of handicrafts such as practical handicrafts and appreciative handicrafts; the other depends on the characteristics, including weaving handicrafts, carving handicrafts, kneading handicrafts, textile handicrafts, printing and dyeing handicrafts, embroidery handicrafts, knitting handicrafts, ceramic handicrafts, lacquer handicrafts, smelting and forging handicrafts, rolling handicrafts, clipping handicrafts and printing handicrafts (Tian Xiaohang, 2007).

Tourism handicrafts are usually daily handicrafts and display handicrafts, including ceramic and lacquer handicrafts, sculpture handicrafts, metal handicrafts, embroidery handicrafts, weaving handicrafts, and flower painting handicrafts, jewelry and jade, and "the scholar's four jewels" (writing brush, ink stick, ink slab and paper), and so on.

9.2.3 The Attributes of Tourism Handicrafts

For tourists, they purchase handicrafts because they value the superb quality of craftsmanship, specifically the valuable work of the hand, the techniques as well as time involved in the production process. These are always seen as the aspects of the authenticity of a handicraft.

Authenticity refers to the authentic life of a community or region. Buying handicrafts may link tourists with the life of destination and enchant their travel experience. More importantly, when tourists come back to home, these authentic handicrafts play a role of evoking a general life rich in meaning.

Authenticity is not static and isolated. Though originally it means expert knowledge and good taste (particularly in art), "authenticity is a socially constructed concept and its social connotation is, therefore, not given, but negotiable" (Cohen, 1988). In this sense, tourist's definition of authenticity also matters.

How to define an authentic craft? These aspects are what tourists always consider: a craft's uniqueness and originality; workmanship; aesthetics; function and use; cultural and historical integrity; person's connection, having produced it with his or her own hands, and materials; local production; shopping experience; genuineness or truth in advertising; and a guarantee of authenticity by way of a label or certificate (Littrell et al., 1993; Kim et al., 2001; Revilla et al., 2003).

Traditional crafts indeed provide a foundation for innovation of tourism souvenirs; only the sustainable development of traditional crafts can make souvenirs creative and novel; thus, innovation of exploitation should be vigorously developed (Zulaikha et al., 2011).

Tourism provides a means of revitalizing traditional crafts, but the key is traditional craft per se that need to be revitalized. Traditional crafts should not miss its essence in the process of production and circulation, particularly many of them are valuable intangible cultural heritage. The purpose of productive protection is not to lose the tradition of manual labor as well as the cultural connotation in it. Also, never replace the manual labor by machine to make the industrial production. However, in the current wave of modernization and industrialization, it should not exclude the participation of machine because machine production can bring out new technology, new materials, and new development. Therefore, how to effectively borrow the power of machines to enable the ecological development of handicrafts has become a topic worthy of further discussion. What would replace industrial civilization must be ecological civilization. Such civilization image and production model are somewhat similar to the return of agricultural civilization. Surely, it is based on high intelligence, new energy, new material and the Internet(Fang Lili, 2017).

9.3 Souvenirs

As discussed earlier, meaning and commodity are the key concepts for understanding souvenirs; however, items that are stumbled upon during travel are used in ordinary time and space but also can recall the experience(as shown in Figure 9-2); in a broader sense, souvenirs refer to the items that can remind travelers of their experience (Swanson et al., 2012).

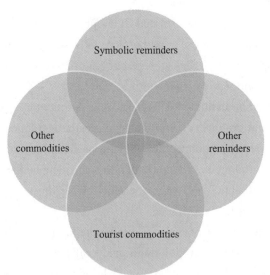

Figure 9-2　Souvenir taxonomies

9.3.1 The Definitions of Souvenirs

The meanings of souvenirs are diverse and cumulative, with much more significance than functions(Graburn, 2000). As a "messenger of the extraordinary" (Gordon, 1986), souvenirs can act as symbolic reminders of events, places, or experiences. Souvenirs are often strategically placed at home where they can best be seen by others. In this sense, souvenirs are a kind of evidence that is useful for social communication, self-conception, and self-expression.

Souvenirs can indicate social status and interpersonal relationship. Tourists use souvenirs to prove to others that they had a travel experience. Souvenirs are the tangible evidence of travel (Graburn, 1987). Evidence is also expressed through souvenir gift-giving. When souvenirs are given to others as a gift, the role they act may not be the experience reminder, but a witness of the interpersonal relationship. Souvenir as evidence is important "both for the tourist and as a means of communicating their experiences with others" (Wilkins, 2011).

Souvenir consumption has close connection with individual's taste and habits, and is an important way to establish his/her self-identity. For individuals, self-identity is also made in the break from daily life such as the life rite. The reason why souvenirs can be a symbol of important events in life is that souvenir is a messenger of the extraordinary, as mentioned above. The purpose of people buying souvenirs is to recollect the travel experience. As tangible evidence of travel, souvenirs are a commemoration of sacred time and space, and an extension of the travel experience. Therefore, tourism becomes an escape from the boring life; leaving profane world, tourists enter the sacred world through a series of life rites; and then they return, they feel new; travel is similar to the religious pilgrimage in which travelers can experience the spiritual death and rebirth (Graburn, 1989). It is natural for people to bring back something commemorated after a sacred trip. Souvenirs, in a sense, just meet the demand.

9.3.2 The Fundamental Types of Souvenirs

There are different classifications of tourist souvenirs with different emphases as follow: ① pictorial images (e.g., picture postcards); piece-of-the-rock (e.g., pinecones, seashells, and rocks); symbols of a destination (e.g., a miniature Eiffel Tower); markers (e.g., T-shirts); and local products (e.g., foods and clothing) (Gordon, 1986); ② photographs, postcards, and paintings of the region; local specialties such as regional food products, wine, and clothing; perfume, electrical goods, cameras, or other similar goods that can be purchased at a discounted price; regional handicrafts and artworks such as carvings, jewelry, glassware; published material on the destination/region, such as books, magazines, and guidelines; items representative of the location/destination, such as key, rings/chains fridge magnets, mugs; hats, caps, or other clothing branded with the destination, hotel, or attraction; nonregional arts and crafts, such as paintings, stuffed animals or toys, ornaments (Wilkins, 2011).

In addition, situational souvenirs that refer generally to wars and disasters (Timothy, 2005), may be put as a single category. For example, after disaster events, those collectible, memorable and beneficial cultural elements can be made into mementos as disaster souvenirs. There are some examples as follows: ① commemorative medals and coins; commemorative coupons and tickets, train and boat tickets; guide maps, manuals, and traffic maps including major cities; books and periodicals related to local tourism which introduce the local customs, features of attractions and legends; scenery pictures, amorous feelings picture albums, bookmarks, postcards, calendars; arts and crafts, local specialties (Zou Delong, 1992); ② ethnic resources; local specialties; commemorative pictures; tourism medals/mascots; handicrafts; art resources (Zhao Peiyan, 2011).

9.3.3 The Attributes of the Souvenirs

The definitions of souvenirs determine that it has a function of communicating and disseminating culture. While in the process of spreading culture, souvenirs can not only promote themselves and increase the sales and profits, but also enhance the overall image of the country or region and further stimulate the development of the tourism destination.

Souvenirs always elicit a coded message about the place or time they come from (Gordon, 1986). Such coded message helps to enhance tourist motivation or produce new motivation toward to the destination and makes a sense of place (as shown in Figure 9-3).

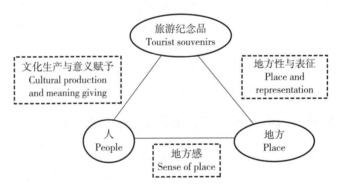

Figure 9-3　An integrated framework for the interaction of "people-souvenir-place"

However, the geographical scale of souvenirs may be not limited to the destinations. Souvenirs may represent a country, a region, a city or a specific attraction or potentially a combination of several of these geographical scales. This nature of souvenirs may bring out a kind of "geographically displaced authenticity" that means "purchasing a souvenir from an area other than the destination being visited" (Hashimoto et al., 2007). For destination retailers, it may present an opportunity to market souvenirs from other places. After all, in time those items may no longer be linked to geographical displaced authenticity but may become elevated to a higher level (of a region or country). In turn, the destination can also adopt a limited marketing strategy by which the local souvenirs are only sold in the location. Tourists who have not been there cannot get the souvenirs. In this way, tourists may make a sense of the geographical authenticity of souvenirs and show more loyalty and satisfaction to the destination.

Aesthetics and utility are also prominent features of souvenirs. The former highlights the aesthetical sensation of the product and its appearance. When consumers perceive that the aesthetics of the product will contribute to attaining social status, feeling happier, rewarding themselves or gaining the admiration of others, they will translate their initial emotional attachment into stronger purchase intentions and commitment (Vilches-Montero et al., 2018). The latter refers to "the convenience, the reasonable price, the quality and the eco-friendliness of a souvenir".

9.4 Specialties

Specialties refer to products that are unique or particularly famous in a place and usually have excellent quality. Generally, these products are agricultural and forestry products or processed products.

9.4.1 The Definitions of Specialties

What makes specialties special? Concerning this question, two criteria are always considered. The first refers to the fact that specialties represent the typical nature of a particular place. The second refers to the fact that specialties are the items or products of distinctive kinds or particular superiority or quality and always increase economic returns.

Specialties are always popular with tourists because they are considered as "iconic" products of a particular place. Specialties are part of the local characteristics of a place. Local characteristics, as a kind of regional comparative advantages, highlight the characteristics of a tourist destination that are significantly different from other regions in terms of nature, history, and culture, as well as the attraction to tourists. And attraction strength depends much on the comparison of the natural, historical and cultural conditions between the tourist residence and the destination. Here the natural conditions mainly refer to the natural environment such as climate, landform, geology and biology in it. With such natural condition, the destination may produce distinctive products and brands such as agricultural and sideline products and "rural brands". The historical and cultural conditions mainly refer to the historical origin, folk culture, exquisite craftsmanship and high popularity of products with which the destination may have local food and "time-honored brands".

In addition, surrounding the discussion of specialties are geographical indication products. Geographical indication products also refer to products that are produced in a specific place. The quality, reputation and other aspects of geographical indication products are essentially determined by the natural and human conditions of the region. But geographical indication products need to be reviewed and approved as geographical name and protected by regional patent. There is special protection of geographical indications and its system also play an important role in protecting the intellectual property rights of geographical indication, improving the quality of local products, promoting rural revitalization, and promoting regional economic development and foreign trade in China.

9.4.2 The Fundamental Types of Specialties

As the main body of specialties, agricultural and forestry products mainly include planting, forestry, animal husbandry, fishery and aquaculture, and so on.

Food is also an important part of specialties, including beverages (mainly tea and wine), dishes (e.g., eight major cuisines), pastries, dried food, and so on.

According to the regulations on the *Protection of Geographical Indication Products in China* (2005), geographical indication products include planted and bred products from a local place; products or its raw materials (mainly or partly) produced and processed according to specific skills in a local place.

9.4.3 The Attributes of Specialties

Specialties are also important for visitors, satisfying their desire for authenticity and distinctive characteristics of a place, because specialties are perceived as products with higher quality, rarity, nutritional values and better reputation and taste. Specialties are always used as a prop for enhancing tourist involvement with the place. This also brings out social proximity that is valued by tourists (Kastenholz et al., 2021). Beyond purchasing specialties, tourists always want to know what history and geography are behind them or what the production methods are and interact with the local producers and people. Social proximity creates a meaningful and memorable experience for visitors. Therefore, as a kind of distinctive endogenous resources, specialties are vital comparative advantages of the location (Ritchie et al., 2003). Involvement and memorable specialty-based experiences can have an impact on the long-lasting loyalty of tourists towards both local products and the location. They thus recommend the local specialties to friends and relatives and share them within the community on the Internet. In addition, specialties also facilitate the local industries, such as the agriculture, forestry, fishery, and dairy industries.

9.5 Tourism Supplies and Consumables

Tourism supplies and consumables mainly refer to the daily necessities, cultural daily necessities and tourism equipment, purchased and consumed in the process of tourism to meet the needs of tourists.

9.5.1 The Definitions of Tourism Supplies and Consumables

Tourism supplies and consumables are tools that have practical functions and are useful in the travel process by providing convenient, safe, and comfortable services to tourists.

9.5.2 The Fundamental Types of Tourism Supplies and Consumables

Tourism supplies and consumables can be divided into cultural daily necessities, including travel daily necessities, entertainment products, stationery, utensils, etc.; technological life products, including tourism electronic products, electrical appliances, personal equipment, sports supplies, etc.; fashion and creative products, including travel clothing, luggage, jewelry, toys, etc.

There are also segmented categories of tourism supplies and consumables. For example, according to the sports categories, sports supplies are subdivided into snow and ice sports tourism supplies, cycling sports supplies, water sports supplies, etc. Outdoor tourism supplies include outdoor clothing, outdoor shoes, camping equipment, backpacks, tools, leisure furniture and so on.

Case 9-1

Case 9-2

In addition, the rapid development of digital technologies such as the Internet of things, artificial intelligence, big data, and cloud computing bring out the integration with tourism equipment, promote the innovation of tourism smart equipment and supplies and launch the smart products of skis, helmets and clothing.

9.5.3 The Attributes of Tourism Supplies and Consumables

In recent years, cultural creativity and technology have been the force to enhance the differentiation of market and product of tourism supplies and consumables. China has promulgated relevant policies, requiring that we should strengthen cultural confidence, enhance the value of commodities by cultural connotations and promote the development of creative tourism products further; then, we need to improve the social influence of excellent products and brands by enriching the variety of commodities, cultivating boutique brands, guiding brand entities to innovate and carry out online marketing, and so on (Ministry of Culture and Tourism of the People's Republic of China, 2021).

Case 9-3

Case 9-4

First, cultural creativity can enable the development of tourism supplies and consumables. Surrounding cultural creativity, creative design, brand authorization and manufacturing, it can lead the consumer demand and the expansion of the consumer market. For example, animation IP carries out joint marketing with tourism supplies brands and launches the same animation products and equipment together, which is not only welcomed by tourists but also the animation fans.

Second, technology can enable the innovation of tourism supplies and consumables. With the development of digital technology, the application of wearable devices and remote sensing satellites in the field of self-service tourism, tourism industry has been in the process of intelligent transformation. These new technologies like "Internet + big data" can reduce the cost of enterprises of tourism supplies and consumables and build a sharing platform for them, which helps optimal allocation of resource and accelerate the formation of the new development model characterized by openness and sharing (Ministry of Culture and Tourism of the People's Republic of China, 2020).

Chapter Review

Tourism commodities are important tourism resources. On the basis of defining the related concepts, this chapter expounds the characteristics, attributes and classification of tourism commodities. Tourism commodities are mainly composed of handicrafts, souvenirs, specialties, and tourism supplies and consumables. The development of tourism commodities is an important indicator of tourism industry that also paves the way to remain committed to the new development philosophy and realize rural revitalization, and inheritance, activation and innovation of intangible cultural heritage. For promoting the high-quality development of tourism, we need to enrich the supply of tourism commodities, expand consumption and extend the industry chain.

Questions for Discussion

1. What is the definition of tourism commodities?
2. What are the attributes of tourism souvenirs?
3. How to understand the contemporary development of handicrafts in our country?
4. What are the characteristics of specialty?
5. Why is cultural creativity important for future development of tourism commodities?

参考文献
References

[1] Beedie P, Hudson S. Emergence of Mountain-based Adventure Tourism[J]. Annals of Tourism Research, 2003, 30(3): 625-643.

[2] Cohen E. Authenticity and Commoditization in Tourism[J]. Annals of Tourism Research, 1988, 15(3): 371-386.

[3] East D, Osborne P, Kemp S, et al. Combining GPS and Survey Data Improves Understanding of Visitor Behaviour[J]. Tourism Management, 2017(61): 307-320.

[4] Gannon M, Taheri B, Olya H. Festival Quality, Self-connection, and Bragging [J]. Annals of Tourism Research, 2019(76): 239-252.

[5] Hu B, Yu H. Segmentation by Craft Selection Criteria and Shopping Involvement [J]. Tourism Management, 2007(28): 1079-1092.

[6] Kim S, Littrell M A. Souvenir Buying Intentions for Self Versus Others[J]. Annals of Tourism Research, 2001(28): 638-657.

[7] Kim S. Audience Involvement and Film Tourism Experiences: Emotional Places, Emotional Experiences[J]. Tourism Management, 2012, 33(2): 387-396.

[8] Leiper N. The Framework of Tourism: Towards a Definition of Tourism, Tourist, and the Tourist Industry[J]. Annals of Tourism Research, 1979, 6(4): 390-407.

[9] Leiper N. Tourist Attraction Systems[J]. Annals of Tourism Research, 1990, 17(3): 367-384.

[10] Lew A A. A Framework of Tourist Attraction Research[J]. Annals of Tourism Research, 1987, 14(4): 553-575.

[11] O'Reilly A M. Tourism Carrying Capacity: Concepts and Issues[J]. Tourism Management, 1986, 7(4):254-358.

[12] Paraskevaidis P, Andriotis K. Values of Souvenirs As Commodities[J]. Tourism Management, 2015(48): 1-10.

[13] Ryan C, Zhang Y M, Gu H M, et al. Tourism, a Classic Novel, and Television: The Case of Cao Xueqin's Dream of the Red Mansions and Grand View Gardens, Beijing[J]. Journal of Travel Research, 2009, 48(1): 14-28.

[14] Sims R. Food, Place and Authenticity: Local Food and the Sustainable Tourism Experience[J]. Journal of Sustainable Tourism, 2009, 17(3): 321-336.

[15] Smith S L J. The Tourism Product[J]. Annals of Tourism Research, 1994(3).

[16] Swanson K K, Timothy D J. Souvenirs: Icons of Meaning, Commercialization and Commoditization[J]. Tourism Management, 2012(33): 489-499.

[17] Turner L W, Reisinger Y. Shopping Satisfaction for Domestic Tourists[J]. Journal of Retailing and Consumer Services, 2001, 8(1): 15-27.

[18] 保继刚,楚义芳.旅游地理学[M].北京:高等教育出版社,1999.

[19] 别金花.都市非物质文化遗产旅游开发与保护[D].上海:上海师范大学,2009.

[20] 陈彦光,王义民.论分形与旅游景观[J].人文地理,1997,12(1):62-66.

[21] 郭来喜,吴必虎,刘锋,等.中国旅游资源分类系统与类型评价[J].地理学报,2000,55(3):294-301.

[22] 李军,陈志钢.旅游生命周期模型新解释——基于生产投资与需求分析[J].旅游学刊,2014,29(3):58-73.

[23] 李蕾蕾,张晗,卢嘉杰,等.旅游表演的文化产业生产模式:深圳华侨城主题公园个案研究[J].旅游科学,2005,19(6):44-51.

[24] 李天元.旅游学概论[M].3版.天津:南开大学出版社,2014.

[25] 李文亮,翁瑾,杨开忠.旅游系统模型比较研究[J].旅游学刊,2005,20(2):20-24.

[26] 李新运,郑新奇,范纯增,等.山东省旅游资源开发潜力评价研究[J].地理科学,1997,17(4):372-376.

[27] 梁保尔,马波.非物质文化遗产旅游资源研究——概念、分类、保护、利用[J].旅游科学,2008,22(2):7-14.

[28] 刘博,张涵.人地互动视角下的旅游纪念品文化生产——多案例研究[J].旅游学刊,2021,36(5):118-129.

[29] 刘益.大型风景旅游区旅游环境容量测算方法的再探讨[J].旅游学刊,2004,19(6):42-46.

[30] 卢凯翔,保继刚.旅游商品的概念辨析与研究框架[J].旅游学刊,2017,32(5):116-126.

[31] 苗学玲.旅游商品概念性定义与旅游纪念品的地方特色[J].旅游学刊,2004,19(1):27-31.

[32] 朴松爱.教育旅游、旅游教育与可持续旅游发展[J].旅游科学,2001(4):40-43.

[33] 申葆嘉.关于旅游发展规划的几个问题[J].旅游学刊,1995(4):34-38.

[34] 宋振春,王颖,葛新雨,等.身体痛苦如何成为情感享受——身心交互视角下的

旅游体验研究[J].旅游学刊,2020,35(10):109-121.

[35] 汪德根,陆林,刘昌雪.体育旅游市场特征及产品开发[J].旅游学刊,2002,17(1):49-53.

[36] 王德刚,王蔚.旅游资源学教程[M].北京:北京交通大学出版社,2011.

[37] 王清廉.旅游资源和旅游景观概念浅析[J].旅游学刊,1988(S1):17-19.

[38] 吴必虎.旅游系统:对旅游活动与旅游科学的一种解释[J].旅游学刊,1998(1):21-25.

[39] 徐菊凤,任心慧.旅游资源与旅游吸引物:含义,关系及适用性分析[J].旅游学刊,2014,29(7):115-125.

[40] 杨振之,陈谨."形象遮蔽"与"形象叠加"的理论与实证研究[J].旅游学刊,2008,18(3):62-67.

[41] 尹泽生,陈田,牛亚菲,等.旅游资源调查需要注意的若干问题[J].旅游学刊,2006,21(1):14-18.

[42] 喻学才.遗产活化论[J].旅游学刊,2010,25(4):6-7.

[43] 周达人.论旅游商品[J].旅游学刊,1988,3(1):49-53.

教学支持说明

为了改善教学效果,提高教材的使用效率,满足高校授课教师的教学需求,本套教材备有与纸质教材配套的教学课件和拓展资源(案例库、习题库等)。

为保证本教学课件及相关教学资料仅为教材使用者所得,我们将向使用本套教材的高校授课教师赠送教学课件或者相关教学资料,烦请授课教师通过电话、邮件或加入旅游专家俱乐部QQ群等方式与我们联系,获取"电子资源申请表"文档并认真准确填写后发给我们,我们的联系方式如下:

地址:湖北省武汉市东湖新技术开发区华工科技园华工园六路

邮编:430223

电话:027-81321911

传真:027-81321917

E-mail:lyzjjlb@163.com

旅游专家俱乐部QQ群号:758712998

旅游专家俱乐部QQ群二维码:

群名称:旅游专家俱乐部5群
群　号:758712998

电子资源申请表

填表时间：_____年___月___日

1. 以下内容请教师按实际情况写,★为必填项。
2. 根据个人情况如实填写,相关内容可以酌情调整提交。

★姓名		★性别	□男 □女	出生年月		★职务	
						★职称	□教授 □副教授 □讲师 □助教

★学校		★院/系	
★教研室		★专业	
★办公电话		家庭电话		★移动电话	
★E-mail（请填写清晰）				★QQ号/微信号	
★联系地址		★邮编	

★现在主授课程情况	学生人数	教材所属出版社	教材满意度
课程一			□满意 □一般 □不满意
课程二			□满意 □一般 □不满意
课程三			□满意 □一般 □不满意
其他			□满意 □一般 □不满意

教材出版信息		
方向一		□准备写 □写作中 □已成稿 □已出版待修订 □有讲义
方向二		□准备写 □写作中 □已成稿 □已出版待修订 □有讲义
方向三		□准备写 □写作中 □已成稿 □已出版待修订 □有讲义

请教师认真填写表格下列内容,提供索取课件配套教材的相关信息,我社根据每位教师填表信息的完整性、授课情况与索取课件的相关性,以及教材使用的情况赠送教材的配套课件及相关教学资源。

ISBN（书号）	书名	作者	索取课件简要说明	学生人数（如选作教材）
			□教学 □参考	
			□教学 □参考	

★您对与课件配套的纸质教材的意见和建议,希望提供哪些配套教学资源：